MORAL RESPONSIBILITY
AND THE PSYCHOPATH

Are psychopaths morally responsible? Should we argue with them? Remonstrate with them, blame them, sometimes even praise them? Is it worth trying to change them, or should we just try to prevent them from causing harm? In this book, Jim Baxter aims to find serious answers to these deep philosophical questions, drawing on contemporary insights from psychiatry, psychology, neuroscience and law. *Moral Responsibility and the Psychopath* is the first sustained, book-length philosophical work on this important and fascinating topic, and will be of deep interest and importance to researchers in these fields – not to mention anyone who has had to interact with a psychopath in their everyday life.

JIM BAXTER is Professional Ethics Consultancy Team Leader at the University of Leeds's Inter-Disciplinary Ethics Applied Centre. His recent research focuses on professionalism in banking and integrity in organisations.

MORAL RESPONSIBILITY AND THE PSYCHOPATH

The Value of Others

JIM BAXTER

University of Leeds

CAMBRIDGE UNIVERSITY PRESS

Shaftesbury Road, Cambridge CB2 8EA, United Kingdom

One Liberty Plaza, 20th Floor, New York, NY 10006, USA

477 Williamstown Road, Port Melbourne, VIC 3207, Australia

314–321, 3rd Floor, Plot 3, Splendor Forum, Jasola District Centre, New Delhi – 110025, India

103 Penang Road, #05–06/07, Visioncrest Commercial, Singapore 238467

Cambridge University Press is part of Cambridge University Press & Assessment, a department of the University of Cambridge.

We share the University's mission to contribute to society through the pursuit of education, learning and research at the highest international levels of excellence.

www.cambridge.org
Information on this title: www.cambridge.org/9781009016391

DOI: 10.1017/9781009025355

First published 2021
First paperback edition 2023

A catalogue record for this publication is available from the British Library

ISBN   978-1-316-51686-7   Hardback
ISBN   978-1-009-01639-1   Paperback

Cambridge University Press & Assessment has no responsibility for the persistence or accuracy of URLs for external or third-party internet websites referred to in this publication and does not guarantee that any content on such websites is, or will remain, accurate or appropriate.

For Bella

Contents

Acknowledgements

This book has been several years in the making, and I am very grateful to Ulrike Heuer and Helen Steward, whose guidance, support and insightful challenges helped me throughout its development. Comments from Gerald Lang, Dorothea Debus and Richard Holton were subsequently hugely helpful in showing me how it could be further improved.

Hilary Gaskin has been a supportive, encouraging and, perhaps most of all, patient guide throughout the editing process.

I am thankful to the two anonymous reviewers of Cambridge University Press, without whose invaluable comments Chapters 1 and 6, in particular, would be in a much poorer state.

Also, thanks to Diana Sofronieva for her insightful comments on an early draft.

I am grateful to the Inter-Disciplinary Ethics Applied Centre at the University of Leeds for supporting my study both financially and through flexibility and understanding. Special thanks go to Chris Megone for his invaluable help and support throughout but also to my other colleagues at the Centre for creating an environment rich with intellectual stimulation and good humour.

Huge thanks go to my parents, Eddie and Rosemary Baxter for, on top of everything else, hours of looking after my children while I struggled to understand psychopaths.

Finally, thanks to my children, Elijah and Shoshana, who have taught me more than anybody else has, particularly about emotions and empathy.

Introduction

Imagine someone to whom other people are truly, thoroughly unimport-ant. This person could do things without concern that would horrify most people. To them, the thought of lying, stealing or committing violence would hold no intrinsic repulsion at all. They would see other people either as obstacles in the way of their goals, or else as tools to be pressed into service, through lying, persuasion, manipulation or threats, to achieve those goals. The ordinarily selfish person prioritises their own needs too much and neglects those of others but could perhaps be confronted with their selfishness and persuaded to change their ways. The person we are considering, however, fundamentally cannot understand why the needs of others should concern them at all, and there is nothing you could do to make them understand. It is as though you are trying to describe colours to someone who can only see in black and white.

Now imagine that this person has acquired this way of seeing the world either purely through their genetic inheritance, or as the result of a childhood characterised by trauma and neglect, or as some combination of these two factors. Having reached this state as an adult, they are stuck there, as recalcitrant to therapy as they are to moral persuasion.

You would perhaps be afraid of such a person. You would probably want to avoid their company. But how would you think they should be treated? If they perform criminal acts, should their unusual psychology affect the way they are dealt with by the law? Should they be *blamed* for the harm they cause (and should they be praised for any apparently good acts they perform)? Would you be inclined to remonstrate with them, or resent them, if they did something thoughtless or cruel? The central idea behind all of these questions is that of moral responsibility. Should this kind of person be held morally responsible for their actions, emotions, attitudes or the states of affairs they bring about? Answering this question would be difficult and it would, I think, force you to consider very carefully exactly what it is to be morally responsible.

You might begin by thinking about other cases of mental abnormality where we are more inclined to think of the person as not being morally responsible, and try to draw a conclusion based on these less controversial cases. Take, for example, those mental conditions which are characterised by delusions. Imagine someone, in the grip of a paranoid delusion, who encounters another person whom they believe to be a persecutor – an alien in disguise, perhaps, bent on the destruction of humanity – and harms this person, in what they wrongly believe is self-defence. In this case we would not, I think, be inclined to hold the mentally ill person fully responsible for their act and the harm they cause. Through no fault of their own, this person misunderstands the nature of their own actions, in a way which is clearly relevant to the way we should react to them and treat them. However, the person in our original description is not suffering from a directly analogous case of misunderstanding. They do not think the people they harm are aliens, and they are not mistaken about the nature of their actions – at least not in the same way, through a straightforward, factual delusion. In this sense, at least, they appear to know what they are doing.

Still, another way of looking at this kind of case might offer us somewhere to begin. In addition to the physical facts of their predicament, the person with a paranoid delusion is apparently mistaken about their *reasons for action*. Among other mistaken beliefs, they believe that they have a reason to defend themselves from a hostile extra-terrestrial. Because of this mistaken belief, they are unable to properly respond to the reasons they do have, such as to avoid harming the person in front of them who is in fact innocent. According to the account of moral responsibility, which I will endorse, it is this inability to respond to the reasons bearing on their choice that renders the person not morally responsible for their actions. However, it is not clear, given this account of moral responsibility, whether we should think of psychopaths as being morally responsible. Psychopaths appear pathologically unconcerned, for example, about the harm their actions cause to other people. But a lack of concern cannot in itself be excusing. What we need to know is whether there is something special about the lack of concern shown by psychopaths, perhaps given the way they acquire that lack of concern, which means we should think of them as lacking moral responsibility for some of their actions.

In this book, I will argue that psychopaths, insofar as they lack responsiveness to a certain set of reasons, are not morally responsible for failing to act on those reasons. I am, of course, not the first person to argue that psychopaths lack moral responsibility. There has been a small but substantial literature on this question, and philosophers have taken several routes to arrive at the same conclusion. It has been argued variously that psychopaths are not responsible because they lack moral understanding,[1] 'moral rationality'[2] or personhood,[3] or because they are incapable of fully fledged reactive attitudes.[4] Within the framework of responsiveness to reasons which I favour, David Shoemaker has argued that psychopaths are not responsible because they are incapable of being motivated to comply with reasons,[5] and Neil Levy has argued that psychopaths lack both responsiveness to reasons and moral knowledge based on their supposed inability to distinguish between moral and conventional transgressions.[6]

On the other side of the debate, several philosophers have argued that psychopaths are indeed morally responsible, again for various reasons. It has been claimed that psychopaths have the cognitive resources that are necessary for responsibility,[7] that their volitional and emotional deficits are not enough to render them non-responsible,[8] that they are capable of forming intentions in a way that justifies ascriptions of responsibility[9] and that they are capable of moral understanding.[10]

My own view is that psychopaths are incapable of responding to some of the reasons that genuinely bear on their actions. However, I do not think this is because of a 'factual' delusion about the nature of the world analogous to the delusions often experienced by schizophrenics, nor do I think it is because of the inability to parse different forms of transgression which would appear to be implied by James Blair's well-known experiments into the 'moral/conventional distinction'.[11] As I argue in Chapter 3, I do not believe these experiments are firm enough ground on which to build an argument of this kind.

My own view is that the primary capacity lacked by psychopaths which is necessary for moral responsibility is the capacity to see others as valuable. Understanding this capacity, and what shapes it, allows us to bridge the apparent disconnect between the deficits experienced by psychopaths, which I will argue, are primarily emotional in nature, and the unresponsiveness to certain reasons which accounts for their lack of moral responsibility.

---

[1] Duff (1977), Fine and Kennett (2004).
[2] Morse (2008). Morse is concerned with criminal responsibility rather than moral responsibility.
[3] Murphy (1972).   [4] Benn (1999).   [5] Shoemaker (2009), Shoemaker (2011a).
[6] Levy (2008). In a later paper, Levy (2014) has also argued that psychopaths are not responsible because, lacking an understanding both of what it means to cause harm or distress to others and of the nature of personhood, they are incapable of performing actions with the necessary type of content.
[7] Zavaliy (2008).   [8] Glannon (1997), Glannon (2008).   [9] Greenspan (2003).
[10] Maibom (2005), Maibom (2008).   [11] Blair (1995), Blair (1997).

This kind of analysis is needed partly because it is not clear what our pre-theoretical intuitions should be about the moral responsibility of psychopaths. This is a point that has been missed by a surprising number of philosophers. For example, R. Jay Wallace includes psychopaths in his list of 'accepted exemptions' from moral responsibility,[12] before going on to try to explain, in the context of his overall theory, why this should be so. My own experience is that it is precisely the difficulty of saying whether psychopaths are morally responsible that makes this an interesting question. I have trouble locating my own intuitions on the subject, and my experience of speaking to people about this suggests that my difficulty is widely shared.

The difficulty of knowing how we should react to, and treat psychopaths, is reflected in a lack of clarity in the criminal law surrounding psychopaths and responsibility, which I explore in detail in Chapter 6. Psychopathy is traditionally excluded from the range of conditions which can form the basis of a successful insanity defence,[13] and personality traits related to psychopathy, such as a lack of remorse, may be taken as evidence of bad character and therefore lead to harsher sentencing. This is perhaps surprising, given the way excuses from responsibility are frequently expressed in criminal tests. For example, the M'Naghton standard refers to 'a defect of reason, from disease of the mind' which leads the person 'not to know the nature and quality of the act he was doing; or that if he did know it, that he did not know he was doing what was wrong'.[14] A strong case could be made that psychopaths suffer from either of the conditions described by the disjuncts of this principle. However, psychopaths are excluded as a result of particular interpretations of the phrases 'defect of reason' and 'he did not know he was doing what was wrong', which may stem more from expediency than from a desire for conceptual clarity.

Perhaps partly because of a wish to justify the existing practice in the criminal law of holding psychopaths fully responsible, the early philosophical literature on psychopathy and responsibility was dominated by a debate about whether the question could be settled a priori, without any reference to the empirical facts about psychopaths. Barbara Wootton[15] was the originator of this view. She claimed that any argument against the responsibility of the psychopath must be circular since the diagnosis of psychopathy itself will be based on facts about criminal wrongdoing, in which case the diagnosis cannot be taken to be an excuse for wrongdoing.

---

[12] Wallace (1994), p. 166.   [13] Bartlett (2010).
[14] M'Naghton case, quoted in Bartlett (2010), p. 35.   [15] Wootton (1959).

Vinit Haksar[16] took the contrary view, on the grounds that psychopathy is a clinical diagnosis which can be made independently, based on facts not connected to criminal wrongdoing.[17]

Wootton's view was perhaps understandable given the unavailability at the time of robust empirical accounts of psychopathy that were not simply based on records of criminal activities. However, following the establishment of clinical tools such as Robert Hare's Psychopathy Checklist (which I will discuss in detail in Chapter 2) the existence of psychopathy as a syndrome of personality, quite separate from any criminal activity in which it might issue, is now quite well established. Many 'successful' psychopaths never come into conflict with the law at all,[18] and Hare's checklist does not depend upon facts about the subject's criminal history for its application. Furthermore, neuroscience is now making significant advances towards identifying an independent neurological basis for psychopathy (see Chapter 2). This raises the possibility of a further means of diagnosis which is independent of any criminal history the subject may have.

Summary of the Argument

If we are to answer the question of whether psychopaths are morally responsible, then we must develop a clear picture of the psychological features necessary for moral responsibility, and of the psychological features which define psychopathy as a type of personality. My overall aim is to show that psychopaths lack some of the features that are necessary for them to be morally responsible. My argument can be summarised as follows:

1. Persons cannot be held responsible for failing to act on reasons that they are unable to recognise as reasons.
2. Psychopaths are unable to recognise reasons for action stemming from the interests, needs and concerns of others.
3. Hence, they are not responsible for failing to act on them.

The aim of Chapter 1 is to defend the first premise of the aforementioned argument, on the basis that moral responsibility is a matter of being responsive to the reasons that bear on one's choices. The literature on

---

[16] Haksar (1965).

[17] In another paper, Haksar (1964) suggests that psychopaths may not be 'choosing agents' – they can recognise moral values but are unable to choose them – and are therefore not responsible.

[18] Hare (1995).

moral responsibility has been dominated by the debate over whether or not moral responsibility is compatible with causal determinism, and providing an answer to this question may not require one to develop a fully fledged theory of moral responsibility. Such theories are, for this reason, quite thin on the ground. There is, however, a strand of theorising within the literature which, unlike other arguments within that debate, purports to explain and justify moral responsibility as a whole. These theories therefore deserve to be considered on their merits as attempts to do this, independent of their success in defeating the challenge from incompatibilism. The strand I have in mind originates with P. F. Strawson. Strawson's discussion of the reactive attitudes is very helpful in displaying the social nature of moral responsibility, and the way it is inherent in a wide variety of attitudes and emotions, not just the Aristotelian notions of praise and blame. Strawson also offers a robust justification of the practices, attitudes and emotions involved in holding people morally responsible. However, in my view Strawson is unable to offer a complete analysis of when it is right to apply, or withhold, judgements of moral responsibility. At the end of the chapter, I argue that an analysis of this kind can be found in the work of philosophers such as R. Jay Wallace, who build on Strawson's work by linking moral responsibility to the idea of responsiveness to reasons.

Chapters 2 to 5 then defend the second premise aforementioned in a number of steps.

In Chapter 2, I develop a picture of the psychopathic personality-type based on the empirical literature. Psychopathy is a complex diagnosis, and there are some controversies about what elements of personality should be considered central to it. Using sources from psychiatry, psychology and neuroscience, I gather evidence of the peculiar deficiencies exhibited by psychopaths, concluding that these are primarily emotional in nature.

In Chapter 3, I consider various interpretations of these deficiencies in terms of moral responsibility, offering as the best interpretation that psychopaths do not recognise reasons stemming from the rights, interests and concerns of other people, due to their inability to recognise sources of value other than themselves.

In Chapters 4 and 5, I seek to bolster and support this interpretation by explaining it in the light of the peculiar emotional reactions of psychopaths that I noted in Chapter 2. In Chapter 4, I draw on literature from the philosophy of the emotions to make the case that psychopaths' emotional deficiencies interfere with their ability to engage evaluatively with the world. In Chapter 5, I argue that empathy has a specific role to play in the development of the ability to see others as valuable.

Finally, in Chapter 6, I begin to explore the implications of my view for the criminal law. The conclusion that some psychopaths are not responsible for some of their acts still leaves unanswered the question of how they should be treated by society. If a psychopath commits a crime, should they be punished for it, and if so, should they be punished in exactly the same way as a non-psychopath should be punished? I also survey some of the controversies that have surrounded this question in the philosophy of law, and argue that current legal practices are on somewhat shaky ground when it comes to the criminal responsibility of psychopaths.

CHAPTER I

Moral Responsibility

1.1 Introduction

The word 'responsibility' in English is used in several different ways. For example, its meaning in the sentence, 'Nigel is a pretty responsible sort of guy' is clearly different from its meaning in the sentence, 'Anastasia is responsible for the death of my rabbit' or 'Hurricane Sandy was responsible for millions of dollars' worth of damage'. On the other hand, while the word has several distinct meanings, it is not merely by coincidence that we use the same word in each of the sentences, or in others in which its meaning is different again. These meanings are related, though distinct. If we are to make enquiries into the nature of responsibility, we would do well first to clarify exactly what sense (or senses) of responsibility we are interested in.

In this initial section, I will try to put the idea of responsibility into focus by examining some of the different ways in which it is used and exploring the relationship between these. This groundwork will be helpful later on because it will allow me to separate out and begin to explicate the idea of *moral* responsibility, which is my primary focus. By the end of this chapter, I will have set out what I believe to be the best available account of moral responsibility. I will then be able to begin to answer the question of whether it is an account which applies to the case of the psychopath.

1.2 Senses of Responsibility

Let me start, then, by identifying some different senses of the word 'responsibility'.

As in the example of Nigel, who is 'a pretty responsible sort of guy', the word 'responsible' is sometimes used to refer to someone who has a particular virtue which manifests in a tendency to be trustworthy, consistent and so on. They are 'a responsible sort of person'; they take their responsibilities seriously; they do not act *ir*responsibly. To describe someone as having responsibility in this sense – *virtue responsibility* – is to praise their character.

There is a very different sense of responsibility which is purely about causation; it has no moral dimension at all. A claim of *causal responsibility* is a claim about the causal history of an event or a state of affairs. The Hurricane Sandy example is an example of mere causal responsibility: it makes no sense to speak of holding a hurricane morally responsible for the damage it causes. Similarly, if a computer virus wipes my hard drive and destroys the only copy of my book manuscript, I might say that the virus was responsible for this destruction, but not in a sense that implied any moral assessment of the virus itself (any moral assessment of the people who created the virus would be additional to this immediate judgement of causal responsibility).

This contrasts with the sense in which the word 'responsibility' is employed in sentences such as 'I hold you responsible for the damage you caused' or 'through his negligence in not holding on to the lead properly, Eric was responsible for the damage caused by his dog'. If a person is responsible in this sense for an action, then the person is liable for various moral repercussions arising from the action. For example, it might be that the person can be either blamed or praised for the action. It might also legitimise other attitudes and emotions, including resentment and indignation. In some cases, it might mean that social sanctions, such as shunning, are appropriate. It might also lead to expressions of disapproval (or approval), remonstration with the person or 'taking them to task'. All of these crucial elements of our social interactions rely on a judgement, whether implicit or explicit, about the person at whom they are directed: that they are *morally* responsible for some relevant action or state of affairs.

This sense of responsibility is what philosophers generally have in mind when they write about *moral responsibility*, and I will hold on to this term for convenience, although it is, of course, not the only sense of responsibility with a moral dimension (consider, for example, the aforementioned 'virtue responsibility').

Moral responsibility has a legal parallel in the idea of criminal responsibility. To say that someone meets the criteria of criminal responsibility in relation to a particular crime is to say that they should answer to the law in respect of that crime. It may be that someone who is causally responsible for a crime may yet not be criminally responsible, for example, because they are too young or because they have a mental illness which exempts them from criminal responsibility (the 'insanity plea'). It is also possible that someone might be criminally responsible without being causally responsible, as in cases of 'strict liability'. It may also be that criminal responsibility and moral responsibility come apart in at least some cases of strict liability.[1]

Nicole Vincent, from whose paper, 'A Structured Taxonomy of Responsibility Concepts', I have taken these labels, also identifies a concept, separate from moral responsibility, which she calls 'capacity responsibility'. This has to do with the capacities people may or may not have which would make them candidates for judgements of moral responsibility. A judgement of capacity responsibility is a judgement of the entity as a whole, not in relation to any particular act or state of affairs. Clearly, there are some entities that are *never* capable of moral responsibility. We might say, for example, that a stone, or a baby, lacks capacity responsibility, in the sense that there is nothing for which the stone or baby is morally responsible. In this sense, the stone or baby lacks whatever capacities allow an entity to be 'in the game' for attributions of moral responsibility in the first place.[2]

However, there are also cases in which people can lack moral responsibility for some things, or types of thing, but not others, because of certain capacities that they lack. The parallel concept of 'capacity' in medical ethics is illuminating here. Judgements about people's medical capacity are, in practice, always judgements about their capacity to do something in particular, for example, to consent to a medical intervention. In many cases, it is likely that moral responsibility operates in the same way. If someone suffers from paranoid delusions, it would not be appropriate to hold them morally responsible for insulting me if I know that one of their delusions has convinced them that I am a persecutor. If, on the other hand, none of their delusions apply to me at all, a judgement of responsibility does seem appropriate. They might, after all, simply not like me. Capacities, then, enter into judgements of moral responsibility for individual acts, as well as judgements of 'capacity responsibility' in Vincent's sense.

Finally, there is a sense of 'responsibility' which is roughly equivalent to 'duty' or 'obligation' – what we might call an *'obligation* responsibility'. To

---

[1] See Chapter 6 for further discussion of the relationship between moral responsibility and criminal responsibility.

[2] There are also controversial cases in this area. For example, there is an ongoing debate within business ethics about whether an organisation is the kind of entity that can ever be morally responsible, that is, which has capacity responsibility in this sense (see French (1979, 1984), Werhane (1985), List and Pettit (2011), Rönnegard (2015)).

say that a referee has a responsibility to ensure that a game is played fairly is just to say that they have an obligation to do so. Sometimes these responsibilities are generated by the roles – social, contractual and so on – which we occupy, but this is not always the case. It makes sense to say that I would have a responsibility to rescue a drowning child if I could do so easily, and this would not be generated by any role I occupy (I would not need to be a lifeguard, for example, or to have any familial or other relationship with the child).

1.3   Moral Responsibility, Praiseworthiness and Blameworthiness

In relation to moral responsibility, I noted that this idea is linked to attitudes including praise and blame. There is clearly a link between the state of being morally responsible and the state of being either *praiseworthy* or *blameworthy* – of being a proper object of praise or blame. But are they merely linked or are they in fact the same thing? It is not clear whether moral responsibility and blameworthiness/praiseworthiness can come apart. Some examples may help to think this question through.

Imagine I am visiting your house and knock over your valuable vase, breaking it. Depending on how this comes to pass, several implications of the event may differ, including your verdict over my blameworthiness or otherwise, how I would feel about it, and whether reparations on my part would be appropriate or not. Here are some possible cases:

Vase 1:   I knock over your vase intentionally because I don't like the vase (or maybe I don't like you).

Vase 2:   I blunder into the vase accidentally because I am not being careful, and I don't really care about your possessions or about the effect of my actions on your feelings.

Vase 3:   I fall over onto the vase because your enemy pushed me into the vase with the intention of breaking it.

Vase 4:   I have a heart attack and fall against the vase, knocking it over.

Vase 5:   Your dog jumps up at me, and, being afraid of dogs, I back into the vase and knock it over.

In Vases 1 and 2, it is quite clear that I am blameworthy for breaking your vase. In Vase 1, it is my intentional act that leads to the vase being broken, and there are no special conditions that should deter you from blaming me for it. In Vase 2, it is my negligence – my failure to act in a way in which I ought to have acted – that leads to the vase being broken, and again there are no special conditions that should deter you from blaming me for it. In both cases, while I may not, in the case as described, feel bad about what I have done, it is clear that I *ought* to feel bad about it, and all other things being equal I am presumably liable for making reparations of some kind.

In Vase 3, it seems clear that I am not blameworthy. In this case, it was not my action that caused the vase to be broken, but your enemy's. I was *used* – and the blame for breaking the vase lies with your enemy, and not me. Nonetheless, I might feel some need to apologise to you. After all, it was my body that caused the vase to break. I was *involved*. However, the appropriate response on your part is surely, 'don't be silly!' rather than, 'apology accepted'. Regardless of my involvement in the scene, it was not my fault, and you should reassure me that there is nothing to apologise for.

Something similar seems to apply in Vase 4. I am not to blame because, again, the vase did not come to be broken through any action of mine. In this case, no one acted. An unfortunate event occurred which resulted in the vase being broken. This time (at a stretch) I can perhaps imagine being moved to apologise for the broken vase (assuming I survive the heart attack of course). You would (I hope!) move even more quickly to reassure me that there is nothing to apologise for.

In all four of these cases, it appears that blameworthiness goes hand in hand with action. In Vases 1 and 2, it is my actions that cause the vase to be broken. In Vases 3 and 4, this is not the case, either because (in Vase 3) it was *your enemy* who acted and I was merely a passive object upon which they acted, or because (in Vase 4) nobody acted.

In Vase 5, I do act – I back into the vase – and my action causes the vase to be broken. Let us assume that my act was voluntary – not that I voluntarily broke the vase, but that I voluntarily moved to get away from the dog. However, not only have I acted without intending to break the vase, but it would also not be right to say that I have acted thoughtlessly or without due care. Is the breaking of the vase, then, an action for which I am blameworthy? Probably not. It is an accident, and it is *my* accident, but it is not one in which I am negligent or careless. It would seem unreasonable for you or anyone else to blame me, given the way I have described the case. Even more than in Vases 3 and 4, however, I would certainly feel the need to apologise, and to offer to make reparation for the broken vase.

What do these cases tell us? First, perhaps that my feeling the need to apologise does not imply that I accept blame for the incident, and also that its being right that I should apologise does not imply that I am blameworthy, or even that you would be justified in accepting my apology. Sometimes, it would appear – at least given the cultural norms that affect my own intuitions – that my proper action is to apologise, and your proper response is to reassure me that there is no need to apologise. It would also appear that, for this to be true, all that needs to be the case is that I have some place in the causal chain resulting in the event in question. This is a very minimal requirement of *causal responsibility*: not that I need to have chosen to act, or even acted at all, in such a way as to bring about the event, but merely that I am involved in some way, even if only in that my body was one of the physical objects involved in the event's coming about.

The really difficult question is where *moral responsibility* fits into all of this. Personally, I find that attempting to test my intuitions about moral responsibility against cases such as Vases 1–5 is of only limited help. In the simpler cases, it seems fairly clear that moral responsibility tracks blameworthiness: I am both morally responsible and blameworthy in Vases 1 and 2, and neither morally responsible nor blameworthy in Vases 3 and 4. In the more difficult Vase 5, I find it hard to discern a clear intuition regarding whether I am morally responsible or not. This is perhaps because moral responsibility is a concept whose meaning and application are actually somewhat unclear. If this is right, then I will have to make a decision about what I take moral responsibility to mean, and it will be reasonable to take this decision at least partly on pragmatic grounds: what definition of moral responsibility is most likely to play a useful role in my overall argument, and confer clarity on the debate that is to come?

In these cases, the vase's breaking is an event, the vase being broken is a state of affairs, and the breaking of the vase is, in some variations at least, an action. Typically, we are responsible for events and states of affairs that are the result of our actions, or sometimes of our failure to perform certain actions. And, again typically, we are responsible for events and states of affairs that are the result of actions for which we are morally responsible. There are exceptions here, as perhaps when we are responsible for an action which leads to an event or state of affairs which we could not reasonably be expected to have included in our deliberation about how to act. Nonetheless, in the typical case, if we are responsible for the act, we are responsible for its consequences – for the events and states of affairs that result from it. At least, if we are to determine whether A is responsible for some given event or state of affairs, then we will need to know what action or failures to act on A's part have led to that event or state of affairs coming about, and we will need to know whether A is responsible for those actions or failures to act (and we may need to know some other things as well). The primary locus of responsibility, in this sense, is actions.

One option, then, is to link moral responsibility to action: if an action is attributable to me as an agent – if it is *my* action – then I am morally responsible for it.[3] In Vase 5, this would mean that I am morally responsible for breaking the vase, because the breaking of the vase is my action – I broke the vase – in contrast to Vases 3 and 4. But I would plausibly not be blameworthy for it. So linking moral responsibility to action broadly fits our intuitions about these cases. However, in these cases it is my control over my actions that is in question. Beginning with Aristotle, lack of control is typically thought to be an excusing condition, with another being ignorance.[4] Equating moral responsibility with action, it turns out, fares better with cases in which lack of control is the excusing condition (including the five 'vase' cases) than with cases in which ignorance is the excusing condition. While filming the movie *The Crow*, the actor Brandon Lee was killed by a bullet from a gun which was fired by an extra – the gun was supposed to contain blanks but somehow a live round had found its way in. It is surely true to say, then, that the extra killed Brandon Lee. But was he morally responsible for doing so? To say that he was is to abandon the idea that ignorance is an excusing condition on moral responsibility since the extra was surely blamelessly ignorant of the most relevant fact in the case – that the gun contained a live round. This would not be disastrous – we would need to talk in terms of blameworthiness and praiseworthiness, at least when discussing matters which touch on the knowledge condition rather than the control condition – but it would put us at odds with the way moral responsibility is typically discussed by philosophers, and it is not clear that there would be any advantage to make up for this.

The better option, I think, is to link moral responsibility closely to blameworthiness or praiseworthiness. We are morally responsible for something if certain conditions (the exact nature of which we have yet to determine) are met, and we are praiseworthy if these conditions are met, *and* praise is due to someone for the thing in question – blameworthy if blame is due. Taking this option allows us to retain the traditional view that there is a knowledge, as well as a control, condition on moral responsibility. However, it does raise two issues which I will deal with in turn before proceeding.

---

[3] There is some ambiguity here around what it means for an action to be *my* action, or to be *attributable to me* as an agent. This depends on one's understanding of action. Whether it is enough simply for me to have performed the action, or whether some further conditions need to be met, I think the result will be too thin a concept to be equated with moral responsibility, as I hope the following discussion shows.

[4] Aristotle (1985), Book ii, chapter 9, section 3.1.

One issue is a potential lack of clarity around the distinction between justifications and excuses. This distinction, which has been much discussed by philosophers,[5] would need to be clarified in any case, but I shall need to make sense of it in the context of an account which links moral responsibility closely to praiseworthiness and blameworthiness. The basic form of this distinction is that if someone has a justification, then they have done nothing wrong, whereas if they have an excuse, they have done something wrong but are not to be blamed for it (and, I would have to add given my understanding of moral responsibility, are not morally responsible for it). When trying to apply this distinction to cases, however, the water becomes muddied very quickly. Did the extra in the Brandon Lee case do anything wrong? The answer to this perhaps depends on how we describe the action in question. It seems odd to say that they did anything wrong *in pulling the trigger*, since that was their job, and they had no reason to think that anything bad would result from it. But did they do anything wrong in killing Brandon Lee? Well, it was surely wrong for Brandon Lee to be killed. Furthermore, if it is supposed to be the case that someone who does nothing wrong by acting in a way which might have been wrong has a *justification*, then this does not seem to be the natural way to talk about this case. The extra was not *justified* in killing Brandon Lee. Better, then, to say that the extra did something wrong in killing Brandon Lee, but that they were not to blame for it. Because I am linking moral responsibility closely to praiseworthiness and blameworthiness, I am therefore committed to saying that they are also not morally responsible for killing Brandon Lee. Since this seems to me a perfectly natural thing to say about the case, I am happy to be so committed.

The other issue raised by the move to link moral responsibility to blameworthiness and praiseworthiness has to do with acts that are neither blameworthy nor praiseworthy in themselves. There are actions which are morally neutral (e.g. going to the shop to buy some milk) and for which it would make no sense to use terms such as 'blameworthy' or 'praiseworthy'. In cases which are *not* morally neutral, moral responsibility on my suggestion would be the state of being the proper recipient of praise and blame. Certain conditions would need to be fulfilled (that the agent is in control of their action, knows what they are doing, etc.) for them to be morally responsible in this sense. In cases which are morally neutral, those conditions still exist, but this does not legitimise praise or blame, because neither praise nor blame is appropriate in morally neutral cases. Am I then to be

5 Austin (1956), Robinson (1996), Gardner (2007) and Botterell (2009).

described as morally responsible for going to the shop for some milk, or not?

On the one hand, I can see that there is something strange about describing someone as *morally* responsible for something which has no moral dimension to it at all. On the other hand, it is possible to describe such a case in a way that exactly mirrors how one would describe a case which did have moral implications. If I went to the shop for orange juice, and picked up a carton marked 'orange juice', which for some reason contained milk, there is a sense (other than causal responsibility) in which I would not be responsible for buying the milk. In fact, not much rides on whether we choose to call this sense 'moral' responsibility or to allocate some other name to it. By definition, nothing of moral consequence depends on attributions of this kind of responsibility in morally neutral cases. However, since what is being described *is* the type of state which justifies praise and blame where there is praise or blame to be justified, and since it is only in cases where praise or blame is appropriate that we are likely to find ourselves discussing this type of state, it at least has the virtue of simplicity to maintain the same term both for cases which have moral dimensions and for cases which do not. I will therefore take this approach.

1.4   Moral Responsibility for Mental Phenomena

I have been talking so far largely about actions, and have also alluded briefly to events and states of affairs. However, we are also, interestingly, often thought to be responsible for mental phenomena, including attitudes, emotions and beliefs. Here, briefly, is an example of each of these mental phenomena: 'Stephen thinks that Johnny takes him for a fool, and demands an explanation.' 'Dave demands an apology from Ray because he believes Ray's anger at Dave is unjustified.' 'Neil takes Chris to task for his racist beliefs.' In each of these cases, the attitude, emotion or belief in question is attributable to the relevant person – it is *their* attitude, emotion or belief. This contrasts with the case in which an attitude, emotion or belief is not really attributable to me – say I have been slandered or misquoted.

Now, as with actions, there will be cases where states of affairs, attitudes, emotions and beliefs are attributable to me, but I am not morally responsible for them. So, in the Vase 5 case, the fact that the vase is broken is a state of affairs that is due to an act of mine, but I am not morally responsible because of the excuse provided by the dog. If Stephen takes

Johnny for a fool because he has (through no fault of his own) mistaken Johnny for someone else who *is* a fool, then he is not morally responsible for his misdirected attitude. If Ray is angry at Dave because he thinks Dave has burned his hat, when in fact *Pete* has burned Ray's hat, and created a plausible situation in which it looks as though Dave burned it, then Ray is not morally responsible for his anger at Dave. If Chris has been brought up in a very isolated community, fed propaganda about the supposed inferiority of some races and not been exposed either to any real members of those races or to any opposing views, then he is (plausibly, I suppose) excused from moral responsibility for his racist views.

Thus, in the case of attitudes, emotions and beliefs, as in that of actions, there are conditions which must be met before someone is morally responsible for the thing in question, and it is only when they meet those conditions that any praise and blame can legitimately be attached to them. The most important question of this chapter is, how should we describe those questions?

I will turn to this question shortly, but first I would like to revisit the different senses of the word 'responsibility' I set out earlier, and consider some relations between them.

1.5 Relations between Senses of Responsibility

First, virtue responsibility appears to be loosely related to both moral responsibility and obligation responsibilities. Someone who has virtue responsibility is likely to recognise that they have certain obligations, and to recognise their moral responsibility (to *take* responsibility) for fulfilling, or failing to fulfil, these obligations. This is partly what we mean when we say that someone is a 'responsible sort of person'. Conversely, when we say someone 'abdicates responsibility', we tend to mean that they either fail to recognise or take seriously their obligations, or to act in a way that suggests that they accept *moral* responsibility for the fulfilment or non-fulfilment of those obligations. This is a good indication that they lack virtue responsibility.

Second, there is clearly a link between causal and moral responsibility. In many cases, it would be strange to say that someone was morally responsible for something while maintaining that they were not causally responsible for that thing. If Lee Harvey Oswald did not fire the gun that killed President Kennedy, then he was not causally responsible for Kennedy's death and therefore could not be morally responsible for it either. However, as some of the brief examples I have given show, it would be wrong to think that causal responsibility is always a necessary condition of moral responsibility. The problem with Eric and his dog is not that Eric caused the damage. The dog caused the damage, but Eric is still responsible for it because he failed in a duty to prevent the dog from doing so. Generally, we tend to think that parents bear at least some of the moral responsibility for the actions, or things caused by the actions, of their children. This is why a parent might apologise on behalf of their child, or offer to pay for damage and so on. We can also be morally responsible for omissions – for things that we fail to do. A driver who fails to signal when turning right is morally responsible for this failure. The driver in this case has not caused anything to happen (this, if you like, is the problem).

Both of these examples also highlight a relation between moral responsibility and obligation responsibilities. We hold the driver morally responsible for failing to signal, partly because we believe they had a responsibility (obligation) to do so, and we hold a dog owner morally responsible for damage caused by their dog when they fail to keep it on a lead, partly because we believe they have a responsibility (obligation) to keep the dog on a lead. The fact that the protagonists in these examples are morally responsible is an indication of the existence of an obligation that each has. However, it does not seem to be the case that being morally responsible, or being in a position to be morally responsible (in cases where the act in question has not occurred yet), for an act is a necessary condition of having an obligation responsibility to perform, or not to perform, that act. Imagine a football referee who sees a player fall over after being tackled in the penalty area, but, though no fault of their own, the referee is unable to see whether the footballer was fouled or not. Perhaps another player passed through their line of sight at the critical moment. Now, it seems to me that this referee is not morally responsible for failing to judge correctly whether a foul has taken place. However, I do not think it is the best explanation of this case to say that the referee does not have an obligation to make this judgement correctly. It seems rather that the obligation stands, but that the referee is not morally responsible for failing to fulfil it in this case.

Perhaps a clearer exception to the close link between obligation responsibilities and moral responsibility is in cases of moral responsibility for supererogatory actions. An ordinary member of the public who rescues someone from a burning building is morally responsible for the rescue, but not because they had any obligation responsibility to do so.

As I have said, the sense of responsibility which is central to this thesis is moral responsibility. It is this concept that is the object of the philosophical work that has already been published on responsibility and psychopaths, and I tried to show in the introduction why it is interesting to ask whether psychopaths can have this kind of responsibility. It is also interesting to note connections to other senses of responsibility in the case of psychopaths, however. First, it is certainly true that psychopaths on the whole lack virtue responsibility. As we will see in Chapter 2, failure to *take* responsibility for one's actions is one of the features by which psychopathy is diagnosed in clinical settings. Harvey Cleckley[6] sets out a series of case studies of psychopaths who manifestly and repeatedly fail to take responsibility – to recognise that they are morally responsible, both for the consequences of their actions for other people, and for their own lives – in any meaningful way. As I have noted, people with virtue responsibility recognise that there are things for which they are morally responsible. Of course, the fact that psychopaths lack virtue responsibility does not in itself tell us anything about whether they *have* moral responsibility (or for what, if anything, they have it): it may be that they do, but that they fail to recognise this.

Second, the link to obligation responsibilities is also interesting. If it were the case that obligations were only possible where the person concerned could be held morally responsible for breaking those obligations, then either psychopaths must be capable of moral responsibility or else they could not have obligations. The latter conclusion would be a surprising one. It would mean, for example, that a psychopathic referee, or a psychopathic teacher, had no obligations at all generated by their role. However, it would also be strange to think that this in itself settled the question of whether psychopaths can be morally responsible. Perhaps, then, the example of psychopaths gives us another reason to doubt that there is such a close link between moral responsibility and obligations.

1.6 Theories of Moral Responsibility

My final task in this chapter is to set out what I think is the most convincing account of moral responsibility available. My view is that this account is, broadly, the one set out by R. Jay Wallace as a refinement of the general framework introduced by P. F. Strawson. I will end this chapter by introducing and explaining this account, beginning with Strawson before moving on to Wallace. In doing so, I will be focusing in particular on what the account has to say about when it is right to hold someone responsible

[6] Cleckley (1941).

for something, and when it is not. This, ultimately, is the question that I am trying to answer for the particular case of psychopaths.

A claim of moral responsibility is, to a great extent, a claim about what should be *done* in relation to the person or other entity who is responsible. Aristotle, in his discussion of voluntary action in the *Nichomachean Ethics*, which is a foundational text in the philosophy of responsibility,[7] takes as central the practices of praise and blame: when someone acts voluntarily, it is proper to praise and blame them. However, it is surely true that several other practices and attitudes are legitimised by moral responsibility. An obvious example is that the appropriateness of rewards and punishment depends on verdicts of moral responsibility. Emotional reactions too can depend on whether we think someone is morally responsible or not. If my friend cooks a meal for me and it makes me ill, I might be upset and even angry towards her. But if it turns out that the food was contaminated by my enemy leaning in through the kitchen window when her back was turned, so that she could not have known what she was serving me, then she is not morally responsible for my illness. I would change my attitude towards her, or if I did not, my continued anger and upset would be misplaced. My emotional reaction to my friend, then, depends on whether or not I judge her to be morally responsible, and the legitimacy of my reaction depends on whether she really *is* morally responsible.

Judging someone to be morally responsible also allows one to call them to account. This might mean that the person who is judged morally responsible is expected to offer an explanation for their actions, for example, or to make amends.[8]

In short, a multiplicity of social practices, emotions, attitudes and behaviours are provoked and apparently justified by (and, one might say, *contain within them*) judgements of moral responsibility, implicit or explicit. The key question for my purposes here, the one which will be essential for my overall project, is this: when are such judgements justified and when are they not?

To say that someone is morally responsible for something (an act, state of affairs, attitude, emotion or belief) is to say that they meet certain conditions in relation to that thing. This may include some claim of causal responsibility (though, as we have seen, there are exceptions to the link between these two ideas). It may also include discussion of the obligations that the person has. In addition to these, however, the conditions of moral

---

[7] Aristotle (1985), 1109b.
[8] See Watson (1996) and Oshana (2004) for discussions of this aspect of moral responsibility.

responsibility are also generally thought to include two other things: a particular kind of control and a particular kind of knowledge. This thought can again be traced to Aristotle, who begins his discussion with the two central claims that 'feelings and actions . . . receive praise or blame when they are voluntary'[9] and that 'what comes about by force or because of ignorance seems to be involuntary'.[10] Substitute moral responsibility for voluntary action and we have the basis of much of the discussion of moral responsibility that has followed. It is interesting to note that Aristotle makes no attempt to explain why it is that ignorance and compulsion, and not other conditions, are thought to be adequate excuses. This is simply taken as given. There are also controversies around the application of these conditions, including the difficulty of determining whether or not someone with a mental illness is in a position of ignorance with regard to the nature of their actions. Psychopathy, as we have seen, is a highly distinctive type of mental illness and one whose implications for moral responsibility is particularly unclear. If I want to answer the question of whether psychopaths are morally responsible, I will need to consider first what the conditions of moral responsibility implied by my favoured theory are, and, second, how these might need to be refined in order to yield an answer for the case of psychopaths.

It is worth noting at this point that the majority of philosophical work on responsibility makes no attempt to offer anything like a comprehensive answer to the questions canvassed above.[11] The very long-running debate about the compatibility or otherwise of free will with determinism, or of a lack of free will with moral responsibility, has not required philosophers to offer a full description of the conditions of application of moral responsibility, nor a justification of the various practices associated with it. Instead, it has to a great extent been confined to questions about the metaphysics of determinism, free will and control. For example, does a lack of alternative possibilities imply a lack of control over one's actions? Or, does determinism imply a lack of alternative possibilities? The aim of the game is to show either that determinism implies that nobody is morally responsible, or else to escape this charge. Thus, the debate is generally

---

[9] Aristotle (1985), 1109b.   [10] Ibid., 1110a. 1–2.

[11] A notable exception is the mid-twentieth-century attempt to explain moral responsibility in utilitarian terms (Brandt (1969), Smart (1969)), according to which responsibility ascriptions are justified by their tendency to produce good outcomes. However, this attempt ultimately fails due to the availability of copious counter-examples in which apparently justified responsibility ascriptions do not lead to good outcomes, or in which apparently unjustified responsibility ascriptions *do* lead to good outcomes.

confined to the *control* condition of moral responsibility – if we can be shown to be in control, in a way that is compatible with determinism, then it follows that our practices of holding people morally responsible escape the very specific charge from determinism, and it is not necessary to look for a more general account of why control (or knowledge, or any other condition) is important in the first place, or of how our practices as a whole might be justified.

Nonetheless, there is a strand within the philosophy of responsibility which, while it too was originally motivated by the need to argue against incompatibilism, has offered a more complete account of what moral responsibility actually is: why it is justified and how it should be applied. In my view this strand of work, which begins with discussion of the 'reactive attitudes' before being refined into a discussion of responsibility in terms of responsiveness to reasons, has broadly got the answers to these questions right. In the remainder of this chapter, I will briefly introduce these ideas before offering my own version of the view in question.

1.7   The Reactive Attitudes

As I have already noted, it is not only the attitudes of praise and blame, and the practices of reward and punishment, that are closely linked to judgements of moral responsibility. There are also a range of emotional attitudes that only seem appropriate if we think of the people at whom they are directed as morally responsible. The strand in philosophy in which these attitudes are taken seriously when talking about moral responsibility begins with P. F. Strawson's 1962 lecture, 'Freedom and Resentment'.[12] This lecture is rich and provocative, and Strawson's argument in it is complex and open to interpretation. Broadly, however, the argument proceeds like this.

Holding people morally responsible, as Strawson rightly points out, is not a simple, unitary practice, but is inherent in a complex, variable set of attitudes which include praise and blame, but also resentment, gratitude, forgiveness, love and hurt feelings, as well as self-directed attitudes such as pride, guilt and shame. These attitudes, which Strawson calls the 'reactive attitudes', are 'something we are given with the fact of human society',[13] and as such are a basic, inescapable part of our nature, though we are capable of withholding them towards specific kinds of people, or in specific circumstances. We do this withholding, first, when actions have been

---

[12] Strawson (2008).   [13] Ibid., p. 25.

performed through ignorance, compulsion, lack of choice and so on. In such circumstances, we do not 'view the agent as one in respect of whom these attitudes are in any way inappropriate'.[14] Rather, we view the specific action as one in reaction to which such attitudes held towards the agent would be inappropriate. Second, we sometimes do withhold reactive attitudes towards the agent as a whole, but only in unusual circumstances, such as when they are under abnormal stress, or under hypnotic suggestion, and are temporarily 'not themselves' in some way, or because they are abnormal in a relevant way (e.g. mentally ill or a child). Finally, we are able to withhold the reactive attitudes voluntarily and temporarily towards someone, 'as a refuge, say, from the strains of involvement; or as an aid to policy; or simply out of intellectual curiosity',[15] and not because of any fact about the person who is the object of the attitudes, or because of any fact about any action which they have performed.

Having set out these three categories of situation in which we are capable of suspending the reactive attitudes, Strawson goes on to claim that no thesis which applies to people indiscriminately – including the thesis which states that moral responsibility is incompatible with causal determinism (the incompatibilist thesis) – either could or should lead us to withhold reactive attitudes in any of these ways. The incompatibilist thesis could not imply that all human interactions would fall into the first category (ignorance, compulsion, lack of choice, etc.) because we ought to be looking for a justification for suspending reactive attitudes towards the agent, not towards the act. Nor could any thesis (including the incompatibilist thesis) ever show that all people are always 'not themselves', or that all agents, at all times, are abnormal (the second category). This leaves only the voluntary suspension of reactive attitudes, which Strawson believes is 'practically inconceivable'[16] as a long-term, general strategy, because of the strain of withholding reactive attitudes in this way, and the way in which attempting to do so would impoverish our lives. Further to this, although Strawson's overall approach is in some sense to eschew discussion of the rationality of responsibility attributions – he claims that the full set of reactive attitudes 'as a whole . . . neither calls for, nor permits, an external "rational" justification'[17] – he apparently does believe that it is rational to hold the reactive attitudes in broadly the circumstances in which it is natural to do so. It could not be rational, according to Strawson, to behave in a way that is so unnatural as to be practically impossible and which, were we to attempt it, would impoverish our interpersonal relationships to the

[14] Ibid., p. 8.   [15] Ibid., p. 10.   [16] Ibid., p. 12.   [17] Ibid., p. 25.

point where they would become unbearable: 'we could choose rationally only in the light of an assessment of the gains and losses to human life, its enrichment or impoverishment; and the truth or falsity of a general thesis of determinism would not bear on the rationality of this choice'.[18]

What does Strawson have to say about the question of when the reactive attitudes are natural, or appropriate, and when they are not? Strawson begins the part of the essay that deals with this question by talking about the types of situation in which we typically withhold reactive attitudes, describing categories of cases in which this usually occurs. The categories that Strawson gives are, I think, open to question. Strawson writes in terms of a distinction between withholding reactive attitudes towards the *act*, and towards the *person*, and includes cases of mental illness in the second category. This is similar to the distinction made by Nicole Vincent between 'capacity responsibility' and what I have called moral responsibility. I noted earlier that this distinction is not a simple one, and it is not entirely clear what to make of Strawson's reading of this. Strawson presumably cannot, for example, mean that suspending reactive attitudes towards the person involves suspending those attitudes in relation to every act by that person, because this is rarely what happens in the types of case described. It is only in very extreme cases of mental illness, for example, that we suspend *all* reactive attitudes in this way. Surely, in most cases, we suspend reactive attitudes towards the mentally ill person only with regard to those actions which we can attribute to the mental illness in some way. To adapt the example I used earlier, if someone suffers from paranoid delusions, it would not be appropriate to resent their insulting me if I know that one of their delusions is that I am a persecutor. On the other hand, if none of their delusions applies to me at all, I might have a different attitude. They might simply not like me, and if so, I might be justified in resenting them. How, in general, would one go about deciding whether to take personally an insult from someone with a psychological or neurological disorder? One might look for evidence that their insult was caused by some delusion that denied them full knowledge or control of what they were doing (e.g. they are paranoid and thought they were insulting their nemesis; in fact, they were insulting their friend). Alternatively, one might look for evidence that they lack control over their actions in some relevant way (e.g. they have a form of Tourette's syndrome which manifests in coprolalia – the condition which causes compulsive swearing). Either way, we would be looking at conditions relevant to the *act*, and not the person

---

[18] Ibid., p. 14.

generally. The capacities of the person are only relevant insofar as they bear on the person's responsibility for the act.

Strawson's general explanation of when and why we hold some people responsible for some actions, though, is that we do so when the actions in question are expressive of 'goodwill, its absence or its opposite', and we do not when they are not:

> If someone treads on my hand accidentally, while trying to help me, the pain may be no less acute than if he treads on it in contemptuous disregard of my existence or with a malevolent wish to injure me. But I shall generally feel in the second case a kind and degree of resentment that I shall not feel in the first. If someone's actions help me to some benefit I desire, then I am benefited in any case; but if he intended them so to benefit me because of his general goodwill towards me, I shall reasonably feel a gratitude which I should not feel at all if the benefit was an incidental consequence, unintended or even regretted by him, of some plan of action with a different aim.[19]

In other words, part of what separates those actions that are appropriate targets of reactive attitudes from those that are not is that the actions in question are expressive of some quality of will on the part of the agent: either goodwill, ill will or an absence of the ordinary level of regard that we demand from people as part of normal human relationships.

One advantage of this suggestion is that it provides a ready explanation for why we hold people morally responsible not only for actions, but also for emotions and attitudes. Goodwill and ill will are themselves attitudes, and other attitudes can be partly constituted by goodwill or ill will. Emotions too can be expressive of attitudes towards others. For example, we might think it praiseworthy that Patti frequently feels compassion for her friends when they are undergoing some hardship or other, implying that she is morally responsible for her emotion, because it is expressive of a general attitude of goodwill towards her friends. In general, for the majority of cases, it seems to me that Strawson's appeal to goodwill and ill will provides a very plausible explanation of why responsibility ascriptions are sometimes justified, sometimes not.

However, it is interesting to note that consideration of how this would apply to psychopaths calls into question the intuition upon which the appeal to qualities of will is based. The problem is that in the vast majority of cases, we can assume that the person in question is perfectly capable of understanding that other people are *due* some degree of goodwill, or at least

---

[19] Ibid., p. 6.

an absence of ill will. Because of this, it makes intuitive sense to hold them morally responsible when they fail to exhibit this quality of will. However, it is not at all clear that psychopaths have the same understanding. In turn, it is not at all clear that they can be held morally responsible when they fail to exhibit those qualities of will. Again, what seems like a solid intuition in the vast majority of cases becomes harder to discern when applied to psychopaths.

1.8   Responsiveness to Reasons

Beginning after Strawson, and partly inspired by Strawson, there have been several attempts to elucidate moral responsibility in terms of the ability to recognise and respond to reasons. My own view is of this kind, and builds on that of R. Jay Wallace, which seems to me to be the most plausible of the responsiveness to reasons views, and the most powerful in terms of its ability to explain and justify our attitudes and practices which imply responsibility ascriptions. In what follows, I will draw on Wallace's account in order to explain my own.

The central insight of the responsiveness to reasons approach is that for an agent to be morally responsible is for them to be able to grasp, respond to, and control their behaviour in the light of certain kinds of reason. Why are we justified in holding someone responsible – in adopting one of the reactive attitudes to them, or in believing some kind of sanction would be appropriate, say – when they exhibit this ability? Wallace's contention, with which I agree, is that we should be looking for a normative answer to this question: specifically, we should be looking for whatever conditions make it *fair* to adopt these attitudes towards them. Now, it cannot be fair to expect someone to act in line with a set of reasons unless they can, first, recognise that those reasons exist, and, second, control their behaviour in such a way that ensures that they do act in line with those reasons. The conditions that one must fulfil in order to be morally responsible, there-fore, are 'the powers of reflective self-control: (1) the power to grasp and apply moral reasons, and (2) the power to control and regulate [one's] behaviour by the light of such reasons'.[20]

These conditions can make sense of the typical cases in which we hold someone responsible for acting in a way in which we are justified in expecting them *not* to act, that is, cases in which they act against an obligation that they have. In such cases, the obligation supplies reasons

[20] Wallace (1994), p. 157.

for them not to act in such a way that breaches the obligation. If they are aware of and understand those reasons, and are capable of controlling their actions to avoid acting against them, and yet they act against them anyway, then we are justified in holding them responsible for doing so.

The powers of reflective self-control can also make sense of omissions – cases where someone has apparently broken an obligation not by performing a certain action, but by *not* performing a certain action which they had an obligation to perform. In such cases, the agent has failed to act in conformity with a genuine reason which they had, which they knew about and were capable of understanding, and which they could have controlled their behaviour to fulfil.

We also, of course, hold people morally responsible for *good* acts, and for refraining from acting badly. In some cases, good acts are simply those acts which the agent was obliged to perform. In these cases, the agent acts in conformity with reasons which are generated by the obligation in question. As long as they knew what they were doing – knew about and understood the reasons in conformity with which they were acting – and were in control of their actions, then any attitudes or practices (praise, for example, although of course praise is not always appropriate for the fulfilment of an obligation) are justified. (Conversely, we can imagine a case in which the agent acts in conformity with the reasons generated by their obligations, but not because they are aware of them and able to control their actions to conform with them, but only, as it were, by sheer luck. In such cases we would, I take it, not hold them morally responsible for doing so, or believe them to be an apt target for any attitudes and practices which would imply them being morally responsible.) In the case where the agent refrains from acting badly, the agent is obliged, and therefore has reason, not to act in a certain way, and indeed does not act in that way, again justifying those attitudes and practices directed at the agent which rely on moral responsibility and which are otherwise appropriate and justified.

Responsibility for supererogatory acts, too, can be explained through this general schema. In these cases, the agent has no obligation to act in the way they do, but we nonetheless think their act is morally worthy, and we hold them responsible for it if they are aware of and understand, and can control their actions in conformity with, the reasons that speak in favour of the supererogatory act. These reasons are not generated by any obligation, but nonetheless must exist in any case in which the agent is to be held responsible for such an act.

A type of case which perhaps puts pressure on the responsiveness to reasons account is the type in which an outcome is predictable but not intended. Imagine, for example, a purely selfish entrepreneur who starts a business solely in order to enrich themself. If they could have generated a significant profit as a sole trader, they would have done so. However, they find that their business will be much more profitable if they take on a few employees. As a result, though this was not their intention, they create several jobs that are beneficial to those they employ. Are they morally responsible for bringing these benefits to the people in question? My own intuition is that they are, and the fact that they are can be explained by the (presumed) fact that they have the powers of reflective self-control with regard to the reasons which bear on their choice, and they act in conformity with those reasons, even if they are not motivated by them. Moral responsibility for a morally worthy act, therefore, would appear to depend on being responsive to the specific reasons that are generated by that act – the considerations that make it morally worthy – even if it does not require that those reasons actually influence the agent.[21]

There is a possible confusion raised by the kinds of cases I have been discussing, which it will be helpful to clear up here. As we saw, Wallace's description of responsiveness to reasons as a condition of moral responsibility has it consisting in 'the powers of reflective self-control: (1) the power to grasp and apply moral reasons, and (2) the power to control and regulate [one's] behaviour by the light of such reasons'.[22] Yet the agent need not lack a *general* rational power of this kind in order to lack moral responsibility for a specific act. For example, in the 'vase' cases, the relevant question is whether I was able to control the specific movement of my body which resulted in the vase being broken. Similarly, one could imagine a case in which I am non-culpably ignorant in a way that excuses my smashing the vase: perhaps due to some comedy of errors, I came to believe that you *wanted* me to smash the vase (let us call this case Vase 6). In that case, I would not be suffering from some general inability to grasp that I had reasons not to destroy other people's property; I would simply be ignorant regarding the particular reasons applying to this specific case.

Thus, the aspect of the global condition of responsiveness to reasons which has to do with knowledge or understanding – the 'ability to grasp

[21] However, see Knobe (2003a and 2003b) for a discussion of how cases like this put pressure on our intuitions about moral responsibility. I should note also that this discussion assumes that one's reasons are, broadly, the facts that bear on one's choices, as opposed to what one *takes* to be the facts that bear on one's choices. Thus, one can believe oneself to have reasons that one does not in fact have, and one can be unaware of reasons that one does have. This view, which I endorse, is subject to some controversy, but defending it would require a lengthy diversion for which I do not have the space. For an opposing view, see Gibbons (2010).
[22] Wallace (1994), p. 157.

and apply' reasons – is continuous with local examples of ignorance or lack of understanding in cases such as Vase 6. The reasons which I cannot 'grasp and apply' might be highly specific to the case in question. Moreover, even in cases where I lack a global power to grasp and apply reasons, it is the specific reasons in specific cases which matter, from the point of view of determining moral responsibility. A general inability to 'grasp and apply' reasons is excusing because it renders the agent non-culpably ignorant of the reasons that bear on individual choices that they make.

Something similar applies in cases in which someone's moral responsibility or otherwise depends on whether they have control of their actions in the case. This includes cases of coercion and of involuntary movement. For example, in the variation of the 'vase' case in which you push me into the vase, I am not morally responsible for breaking the vase because I am not in control of the action which leads to the vase being broken. More generally, someone who lacks control over their bodily movements (say because they suffer from a neurological condition involving violent 'tics') might lack moral responsibility for a broad range of things resulting from those movements. But what matters from the point of view of determining whether that person was responsible for smashing the vase is whether they were in control of specifically those movements which resulted in the vase being smashed.

Both the 'knowledge' and 'control' conditions of moral responsibility, then, can apply either to specific actions, or generally to an agent in a way which renders that agent morally responsible (or not) for a broad range of actions, and the agent's position with respect to the reasons that bear on their actions is what makes the difference between responsibility and non-responsibility. The agent is either in a position to engage with these reasons in their actions or they are not, because of conditions that apply either specifically to the case in question or generally across a range of cases. Wallace's formulation of responsiveness to reasons has to do with 'general rational powers', and so is focused on the latter conditions. However, given that the former conditions also have to do with whether the agent *can respond to* the reasons that bear on their choice, I see no reason not to refer to these conditions also in terms of responsiveness to reasons. Therefore, I will use the term to refer to both types of condition in this thesis, distinguishing when necessary between *global* responsiveness to reasons and *local* responsiveness to reasons.[23]

---

[23] The use of the word 'global' should not be taken to imply that someone lacking one of these conditions must be unresponsive to *all reasons*. Clearly, it is possible for an agent to possess general qualities which make one unable either to recognise or to control one's behaviour in the light of some reasons or kinds of reason, but not others. Indeed this is precisely my conclusion in this book.

The idea of 'culpable ignorance' mentioned above would also bear some exploration. When one acts from ignorance, but one ought not to be ignorant, is one morally responsible only for being ignorant, or also for the act that was done from ignorance? Wallace states that excuses arising from ignorance 'may not be accepted at all if the ignorance that makes what one did unintentional is itself culpable'.[24] However, this turns out not to be a complete description of what he has in mind:

> In that case it will be taken not for a valid excuse, but for evidence of one of a different family of moral faults that includes negligence, carelessness, forgetfulness, and recklessness. Thus, if [on the way to the refrigerator, I tread on the hand of] a baby I am supposed to be looking after, then I am presumably under an obligation to keep track of where the child is and what he is up to, and so my ignorance that I would be treading on the child's hand by going to the refrigerator would not excuse my treading on his hand. More precisely: it might excuse me from responsibility for directly treading on the child's hand, but only by making me vulnerable to the different charge of negligence, which led to the hand's being damaged.[25]

However, it seems to me that Wallace's first description of the case is actually more accurate than that following the phrase 'more precisely'. Surely in this case, I am indeed morally responsible for treading on the child's hand, and not just for the negligence which led to my treading on his hand. The fact that I have a specific responsibility to look after the baby in this case means that, although I may not be aware of the presence of the baby's hand, and the reason this supplies which bears on my choice to put my foot there, I *can reasonably be expected* to be aware of this. We are, it seems, morally responsible for failing to act on those reasons, and only those reasons, of which we can reasonably be expected to be aware. (This result has implications for my broader project, since to show that psychopaths are not morally responsible for failing to act on a certain class of reasons will involve showing, not just that they are unaware of these reasons, but also that they cannot reasonably be expected to be aware of them.)

One important implication of the responsiveness to reasons account is that one can be responsible for some consequences of one's actions, and not for others, depending on what particular reasons bearing on that act one is responsive to. In fact, one can be responsible for an act construed in one way and not for the same act construed in another. Imagine a slapdash chef serves undercooked seafood to a number of different customers. Unknown

---

[24] Wallace (1994), p. 138.   [25] Ibid.

to them, one of their customers is a terrorist, who is planning the next day to carry out a number of murders. As a result of the slapdash chef's undercooking the seafood, all of the customers are incapacitated with severe food poisoning, and the terrorist's murders do not go ahead. In this case, the chef is morally responsible for harming their customers, because they can reasonably be expected to be aware of the reasons that speak against harming customers, and are capable of controlling their actions in conformity with those reasons. Similarly, they are morally responsible for harming and incapacitating the terrorist. They are not, however, morally responsible for preventing the murders since, not knowing that their customer is a terrorist, they are not aware – and cannot be expected to be aware – of the reasons bearing on this (preventing the murders) as a construal of his actions in serving undercooked seafood to this particular customer.

In my modified, 'neo-Wallacean' version of the responsiveness to reasons view, being morally responsible for an act is a matter of being responsive (globally and locally) to the reasons that bear on that act. This account allows us to see why qualities of will are important indicators of moral responsibility. If we are unable to control our behaviour in the light of the reasons that bear on an act, then we have not exercised the kind of choice to perform that act that would demonstrate a quality of will, either good or bad, or the absence of a quality of will that was rightly expected of us. However, in some cases (the selfish entrepreneur is an example), I would be able to exhibit the powers of reflective self-control in the choice without having a relevant quality of will, or lacking a quality of will that was expected of me. Thus, the link between moral responsibility and qualities of will is indirect and defeasible. We would expect qualities of will to figure in very many cases of moral responsibility, but not in all, and indeed this is what consideration of cases reveals.

For convenience, I have so far in this section been talking about moral responsibility for actions, but it is worth noting that the responsiveness to reasons account can also make sense of the other things for which I argued, in Section 1.4, that we can be morally responsible, namely, states of affairs, attitudes, emotions and beliefs. There are reasons that speak in favour of or against our bringing about states of affairs, having certain attitudes and emotions, and holding certain beliefs. For each of these, responsiveness to reasons represents a plausible way of distinguishing between cases where we are or are not morally responsible, in the same way as for actions. So, to develop the three cases I outlined when discussing this issue earlier:

(1)   If Stephen knows Johnny well, he is responsive to facts about Johnny's character, which generate reasons which bear on Stephen's choice about whether or not to take him for a fool. If he does not know Johnny, then he is responsive to reasons that bear generally on the choice one has to take someone for a fool when one does not know the person in question. If, however, he has (through no fault of his own) mistaken Johnny for someone else who *is* a fool, then he is responsive to none of these reasons – to the reasons that bear on this particular case.

(2)   If Dave has burned Ray's favourite hat, and Ray knows about it, then Ray is responsive to the reasons that speak in favour of his being angry with Dave. The same is true if Dave has not burned the hat or done anything to incur Ray's wrath, and Ray is well aware of the situation. However, if Pete has burned Ray's hat, and created a plausible situation in which it looks as though Dave burned it, then Ray is not responsive to the actual reasons for and against anger directed at particular people with regard to the burned hat.

(3)   If Chris's racist beliefs are simply the result of his own irrational hatred and prejudice, then he is responsive to the reasons that bear on whether one should hold such beliefs. If, however, he has been brought up in a very isolated community, fed propaganda about the supposed inferiority of some races and not been exposed either to any real members of those races or to any opposing views, then he is not responsive – because he cannot reasonably be expected to respond – to the relevant reasons and is therefore (plausibly) not morally responsible for holding beliefs that are contradicted by those reasons.

The idea of responsiveness to reasons offers what I think is the best analysis of how we, as a matter of fact, naturally and instinctively arrive at ascriptions of responsibility. This is why it gives the most intuitively plausible results in the range of cases I have been discussing. It is the best analysis of what we mean when we say that someone *is* morally responsible for something, which is distinct from their being blameworthy or praiseworthy, but also from that thing's merely being attributable to them as an agent, since there are many cases in which an act, say, is attributable to someone as an agent, without their being responsive to the reasons that bear on that act. Vase 5 would plausibly be an example of this. In this case, the act of breaking the vase is an act which is attributable to me as an agent, and I am aware of the reasons which bear on that act, including the fact that it is your vase and an expensive one. However, I did not in this instance have the power to regulate my behaviour by the light of these reasons, and therefore I lack local responsiveness to reasons in regards to the act of breaking the vase.

The responsiveness to reasons account shows how the distinction between those who are morally responsible and those who are not is related to the question of what we hold people responsible *for*. We hold people responsible either for acting on (or holding beliefs based on, etc.), or for failing to act on (or to hold beliefs based on, etc.) reasons of which they can be expected to be aware, and to which they can be expected to control their actions (beliefs) in response. If we do not hold someone responsible for failing to respond to a particular reason or set of reasons in this way, it is because they could not reasonably be expected to respond to that particular reason or set of reasons, either because of local conditions in the case, or because they are not globally responsive to a set of reasons that includes this particular set of reasons.

Building on this, the responsiveness to reasons account also provides what Strawson's account alone cannot provide: not simply a justification for targeting the practices and attitudes involved in holding people responsible wherever happens to be natural, but a justification for targeting them precisely where we do naturally target them. If holding people responsible implies believing them to be responsive to reasons, then when we hold someone responsible who is not responsive to reasons, we are being irrational, and we are treating them unfairly (assuming we are aware, or should be aware, of the fact that they are not responsive to reasons). But when we hold them responsible and they *are* responsive, the attitudes we hold, and the practices we engage in, have the chance of being justified, assuming they are themselves sensitive to the relevant set of reasons arising from whatever the person at whom they are directed has done.

Let us explore how this works for the reactive attitudes, using anger as an example. If A is morally responsible for φ-ing, an action which they had an obligation not to perform, then B may be justified in being angry with A for A's φ-ing, assuming B is in a position to be angry with anyone for φ-ing. This is because A either was, or should have been, aware of the reasons arising from their obligation not to φ. It is fair to expect A to take proper account of reasons arising from obligations which they genuinely have, if they are responsive to those reasons, and anger can be partly a matter of believing someone not to have taken proper account of reasons arising from their obligations. (That anger has cognitive content is a controversial idea, but it is one with which I agree and for which I will argue in Chapter 4.) Thus, particular reactive attitudes can be justified in the sense that the beliefs upon which they depend are justified beliefs, and part of what makes them justified beliefs is the fact that the person concerned is responsive to the reasons that bear on whatever it is about that person that is prompting the reactive attitude (i.e. they are morally responsible for it).

A similar story can be told about practices that depend upon responsibility ascriptions. So, for example, having justification for punishing someone for a crime may depend on having a justified belief that they are morally responsible for that crime. Whatever it is that justifies punishment (and there are of course conflicting accounts of this), the reasons justifying punishment of the individual will be related to the reasons to which the person must be responsive if they are morally responsible. If they did not have the powers of reflective control in regards to the crime, then punishing them is unjustified because the reasons that would normally justify punishment do not apply.

In short, the justification for each case of performing a practice or holding an attitude which is involved in holding people responsible is to be found in that particular practice or attitude, and is sensitive, in the right kind of way, to considerations about the person whom one is holding responsible, and whatever it is one is holding them responsible for. Strawson's point about the psychological strain and impoverishment of relationships which would result from abandoning the reactive attitudes is a plausible additional justification of them taken as a whole, but this is not the whole justification. The refinement offered by the responsiveness to reasons approach is therefore an improvement on Strawson's account.

1.9   Conclusions

In the latter part of this chapter, I have set out a 'neo-Wallacean' account of moral responsibility as consisting in the ability to recognise and understand reasons, and to control one's behaviour in conformity with those reasons.

The particular consequence of the account I have endorsed, which is relevant to the central argument of this book, is that someone cannot be held morally responsible for failing to act on reasons which they are incapable of recognising as reasons. As I have argued, to be morally responsible for an action, it must be the case that one can reasonably be expected to recognise those reasons. Whatever makes it the case that one can reasonably be expected to recognise a reason, one condition must surely be that one is capable of recognising that reason or, if not, that the conditions which make it the case that one cannot recognise the reason are not themselves within one's control. This second condition excludes cases where someone has, either intentionally or through negligence, brought it about that they are incapable of recognising an important reason – for example, I have blindfolded myself while driving my car and, as a result, cannot see the child in the road or recognise that I have a reason to apply the brakes. As we will see in later chapters, this is relevant to the case of psychopaths because, if psychopaths are to be judged non-responsible, the conditions which lead to their unresponsiveness to reasons must not be under their control in an analogous way.

I will go on to argue that psychopaths are indeed unresponsive to a particular class of reasons in a way that renders them not morally responsible for failing to act on those reasons. However, before we can see why this is, we first need to have a good understanding of what is unusual about psychopaths, and particularly of what it is about them that might lead us to doubt that they are morally responsible for the normal range of actions. Developing this understanding is the aim of Chapter 2.

CHAPTER 2

Psychopathy

2.1 Introduction

In the Introduction, I gave a very brief sketch of the psychopathic personality type, incorporating such features as remorselessness, cunning and selfishness. The function of this chapter is to flesh out this picture. In doing so, I will draw on literature from psychology, psychiatry and neuroscience. Some of these areas of study are better developed than others, and as with most scientific fields there are controversies about some central questions. It will not therefore be possible to give definitive answers to most of the questions which we would want to ask about psychopaths. However, it seems clear that an enquiry about the moral responsibility of psychopaths, a category of person which exists in reality, should be informed by empirical evidence as far as possible, and to this end I will present my own interpretation of the evidence as it stands.

2.2 Diagnosis

The serious study of the phenomenon of psychopathy as it is now understood begins with the psychiatrist Harvey Cleckley's seminal 1941 study, *The Mask of Sanity: An Attempt to Clarify Some Issues about the So-Called Psychopathic Personality.*[1] Prior to this, in the nineteenth and early twentieth centuries, there had been a number of attempts to describe those psychological conditions that were associated neither with delusions of any kind nor with intellectual impairment, and yet which affected the subject's social functioning. Indeed, the term 'psychopath' was originally intended to cover *all* members of this very broad category, which is why the word's etymological meaning is so vague: literally, 'psychopath' means nothing more specific than 'diseased mind'. Other terms, including the

[1] Cleckley (1941).

36

'moral insanity' generally thought to have been coined by James Cowles Prichard,[2] and the 'moral imbecility' favoured by Henry Maudsley[3] and Havelock Ellis,[4] are slightly more specific, but still include a much greater variety of phenomena than would now be categorised as psychopathic. Prichard's concept of moral insanity, for example, included mental conditions that would today be classed as depressive or bipolar.[5]

Cleckley, a practising psychiatrist who had worked in an asylum for many years before writing his book, used the term 'psychopath', apparently derived from 'the vernacular of the ward or the staff room',[6] to refer to a class of psychiatric patients who, having been committed to the asylum because of a clear inability to function within society – manifesting in a series of typically petty and impulsive criminal acts – failed to show any evidence of psychosis or neurosis once admitted. These patients, though apparently lucid and rational, had failed 'to translate [their] apparent rationality into the successful conduct of life'.[7] Cleckley combined detailed case studies of thirteen such patients, with a careful description and analysis of what he saw as the common condition which afflicted them. He characterised this condition as a 'pathologic general devaluation of life, a complex deficiency, confusion, or malfunction in what chooses aims and directs impulse',[8] and coined the term 'semantic disorder' to refer to the absence of *meaning* he perceived in the worldview of his patients.

Stemming from the 'general devaluation', Cleckley identified a number of observations about psychopathic lifestyle and personality, which were later adopted by R. D. Hare as the basis of his Psychopathy Checklist (PCL) and its later revised version (PCL-R).[9] Since this checklist is the central diagnostic tool for psychopathy, and can therefore be taken to define the concept of psychopathy as it is applied in clinical contexts, it is worth reproducing it in full here (Table 2.1).

The checklist is applied by clinicians on the basis of file information and – usually – a semi-structured interview with the subject.[10] The subject is given a score of 0, 1 or 2 against each of the 20 items, reflecting the extent to which he

---

[2] Pritchard (1835).   [3] Maudsley (1873), Maudsley (1874).   [4] Ellis (1890).
[5] A very helpful discussion of the diagnostic history of psychopathy and similar conditions is provided by Ward (2010).
[6] Cleckley (1941), p. 20.   [7] Ward (2010), p. 21.   [8] Cleckley (1941), p. 172.
[9] Hare's construct of psychopathy is generally thought to have 'drifted' somewhat from Cleckley's description. Hare and Neumann (2008) are happy to accept this claim, noting among other factors the relatively small sample size of Cleckley's work compared to Hare's own. Nonetheless, Hare's PCL-R retains significant similarity to the phenomenon described by Cleckley.
[10] According to Hare (1998), 'the PCL-R can be scored on the basis of file information alone, provided that the material contained in the files is extensive and detailed, and that the rater acknowledges the limitations of the procedure'.

Table 2.1 *The Hare Psychopathy Checklist, Revised Version (PCL-R)*[11]

Factor 1	
Interpersonal	**Affective**
1. Glibness/superficial charm	6. Lack of remorse or guilt
2. Grandiose sense of self-worth	7. Shallow affect (genuine emotion is short-lived and egocentric)
4. Pathological lying	8. Callousness; lack of empathy
5. Conning/manipulative	16. Failure to accept responsibility for own actions

Factor 2	
Lifestyle	**Antisocial**
3. Need for stimulation/proneness to boredom	10. Poor behaviour controls
9. Parasitic lifestyle	12. Early behaviour problems
13. Lack of realistic/long-term goals	18. Juvenile delinquency
14. Impulsivity	19. Revocation of conditional release
15. Irresponsibility	20. Criminal versatility

No factor	
11. Promiscuous sexual behaviour	17. Many short-term marital relationships

or she demonstrates the given trait. A score of 30 or more overall (out of a possible 40) is typically used as the cut-off point for a diagnosis of full-fledged psychopathy.

It is notable that, while many of the items in the PCL-R are directly observable facts about the subject's lifestyle and behaviour (e.g. 'juvenile delinquency' and 'promiscuous sexual behaviour'), others refer to personality traits which must be inferred by the person applying the checklist (e.g. 'callousness, lack of empathy', and 'grandiose sense of self-worth'). The apparent element of subjective judgement introduced by this aspect of the PCL-R worried the compilers of the American Psychiatric Association's Diagnostic and Statistical Manual (DSM), which is currently in its fifth edition (DSM-V).[12] This manual, which is the global standard diagnostic tool for psychiatrists, stipulates that classification in psychiatry should not

[11] Ibid. and Gacono (2005). This table shows the four factors forming the structure of the current clinical version of the checklist, but also shows how these factors relate to the two factors of Hare's original construct. The numbering is that given to the twenty items in the checklist as used in clinical settings.
[12] American Psychiatric Association (2013).

include reference to underlying causes or inferred psychological traits. For this reason, the DSM's compilers did not adopt Hare's construct, replacing it instead with 'Antisocial Personality Disorder' (APD), which is applied on the basis of observed behaviour only. As Minzenberg and Siever note, DSM 'criteria for APD consist almost exclusively of behavioural indicators, neglecting the affective-interpersonal features that appear to reflect much of the notion of a distinct personality type as described by Cleckley'.[13] Though the DSM states that APD 'has also been referred to as psychopathy, sociopathy, or dissocial personality disorder',[14] it is clear that Hare's construct of psychopathy and APD are not the same thing. Importantly, APD bears significant relation to Factor 2 of PCL-R, as opposed to Factor 1.[15] The emphasis on quantifiable behavioural tendencies has had the effect of creating a new construct that shares many of the elements of psychopathy, but favours those of the lifestyle/antisocial type over those of the interpersonal/affective type. Given the similarities and differences between the two constructs, APD is often seen as a rival to PCL-R.

I will take the PCL-R diagnosis to be the central one. This decision is partly based on including three interrelated worries about the usefulness of APD as a construct in grounding judgements of responsibility. First, since the question of responsibility will depend on judgements about the psychological make-up of individuals – about their rational and emotional deficits and so on, a diagnosis which makes explicit reference to these psychological features is likely to provide a stronger ground for such judgements, and APD does not make such reference. Second, PCL-R has been proven to be a better predictor of behaviour, including criminal recidivism,[16] than APD. In addition, APD applies to a much wider class of people than PCL-R. For example, according to some studies, the majority of prison inmates have APD,[17] whereas considerably fewer of them have been diagnosed with PCL-R.[18] In civil populations too, there is 'a prevalence of APD ... that is at least three times the prevalence of psychopathy (based on the PCL-R and PCL)'.[19] Together, these facts suggest that PCL-R picks out a much more tightly defined set of personality traits, whereas the antisocial behaviour of those diagnosed with APD may have its roots in more disparate aspects of personality, or in environmental or social factors. Though there will be considerable variation even within the PCL-R diagnosis of psychopathy, the more closely related the

---

[13] Minzenberg and Siever (2006), p. 251.   [14] American Psychiatric Association (2013), p. 645.
[15] Hare and Neumann (2010).   [16] Hemphill et al. (1998).   [17] Hare (1995), p. 25.
[18] Around 20% according to Hare (1995), p. 87, though there were only around 7.7% of male prisoners and 1.9% of female prisoners in the sample of Coid et al. (2009).
[19] Hare and Neumann (2010), p. 131.

individuals picked out by that diagnosis, the more likely are judgements of responsibility to apply to a greater number of those individuals. Third, there is reason to question whether a diagnosis of APD truly functions as an *explanation* of behaviour in the same way that a PCL-R diagnosis of psychopathy does. Indeed, since the diagnosis of APD is based entirely on observed behaviour, and the diagnosis does not include inferred personality traits, it is difficult to see how a person having APD can explain their behaviour in a non-circular way. Discussions of attenuated responsibility owing to mental disorders often use the language of explanation (e.g. 'he killed her because he's a schizophrenic'). If this option is not available in the case of APD, a discussion about responsibility may have trouble getting off the ground. Interestingly, this relates to Barbara Wootton's attempt to settle the question of psychopaths' responsibility a priori that was discussed in the Introduction. It may be that the charge of circularity that Wootton brought against any attempt to prove non-responsibility on the basis of a diagnosis of psychopathy, which fails when PCL-R is used, might have more traction in the case of APD.

One final pragmatic reason for favouring PCL-R is that it is the dominant diagnostic tool used by researchers examining the psychological and neurological mechanisms underlying psychopathy. The vast majority of the literature in these fields uses PCL-R to identify research participants. This may be partly because of the worries mentioned earlier. Though PCL-R, like APD, is not immune to worries about aspects of its validity as a construct,[20] it is seen by most psychopathy researchers as the most useful diagnostic tool available.[21] It is therefore possible to build up a more detailed and nuanced picture of what is at stake using PCL-R rather than APD.

2.3 Emotional Deficiencies

It is immediately noticeable how many of the items in the PCL-R might be explained by means of specifically emotional deficiencies. A lack of remorse or guilt, shallow affect and callousness/lack of empathy all naturally fit into the category of emotional deficits. Glibness and superficial charm perhaps suggest a lack of deep emotional engagement. Many of the items which involve manipulating or generally mistreating others – pathological lying,

---

[20] See, for example, the correspondence on psychopathy and anti-social behaviour in the *British Journal of Psychiatry* 191 (2007), pp. 357–65.
[21] For example, Blair et al. (2005).

cunning/manipulative, parasitic lifestyle, criminal versatility – might be thought to be the result of an emotional lack, particularly a lack of empathy, or of fear or guilt, emotions which, it might be thought, regulate our behaviour and prevent us from harming or taking advantage of others when it might otherwise be in our interest to do so. There are also a number of aspects of lifestyle in the list, which look like the results of a general deficiency in behavioural regulation: failure to accept responsibility for one's actions, lack of realistic/long-term goals, irresponsibility, juvenile delinquency, early behaviour problems, revocation of conditional release, and many short-term marital relationships. Recent developments in neuroscience suggest that a function performed by emotions is to shape our lives by imposing checks on certain forms of behaviour, and encouraging others.[22] If this is true, then a mental condition which lacks the emotional richness of ordinary human life might plausibly be expected to result in impulsivity and poor behaviour control, which might in turn manifest in the aspects of lifestyle referred to earlier. All of this points to a disorder which is essentially emotional in character. As we will see, this suggestion is backed up by neurological evidence: the parts of the brain affected in people with psychopathy are primarily the parts involved in emotional processing.

2.4 A Distinct Condition?

If psychopathy is a construct made up of twenty separate personality and behavioural traits, one might wonder whether we are discussing a distinct condition at all. It might be that 'psychopath' is simply a word for someone who, for disparate reasons, happens to demonstrate a large number of these traits to a high degree. Indeed, it is generally accepted that psychopathic traits, in common with those associated with other personality disorders, exist on a continuum. That is, these traits are not unique to psychopaths, but are found also in the general population to a greater or lesser extent. We all know people who lack empathy, or are impulsive, or have trouble working towards long-term goals. We may indeed observe some of these traits in ourselves at times. On the other hand, it is apparently the case that psychopathic traits tend to cluster together, suggesting that they are related, or perhaps the product of an underlying cause. Interestingly, a large-scale study[23] found that all of the factors in the PCL-R construct correlate positively with a single, 'superordinate' factor, suggesting that the lower-order factors are

---

[22] See, for example, Damasio (2006).   [23] Hare and Neumann (2008).

related by a common theme, which Hare and Neumann characterise as 'the broad dissocial nature of psychopathic traits'.[24]

Perhaps the best reason for regarding psychopathy as a distinct condition is given by the promising attempts (to which I will turn shortly), to identify a neurological basis for the disorder. Antonio Damasio,[25] for example, discusses several cases where lesions to the amygdala and frontal regions of the brain have resulted in symptoms very close to those found in psychopaths. Coupled with the numerous studies showing reduced activity in these same regions in psychopaths' brains, it is plausible to suppose that (partly genetically determined) reduced *functioning* in specific brain regions, as well as that which is the result of injury, might be the *cause* of psychopathic symptoms (rather than reduced *activity* being merely a *correlate* of these symptoms). If the cluster of symptoms associated with psychopathy has a single neurological cause, or a small set of closely related causes, then it is not a mere cluster of unrelated traits arising from a random distribution.

Nonetheless, it is important to remain aware of the fact that not all psychopaths are alike, and not every psychopath will demonstrate every item in the PCL-R to a high degree. This has important consequences for the question of moral responsibility. Discussions of moral responsibility can sometimes give the impression that it is a binary concept – one is either morally responsible or one is not. However, this is probably not the case. The law recognises not just a complete *lack* of responsibility, but also *diminished* responsibility, and it is likely that this idea has an ethical parallel, so that there are degrees of moral responsibility in some cases. If I am a minor shareholder in a company that dumps hazardous waste in the sea, I am presumably not as responsible as the executive who ordered the dumping, but I am also plausibly more responsible than someone who has nothing at all to do with the company (is not aware of the dumping, and so on). It may also be the case that the degree of moral responsibility I have for an action tracks other concepts, such as my understanding of the facts, or of the reasons bearing on decisions I have made. If so, conclusions about the moral responsibility of psychopaths may not apply to all psychopaths equally. This fact will need to be borne in mind when considering arguments in the following chapters. It might be thought that psychopaths will lack responsibility *insofar as* they lack the relevant traits, with only the most 'hard-core', high-scoring psychopaths, or perhaps only those psychopaths lacking the relevant traits to a very high degree, lacking moral responsibility

---

[24] Ibid.   [25] Damasio (2006).

completely. However, we should not leap to the conclusion that degrees of responsibility will straightforwardly track degrees of possession of the relevant attributes. It might be that possession of a given attribute to *any* degree is enough of a window to allow responsibility to enter the picture.

2.5 'Successful' and 'Unsuccessful' Psychopaths

A further complication affecting the diagnosis and classification of psychopathy is the possibility that there may be distinct sub-types of the overall condition. Gao and Raine[26] and Lilienfeld et al.[27] present fascinating reviews of studies which have sought to distinguish between 'successful' and 'unsuccessful' psychopaths, and to identify differences between these two groups at the levels of psychology and neuroscience. Successful psychopaths are defined as those who have little or no history of criminal conviction and incarceration, in contrast to unsuccessful psychopaths who do have such a history. In fact, the vast majority of our evidence concerning psychopaths comes from the latter group, because of the relative ease of identifying and gaining access to psychopaths among prison populations. The problem is that, as Gao and Raine point out, 'our research knowledge based on incarcerated psychopathic offenders may not be generalisable to psychopaths in the general population'.[28]

At the time of writing, successful psychopaths are still relatively under-researched and, as Lilienfeld et al. point out, 'the amount of popular speculation devoted to successful psychopathy dwarfs the modest research base bearing on its correlates and causes'.[29] Furthermore, what research there is has reached mixed conclusions. Nonetheless, some patterns have begun to emerge. According to Gao and Raine's tentative interpretation of the studies, all psychopaths have deficits in emotional processing and emotional empathy. However, successful psychopaths may have intact (or in some cases even enhanced) information processing, fear conditioning and *cognitive* empathy (i.e. the ability correctly to identify others' emotions), correlating with intact (or enhanced) orbitofrontal cortex and amygdala function.[30] These differences are accompanied by a disposition among successful psychopaths towards white-collar crime, as opposed to blue-collar crime, and towards relational aggression, as opposed to physical aggression. Both the psychological features and the behavioural

---

[26] Gao and Raine (2010).   [27] Lilienfeld et al. (2015).   [28] Gao and Raine (2010), p. 196.
[29] Lilienfeld et al. (2015), p. 299.   [30] For example, Yang et al. (2005), Yang et al. (2011).

dispositions, plausibly, contribute to successful psychopaths' greater ability to keep themselves out of prison.

In the scientific literature, research such as that summarised by Gao and Raine has led to a debate about the classification of psychopathy, with Cooke and Mitchie[31] proposing that the behavioural (Factor 2) aspects of Hare's checklist should be considered a contingent effect of psychopathy, rather than a constitutive element of it.

For their part, Lilienfeld et al. identify three possible interpretations of the research evidence relating to successful psychopaths:

> First, the *differential-severity model* proposes that successful psychopathy is simply a mild expression of clinical psychopathy. This model presumes that psychopathy is a unitary construct and that successful and unsuccessful psychopathy differs in intensity. Second, in the *moderated-expression model*, successful psychopathy is viewed as a *forme fruste*—an atypical manifestation—of psychopathy whose less savory behavioral manifestations have been tempered by protective factors, such as intact executive functioning, intelligence, or effective parenting. This model similarly posits that psychopathy is a unitary construct, but it also assumes that successful psychopathy is associated with one or more variables (extraneous to psychopathy itself) that buffer individuals against maladaptive outcomes. Third, in what we call the *differential-configuration model*, successful psychopathy is characterized by a different constellation of personality traits, such as boldness and conscientiousness, than is unsuccessful psychopathy. In contrast to the first two models, this model presumes that psychopathy is an amalgam of two or more distinct traits rather than a unitary construct and that successful and unsuccessful psychopathy differ in their constituent traits.[32]

Summarising the research, Lilienfeld et al. find some support for the second and third interpretations, but not for the first. If their conclusions are correct, successful psychopathy is either (1) essentially the same condition as unsuccessful psychopathy, but with some of its rougher edges smoothed by the presence of other factors such as those listed, or (2) a different, but obviously closely related, condition.

It is useful to consider what the implications of these controversies might be for moral responsibility. Sifferd and Hirstein[33] argue that only unsuccessful psychopaths can be said to have reduced moral responsibility, on the grounds that successful psychopaths have unimpaired executive function and are capable of contravening moral norms intentionally. This conclusion is not unavoidable however: if, as many philosophers have

---

[31] Cooke and Michie (2001).   [32] Lilienfeld et al. (2015), p. 299.   [33] Sifferd and Hirstein (2013).

argued, the emotional deficits of psychopaths are in themselves enough to deliver a verdict of non-responsibility, then this verdict will apply equally to successful and unsuccessful psychopaths. One characteristic which is not generally thought to differ between successful and unsuccessful psychopaths is their lack of emotional empathy, as opposed to cognitive empathy.[34] If this lack of empathy is indeed shared by successful psychopaths as well as unsuccessful ones, and is the result of factors beyond their control, such as neurodevelopmental factors, then this may be enough to ground a verdict of non-responsibility. I will return to this point in Chapter 5.

2.6 Psychopathy and the Brain

Recent attempts to establish a neurobiological basis for psychopathy have proved somewhat fruitful. On the other hand, the techniques used to examine structural and functional aspects of the brain are still developing rapidly, the relationship between different regions of the brain and different psychological phenomena is only partly understood, and the business of relating personality traits to neurological phenomena is a complex one. Therefore, any conclusions drawn from neurological studies must be highly tentative. Still, it is possible to discern patterns in the results, which are worth discussing here. Overall, a picture is beginning to emerge of a neurodevelopmental disorder with a significant genetic basis, though there are probably environmental factors involved in producing its full clinical manifestation.[35]

Studies have been carried out investigating two separate aspects of the neurology of psychopaths: brain activity and brain structure. These are importantly distinct because they point towards two distinct overall types of conclusion. On the one hand, to show that psychopaths have particular patterns of activity in the brain, perhaps when performing tasks of a particular kind, is broadly to provide evidence that they are using some regions of the brain more than, or instead of, others. This might lead one tentatively to conclude, for example, that psychopaths tend not to engage their emotions as much when performing certain tasks, compared to normal agents. It says nothing about *why* this is the case. Showing that

---

[34] Gao and Raine (2010), p. 204.
[35] Gao et al. (2009). In this section, I will be relying heavily on this and another review of the neuroscientific literature: Seara-Cardoso and Viding (2014). Blair (2010) provides a further useful review of studies, focusing on those concerned with structural and functional differences, and the particular issue of instrumental versus reactive aggression.

psychopaths have differently *structured* brains, on the other hand, provides evidence that aspects of their psychology might have a particular neurological *cause*. If a psychopath's brain shows reduced volume in a region associated with a particular kind of emotional processing, then it might be possible to conclude that unusual patterns in their experiencing of the relevant kind of emotion are due to their not having the same neurological resources as normal agents. This in turn might lead them to compensate by engaging other regions of the brain when performing tasks for the completion of which normal agents would be likely to engage their emotions, which might manifest psychologically through the use, for example, of cognitive strategies rather than emotional ones. Ultimately, this may have implications for things such as understanding and value, which are interesting in relation to moral responsibility. However, it is worth reiterating that such conclusions would only be tentative given the inexactness and incompleteness of the science in this area.

Seara-Cardoso and Viding[36] reviewed studies which used functional magnetic resonance imaging (fMRI) technology to assess whether psychopaths (diagnosed using PCL-R) showed decreased activity in specific areas in the brain correlating with their performance of specific tasks, split into three groups: tasks designed to stimulate emotional processing in general, tasks designed to provoke empathy and moral judgement tasks.

Turning to the basic emotional processing studies first, Seara-Cardoso and Viding reviewed studies that involved different tasks: tasks involving passively observing photographs designed to stimulate particular emotional responses;[37] memory tasks involving remembering words that have either a neutral or a negative emotional valence;[38] tasks involving the recognition of faces that have either an emotionally neutral or emotionally aroused expression[39] and tasks involving passively observing faces, again with expressions that are either emotionally neutral or emotionally aroused.[40] The studies primarily examined brain regions associated with emotional processing, including the amygdala, the anterior insula and various portions of the prefrontal cortex. They found that psychopaths showed consistently less activity in these brain regions when performing these tasks, compared with non-psychopathic controls.

The studies designed to find neural correlates to empathy-based tasks again used a number of such tasks, including observing pictures of people apparently in pain,[41] observing videos of people's hands in situations with

[36] Seara-Cardoso and Viding (2014).   [37] Muller et al. (2003).   [38] Kiehl et al. (2001).
[39] Deeley et al. (2006).   [40] Decety et al. (2014).   [41] Decety et al. (2013b).

emotional implications (e.g. a hand being hit, or caressed, by another hand),[42] and trying to guess the emotional state of protagonists in a cartoon story.[43] The brain regions studied included the amygdala, anterior insula, inferior frontal gyrus and dorsal anterior cingulate, all of which are associated with empathy-related tasks. Again, psychopaths showed consistently lower levels of activity in these regions when performing the tasks relative to non-psychopathic controls.

Two specific results are interesting enough to be worth noting here. First, Decety et al.[44] showed a group of psychopaths pictures of people apparently in pain, and found, as expected, reduced activity in relevant brain regions in these subjects relative to controls. However, in a follow-up study,[45] it was found that manipulating the instructions given to subjects had an effect on the level of brain activity displayed. When instructed to imagine the person in the picture being in pain, they continued to display reduced activity. However, when asked to imagine *themselves* in similar pain, they showed *increased* activity. This suggests that psychopaths' own pain may even be more salient to them than normal subjects' own pain is salient to them, while others' pain is less salient to the psychopath.

Another interesting result was discovered in Sommer et al.'s study.[46] When trying to guess the emotional state of a cartoon character, as well as showing reduced activity in brain regions associated with emotional processing (superior temporal sulcus, supramarginal gyrus, frontal gyrus), the psychopathic group showed increased activity in regions associated with 'processing the value of an outcome and mentalising efforts'.[47] This, conclude Seara-Cardoso and Viding, 'may reflect additional efforts in computing the emotion attribution due to an inability to automatically simulate the emotional state of the cartoon character'.[48] This suggestion, which invites us to imagine psychopaths using inductive reasoning to arrive at a conclusion about the mental state of a person ('I've seen people pull facial expressions like that before, when they were in pain . . . so that's probably what's going on here') where a normal agent would simply *see someone in pain*, raises interesting questions about what it is to empathise with someone. To acquire knowledge about their mental state? To perceive them directly as experiencing a particular mental state? To feel some of what they are feeling? We might also ask what implications not having access to the full range of processes of this kind would have for a person's

---

[42] Meffert, et al. (2013), Decety et al. (2013a).   [43] Sommer et al. (2010).
[44] Decety et al. (2013b).   [45] Decety et al. (2014).   [46] Sommer et al. (2010).
[47] Seara-Cardoso and Viding (2014), p. 5.   [48] Ibid.

attitude and behaviour toward others. I will return to these questions in Chapter 5.

The final set of studies reviewed by Seara-Cardoso and Viding concern psychopaths' brain states when engaging in moral judgement tasks. In these tasks, psychopaths were presented with a series of moral 'dilemmas' (in fact, strictly speaking these were not dilemmas but situations requiring a difficult moral judgement to be made by a protagonist – the experimental subject is asked what the protagonist should do in the situation). The results from these experiments were also extremely interesting. Glenn et al.[49] found that, when presented with (a) moral dilemmas designed to illicit strong emotional reactions, (b) moral dilemmas designed not to illicit strong emotional reactions and (c) non-moral dilemmas, psychopaths showed no significant difference from non-psychopathic controls in their responses to the dilemmas. However, the psychopaths showed less activity than the non-psychopaths in brain regions associated with emotional processing (amygdala, medial prefrontal cortex, posterior cingulate and angular gyrus) when considering the emotional dilemmas, and increased activity in brain regions associated with cognitive control (dorsolateral prefrontal cortex). Very similar results were also shown by Pujol et al.[50] As with the empathic tasks, these results suggest that psychopaths may be pressing into service non-emotional, cognitive processes in order to per-form tasks which normal agents would perform using emotion. Moreover, given the fact that the psychopaths did not differ from the non-psychopaths in the actual responses given to the dilemmas, it would appear that this strategy is successful, at least for the range of moral dilemmas included in the experiments. The relative lack of emotional engagement shown by the psychopaths was not a disadvantage in performing the tasks.[51] This is suggestive in relation to psychopaths' ability to make moral judgements. In Seara-Cardoso and Viding's words, 'these results suggest that moral judgment ability may be spared in individuals with psychopathy but that they may use different strategies, or different brain regions, to compute their judgments'.[52] Philosophers should be more cautious, however: similarity in the verdicts given does not prove that the psychopaths in the studies were indeed making moral judgements. We might tentatively conclude, however, that at least for the range of scenarios

[49] Glenn et al. (2009).   [50] Pujol et al. (2012).
[51] Neither was it apparently an advantage: the balance between emotional and cognitive resources dedicated to the moral judgment task by different subjects simply made no difference to the answers given.
[52] Seara-Cardoso and Viding (2014), p. 6.

tested, the psychopathic subjects were capable of either making, or successfully *faking*, normal moral judgements.

Summarising the studies in their review, Seara-Cardoso and Viding state that 'although the direction of the findings is not entirely consistent across studies, overall, these studies seem to point to reduced response in regions typically associated with affective processing and increased activity in regions typically associated with cognitive control during processing of emotional and salient stimuli'.[53]

Interestingly, many of the studies that were reviewed used 'community samples', that is, psychopaths drawn from the general population – not only from prisons and psychiatric institutions. The conclusions canvassed, therefore, would appear to apply to 'successful' as well as to 'unsuccessful' psychopaths. This would still be consistent with the idea that these two categories represent distinct personality types, but with overlapping emotional deficits.

In Gao et al.'s earlier review,[54] studies that focused on investigating possible structural and functional correlates associated with psychopathy (diagnosed using PCL-R) were chosen. As noted earlier, work of this kind suggests a neurological cause of psychopathic traits, as opposed to merely supporting the hypothesis that psychopaths use different psychological strategies when performing different tasks. As such, it is particularly interesting in the context of the present enquiry. Nonetheless, it should be emphasised that identifying an associated structural or functional deficit in psychopaths is not the same as identifying a genetic cause of psychopathy, since brain structure and function develops from childhood onwards. It could be that structural and functional abnormalities in adult psychopaths are the result of abnormal neurological development, rather than an abnormal genetic inheritance.

Past support for an underlying role of functional connectivity in the manifestation of psychopathic traits has come from research involving subjects who have suffered injury to specific brain regions, and as a result have developed traits similar to those found in psychopaths. The phenomenon of 'acquired sociopathy' in patients suffering damage to the ventro-medial prefrontal cortex (vmPFC) was explored in a seminal study by Eslinger and Damasio.[55] More recently, using advanced brain imaging techniques such as voxel-based morphology, researchers have turned to psychopathic subjects who have not suffered from brain injury, and

---

[53] Ibid., p. 7.   [54] Gao et al. (2009).   [55] Eslinger and Damasio (1985).

attempted to discover whether they too have structural deficits in comparison to non-psychopathic controls.

A correlation between high scores on PCL-R and reduced volume in the vmPFC has been shown repeatedly, for example, by Yang et al.,[56] Muller et al.[57] and de Oliveira-Souza et al.[58] A significant correlation between psychopathic traits and reduced volume in the amygdala has also been shown by Yang et al.[59] Both regions are associated with emotional processing. Yang et al.[60] also distinguish between successful and unsuccessful psychopaths, finding differences in the specific regions affected. In the words of Gao et al., 'findings suggest that neuropathological characteristics such as abnormal hippocampal asymmetry and reduced prefrontal grey matter volume may contribute to the emotional dysregulation and poor fear conditioning in unsuccessful psychopathic people, and consequently render these people less sensitive to environmental cues predicting danger and capture'.[61] This interesting result suggests that the lack of prudence exhibited by unsuccessful psychopaths may have a separate neurological basis from the lack of moral sense found in both successful and unsuccessful psychopaths.

Overall, the evidence appears to suggest that several brain regions associated with the emotions are typically underdeveloped in people with psychopathic tendencies:

> Overall, brain imaging studies have suggested that: the orbitofrontal, ventromedial prefrontal, and the cingulate cortex are crucial in decision-making, behavioural control, and emotional regulation, and that deficits in these regions may contribute to features such as impulsivity and impaired moral judgment in psychopathic people; and, the medial temporal regions, particularly the amygdala and hippocampus, are critical for emotional processing, and thus, when impaired, predispose to a shallow affect and lack of empathy in psychopathic people. Findings also suggest that no one single region, when impaired, will result in psychopathy.[62]

This evidence is particularly important because it points towards underlying neurological deficits as a possible *cause* of psychopathic traits. In particular, this has potential implications for moral responsibility: if the structure of one's brain predisposes one to have certain psychological traits, and if the structure of one's brain is largely established by adulthood,[63]

---

[56] Yang et al. (2005).   [57] Muller et al. (2008).   [58] de Oliveira-Souza et al. (2008).
[59] Yang et al. (2009), Yang et al. (2010).   [60] Yang et al. (2005).   [61] Gao et al. (2009), p. 814.
[62] Ibid., p. 815.   [63] Stiles and Jernigan (2010).

then we might be less inclined to hold people with the relevant psychological traits responsible for the possession of those traits. If those traits turn out to be incompatible with moral responsibility themselves, then it becomes much more plausible to conclude that people who possess them to a high degree are not morally responsible at all.

2.7 Are Psychopaths Treatable?

That psychopaths are 'untreatable' is a commonly held view going back to the earliest days of its identification as a condition. Cleckley, writing in 1941, confessed his own 'inability to achieve successful results with any regularity in dealing with severe cases' of psychopathy, but noted that 'it is hardly accurate to say that treatment of psychopaths has been given a reasonable trial'.[64] Reading recent reviews of the scientific evidence regarding treatment, it is striking how little the prevailing view has changed since Cleckley's time, in both respects. Nonetheless, there is now a growing literature describing attempts to evaluate the effectiveness of various therapeutic interventions in treating psychopathy, including various forms of group therapy and cognitive behavioural therapy. Several reviews have been published with the aim of assessing the overall evidence for effectiveness.

One thing on which all of these reviews are agreed is that the evidence is inconclusive. This is partly because there is still a paucity of studies in this area, and partly because many of the studies that do exist have significant methodological problems. This can be illustrated by considering a metaanalysis by Salekin.[65] In it, Salekin expresses optimism about the prospects for finding effective treatments for psychopathy, based on a number of studies which appeared to show encouraging results. Salekin himself acknowledges the methodological limitations of many of these studies. However, as Harris and Rice have ably shown, these limitations are too severe for Salekin's optimism to be warranted.[66] Harris and Rice's review discusses these problems in detail, drawing attention to numerous instances of apparent misinterpretation of studies on Salekin's part, concluding that the only studies included in Salekin's paper with properly controlled conditions, and which produced clear results, actually showed that the condition of the psychopaths involved in the studies *worsened* when they were subjected to the treatment in question.

---

[64] Cleckley (1941), p. 534.   [65] Salekin (2002).
[66] Harris and Rice (2006). See also Salekin et al. (2010).

This apparent iatrogenic[67] effect of some treatment approaches is a remarkable result of several studies. Harris and Rice conclude their paper by recommending that attempts to treat psychopaths should be approached with caution, because of this issue, which is also found in studies other than those included in Salekin's review. It is, of course, a serious problem for those working with psychopaths, which in turn causes a problem for anyone wishing to develop and evaluate new treatments. If the effect of some treatments may be to make psychopaths more likely to commit criminal and violent acts in future, the risks of treatment are severe, and studies may have difficulty getting off the ground.

Probably the most widely discussed set of results to show this effect was produced by the Oak Ridge Social Therapy Unit which, during the 1960s and 1970s, tried radical and experimental therapeutic techniques with psychopaths and other criminals, which would have no chance of obtaining ethical approval today.[68] At their most extreme, these techniques included groups of naked inmates being shut in an 8 foot by 10 foot windowless box, the 'Total Encounter Capsule', for weeks at a time, being fed only liquid food through a hole in the wall, and being administered occasional doses of LSD.[69] Some inmates were forced to take part in group therapy sessions, and inmates who were judged to be at risk of suicide were handcuffed to other inmates who were given responsibility for their well-being. The psychiatrists running the programme reported that inmates taking part in it showed greatly improved ability to relate to each other empathically, and to articulate their own feelings.

After the closure of the programme, data from it were used as part of a longitudinal study, which compared immediate outcomes of the therapy for individuals with information about those individuals' recidivism, and particularly long-term recidivism.[70] In the results of this study, 'treatment was associated with lower violent recidivism for non-psychopaths but with *higher* violent recidivism for psychopaths'.[71] The authors concluded that the therapeutic techniques were indeed successful in improving subjects' understanding of others' emotions, ability to take others' perspective, facility with emotional language, general social skills and ability to delay gratification. For the non-psychopaths, these effects facilitated better socialisation and reduced the tendency to violence; for the psychopaths, the authors speculated, because they did not address their underlying

---

[67] That is, exacerbating of the condition being treated.   [68] Harris and Rice (1992).
[69] Barker and Mason (1968), Barker et al. (1969), Barker and McLaughlin (1977), Barker (1980).
[70] Rice et al. (1992).   [71] Harris and Rice (2006), p. 556 (italics authors' own).

motivations, they simply equipped the subjects more effectively to manipulate others. Polaschek and Daley,[72] however, question this interpretation, arguing that increased ability to manipulate others would not necessarily have led to more violent recidivism, and might instead be more likely to have equipped the psychopaths to achieve their goals in ways that did not require violence, and which made them less likely to be caught. Instead, they point to the more coercive elements of the programme, as well as the LSD, speculating that these techniques might have harmed the psychopaths in a way which led to a decline in their future behaviour. Whatever the correct interpretation of these results, however, the fact is that several other studies have shown a similar iatrogenic effect.[73] Both Harris and Rice and Reidy et al.[74] conclude on the basis of their reviews that this effect is significant enough to warrant caution in attempts to treat psychopaths.

Harris and Rice are unencouraged by the overall evidence for psychopaths' responsiveness to treatment, concluding that, 'in short, the few available empirical results regarding the effectiveness of treatment with psychopathic offenders are dismal'[75] and 'there is no evidence that any treatments yet applied to psychopaths have been shown to be effective in reducing violence or crime'.[76] Reidy et al. show some guarded optimism about certain forms of treatment, concluding that 'the state of the literature precludes the ability to speculate with great confidence about the amenability of psychopathic violence to treatment', but that 'we believe that there is good preliminary evidence to suggest that although they are more treatment resistant likely requiring more resources and dosage, a specifically and carefully crafted intervention may be effective in reducing violence by psychopathic individuals'.[77] Polaschek and Daley are also guardedly optimistic, concluding that 'recent scientific evidence is tentatively encouraging',[78] and recommending in particular intensive treatment of high-risk individuals in isolation from other offenders, since (1) there is some evidence that they will respond better to such treatment, and (2) they have a tendency to disrupt treatment with broader groups, making that treatment less effective overall. Felthous allows no firm conclusion, on the basis that 'evidence for treatment amenability or non-amenability of psychopathic disorders has yet to be proven by research'.[79]

[72] Polaschek and Daly (2013).
[73] Craft et al. (1964), Seto and Barbaree (1999), Hare et al. (2000), Chakhssi et al. (2010).
[74] Reidy, et al. (2013).   [75] Harris and Rice (2006), p. 557.   [76] Ibid., p. 568.
[77] Reidy, et al. (2013), p. 536.   [78] Polaschek and Daly (2013), p. 600.
[79] Felthous (2011), pp. 404–5.

A common feature of the majority of the studies included in these reviews, which should be noted for our purposes here, is that they have the specific aim of reducing criminal recidivism, and often violent recidivism, and the focus of evaluations of these treatments is on their effectiveness in meeting this aim. This is unsurprising given the pressing social need for any means of reducing violent and criminal behaviour in these high-risk individuals. However, it does mean that little attention is paid to the question of whether any effectiveness is due to a change in the underlying traits that produce the behaviour in the first place. In short, evidence that a particular treatment programme prevents psychopaths from committing violence is not necessarily evidence that it does so by making them less psychopathic. Even the most optimistic reviewers, Polaschek and Daley, accept this point, noting that 'it may . . . be premature to conclude that the treatment of PCL-psychopaths cannot effect changes in personality traits', but only because 'these questions have rarely been asked in treatment research and are difficult to investigate given the limitations in available dynamic measures that directly reference these traits'.[80]

One way in which treatment of psychopaths might make them less likely to reoffend without changing their psychopathic traits is by affecting other disorders which co-occur with psychopathy in many individuals. Felthous emphasises this point strongly, since the studies in his review which show the most encouraging results are those that attempt to treat these 'co-morbid' disorders, including 'schizophrenia, affective disorders, substance use disorder, anxiety disorders, post-traumatic stress disorder, sexual disturbances and paraphilias and organic brain syndromes',[81] rather than psychopathy itself. Because the evidence base for treatment of these disorders may be better established than that for treatment of psychopathy, Felthous recommends focusing on this avenue for treatment.

One notable area where there does seem to be somewhat better evidence for the reduction of violent reoffending is with psychopathic youths. For example, of the eight studies of treatment programmes with young offenders included in Salekin et al.'s review,[82] six showed some evidence of effectiveness. A notable example is the Mendota Juvenile Treatment Centre (MJTC) which used a non-punitive approach, subjecting non-compliant subjects to increased individualised treatment contact instead of sanctions or expulsion, and basing treatment around a kind of token economy. Longitudinal evaluations of this programme found that psychopathic subjects, as well as non-psychopaths, were significantly less likely to

---

[80] Ibid., p. 600.   [81] Ibid., p. 403.   [82] Salekin et al. (2010).

reoffend than controls.[83] Most significantly, a later evaluation found that treatment at the MJTC led specifically to reductions in callous/unemotional, narcissistic and impulsive personality traits.[84]

In conclusion, while reviewers of the scientific evidence for the efficacy of treatment of psychopaths differ somewhat in their overall conclusions, the general consensus is that there is relatively little scientifically rigorous evidence for effectiveness. Some commentators express optimism about some forms of treatment, but only cautious optimism. Where there is evidence for effectiveness, there is little reason to think that treatment is effective in altering underlying psychopathic traits, rather than simply changing behaviour, or improving co-morbid disorders. The exception is with younger psychopaths, where there is slightly more reason to think that treatment can be effective, not just at changing behaviour but at changing underlying traits as well. On the other hand, there is some evidence that some forms of treatment, which are effective with non-psychopathic subjects, may actually be counter-productive when carried out with psychopaths.

2.8 Conclusions

We have seen in this chapter that the psychopathic personality is characterised primarily by emotional deficits, which may to some extent be caused by underlying abnormalities in their brain structure, and which manifest in forms of behaviour that can be described as antisocial or amoral.

I believe these factors provide the foundations for a verdict of non-responsibility, but before this verdict can be confidently made, there is considerable ground to cover. In Chapter 3, I will interpret the conclusions of this chapter, particularly focusing on their implications for the ability of psychopaths to recognise the value of others. Ultimately, I think the *in*ability of psychopaths to recognise this value provides good grounds for thinking that they are incapable of recognising a broad category of reasons, and therefore that they are not morally responsible for failing to act on reasons which belong to that category.

---

[83] Caldwell et al. (2006), Caldwell et al. (2007), Caldwell (2011).   [84] Caldwell et al. (2012).

CHAPTER 3

Psychopathy and Moral Responsibility

3.1 Introduction

I have now outlined my understanding of what moral responsibility is, and made some observations about what I take to be the central psychological deficits which characterise psychopathy. I turn in this chapter to the central question of the book, namely whether psychopaths are morally responsible. More precisely, I am interested in what kinds of action, attitude, emotion and so on psychopaths are capable of being morally responsible for. In the second part of the chapter, I will identify a category of actions (etc.) for which I believe psychopaths are not capable of being morally responsible. However, before I turn to this part of the project, I will assess some prominent arguments both for and against psychopathic responsibility. I will concentrate on those arguments which are rooted in the two connected fields of thought concerning moral responsibility, which I surveyed in Chapter 1: the reactive attitudes view and the reasons-responsiveness view.

3.2 Psychopathy and the Reactive Attitudes

As set out in Chapter 1, my view of moral responsibility is based on the reasons-responsiveness model, which in turn draws heavily on the insights expressed by P. F. Strawson in 'Freedom and Resentment'.[1] There have been some attempts to settle the question of psychopathic responsibility using these insights, and it will be worthwhile discussing these attempts here. Probably the most fully Strawsonian discussions of psychopathic responsibility are those by Piers Benn and Gwen Adshead, and I will concentrate on these discussions in this section.

[1] Strawson (2008).

As we have seen, Strawson's account of 'participant reactive attitudes' in 'Freedom and Resentment' is intended as a way of sidestepping the debate between compatibilists and incompatibilists about determinism and moral responsibility. His major claim is that the set of attitudes which embody our practices of holding people responsible is not, and should not be, prey to general theoretical convictions such as a belief in the truth of determinism. Thus, Strawson attempts to show, against the incompatibilist position, that we are sometimes justified in holding people morally responsible for their actions, but he attempts to do so without solving the theoretical problem of the supposed incompatibility of moral responsibility and determinism. Instead, he proceeds by illuminating the nature of the normal social practices involved in holding someone morally responsible, so that it becomes clear in his view that they do not require external justification. As part of this project, he sets out a typology of cases in which it would be acceptable and normal to withhold reactive attitudes; for example, towards children or animals, or people who are in the grip of ignorance or compulsion. In these cases, the actions in question are not expressive of either 'ill will or indifferent disregard',[2] and hence we are justified in holding the agents morally responsible. As I noted in the introduction, however, the case of psychopaths is notable for pulling our intuitions in two directions simultaneously. It is particularly unclear how we should react to someone who may not be capable of understanding that other people are due a particular quality of will. The question of what kind of reactive attitudes, if any, we should hold towards psychopaths is therefore a difficult one.

While Strawson does not mention psychopaths specifically, there are hints in 'Freedom and Resentment' as to what he might think about them. The most promising clue is in Strawson's list of those excluded from being a target of reactive attitudes, in which he includes both 'the extreme case of the mentally deranged' and the case of the 'moral idiot'.[3] Either of these categories might be thought to include psychopaths. However, this idea is not in fact suggested by Strawson's discussion. More likely, Strawson intends these terms to pick out individuals whose mental condition more obviously includes them in one of the traditional (Aristotelian) categories of exemption from moral responsibility – lack of control and lack of knowledge. Thus, someone who is 'mentally deranged' in a way that exempts them from moral responsibility would need to be significantly mistaken about the facts bearing on

---

[2] Ibid., p. 15. [3] Ibid., p. 13.

their choices (e.g. because they suffer from paranoid delusions). A 'moral idiot', on the other hand, might be understood as someone who fails to have a competent grasp of moral concepts and their application. Psychopaths do not fit easily into either of these categories. Most importantly, from a Strawsonian point of view, they are typically quite capable of both ill will and indifferent disregard towards others. Indeed, they are somewhat expert at this. It might seem, therefore, that psychopaths are apt targets of Strawsonian reactive attitudes.

Piers Benn has tried to show that this is not the case. In 'Freedom, Resentment and the Psychopath',[4] he sets out an interpretation of the reactive attitudes as essentially 'communicative'. For Benn, Strawsonian participant reactive attitudes should be understood as acts of communication with the person towards whom the attitude is held. If someone has wronged me (for example), and I resent them for it, I thereby have the capacity to create two things in the person who wronged me: first, the understanding of what they have done wrong; second, the motivation to act on this understanding (by making amends, or changing their ways in the future and so on). This second aspect is achieved through the creation of self-directed reactive attitudes such as guilt, shame or remorse. Now, psychopaths, as we saw in Chapter 2, appear to be incapable of genuinely holding these self-directed reactive attitudes. Insofar as our own reactive attitudes such as resentment have a supposed role to play[5] in bringing about these attitudes, this role is frustrated when they are directed at psychopaths. In terms of attitudes, it seems, psychopaths simply do not speak our language. This analysis leads Benn to a more general conclusion: 'only creatures able to form participant attitudes are proper objects of such attitudes on the part of others'.[6] Psychopaths are able to hold attitudes, of course, but these attitudes are not *participant* in the way Benn understands this term, and therefore we go wrong when we hold such attitudes towards them.

---

[4] Benn (1999).
[5] It is a little unclear how this idea of a role should be cashed out. It is presumably not the case that we are always supposed to be *intending* to communicate anything to the object of our resentment, since (for one thing) resentment can sometimes be unexpressed and is no less justified for that. It is also presumably not the case that the communicative role described by Benn is supposed to be the only role resentment has. Indeed, it is probably not the only communicative role it has: one role of expressing our resentment might be to communicate to others something about what type of a person the object of the resentment is. There might also be some use in simply organising our own thoughts about what attitudes we should have towards the person in future. Nonetheless, it is plausible that one of the *uses* that resentment has is to communicate something to its target, and that this might be one way in which resentment can be *valuable*.
[6] Benn (1999), p. 34.

From this, Benn draws a tentative second conclusion which he describes as 'illiberal'. Endorsing a point made by Jeffrie G. Murphy,[7] he suggests that, to the extent that our moral treatment of others is motivated by 'Kantian' considerations of respect for autonomous persons and a duty to treat them as ends in themselves, we would be justified in withholding this treatment from psychopaths. Of course, we might also be motivated by non-Kantian considerations such as 'sympathy and virtue',[8] but we would not see psychopaths as *persons* or 'as having a full set of rights'.[9] Here we see why Benn describes this view as 'illiberal': if psychopaths do not have 'a full set of rights', then we might be justified in treating them in ways it would be unacceptable to treat other human beings. We might conclude, for example, that we are justified in pre-emptively detaining psychopaths on the basis of their high PCL-R scores. We would do well to think very carefully before endorsing a theory with implications of this kind.

Should we accept Benn's two conclusions? One reason to hesitate might be the thought that Benn's discussion seems to have drifted somewhat from the central ideas of Strawson's original paper. What Strawson is at pains to stress above all is the unavoidability, the 'given-ness', of the reactive attitudes. At one point, Strawson compares our attachment to the reactive attitudes to our attachment to the process of inductive reasoning. A theoretical conviction of the truth of determinism, he thinks, could no more force us to suspend in practice our reactive attitudes than a theoretical conviction of the impossibility of logically supporting induction could force us to stop practising induction. For Strawson, 'a sustained objectivity of inter-personal attitude, and the human isolation which that would entail, does not seem to be something of which human beings would be capable, even if some general truth were a theoretical ground for it'.[10] If this is right, simply withholding reactive attitudes towards psychopaths in the way recommended by Benn's first conclusion would seem to be easier said than done.

However, while Strawson may be right that it would be 'practically inconceivable'[11] to suspend reactive attitudes towards everybody at all times, it is surely not the case that we are incapable of suspending reactive attitudes towards particular classes of people. History is full of examples of groups being systematically dehumanised, perhaps most notoriously the Jews (as well as other groups) in Nazi Germany. While this process began with the stirring up against the Jews of reactive attitudes such as

---

[7] Murphy (1972).   [8] Benn (1999), p. 38.   [9] Ibid.   [10] Strawson (2008), p. 12.
[11] Ibid., p. 3.

anger and resentment, it ended with an attitude that is much closer to what Strawson describes as 'the objective attitude'. The Jews were seen as merely a problem to be dealt with. This comparison brings out very starkly the acknowledged illiberality of Benn's suggestion, though it should also be acknowledged that of course nothing akin to the Nazis' treatment of the Jews is automatically implied by that suggestion. However, the historical example shows that it does seem to be quite possible for people to persuade themselves to treat all classes of people as less than fully fledged persons.

There is, however, reason at least to doubt the legitimacy of Benn's move from his first conclusion to his second. This move rests on his endorsing a Kantian view of obligation:

> The guiding thought here is that morality is that set of principles that rational agents could freely agree to observe, on condition that everyone else observe them as well. And commitment to such an agreement entails a commitment to reciprocity. If certain individuals are incapable of understanding the need for reciprocity, or of entertaining the moral feelings that normally motivate its observance, then for that reason they exclude themselves from the agreement, and may be treated in ways in which normal people may never treat one another.[12]

In their response to Benn,[13] James Harold and Carl Elliott resist Benn's 'illiberal' move, implicitly also rejecting the Kantian view on which it is based. They make their point by drawing a distinction between moral *agents* and moral *patients*. Accepting that psychopaths are not moral agents, and they should not be held morally responsible, does not entail accepting that they are not moral patients, to whom we have direct duties, and who might hold a set of rights. For example, we do not think of babies as being fully fledged morally responsible agents, but we clearly do think of ourselves as capable of having direct duties towards them, and of them as having rights. Indeed, it is also very likely that we have direct duties towards animals. Even if we accept Benn's first conclusion, that psychopaths are not morally responsible agents, the proper way to treat them may be determined by more than 'sympathy and virtue'.

Patricia Greenspan[14] offers an alternative interpretation of Strawson's account, concluding that psychopaths are not excluded from the community of responsible agents in virtue of their social disconnectedness. Greenspan points out that psychopaths are not entirely incapable of reactive attitudes themselves:

---

[12] Benn (1999), p. 38.   [13] Harold and Elliott (1999).   [14] Greenspan (2003).

Psychopaths do not lack all varieties of interpersonal attachment . . . though their relationships are in many ways inconsistent and superficial. They do seem to establish at least deficient interpersonal relationships of the rough sort that Strawson described as based on mutual reactive attitudes. The problem is that their reactive attitudes (and their awareness of others' reactive attitudes) apparently do not generate motivating attitudes, including guilt and other self-directed forms of blame, that manifest themselves as needed to inhibit impulses to act.[15]

We can see Greenspan's position as implying that reactive attitudes are not essentially, not always, communicative, as Benn insists they are. While it may be inappropriate to hold a reactive attitude towards a psychopath when that attitude is directed at influencing the self-motivating attitudes of its object, not all reactive attitudes need to be like this, and there may therefore be some attitudes that can still appropriately be held towards psychopaths. For Greenspan, such 'non-retributive' attitudes include 'reactive attitudes based on hatred rather than anger (e.g. disgust or contempt)',[16] but they might also include some forms of resentment. Returning to Strawson's original analysis, Greenspan argues that what justifies taking one of these attitudes towards someone is that their actions manifest 'bad qualities of will'. Because psychopaths *intend* their actions, and even intend the harm that those actions cause, we are justified in ascribing bad qualities of will to them, and therefore in holding non-retributive attitudes towards them. On this basis, and if we suppose that what makes psychopaths morally responsible or not is a matter of our being justified in holding reactive attitudes towards them, then psychopaths' responsibility can be said to be diminished, but not completely ruled out.

Thus, the dispute between Benn and Greenspan, and the question of whether psychopaths ought to be held morally responsible under a Strawsonian framework, would appear to hinge on whether we accept Benn's analysis of the 'communicative' role of the reactive attitudes. Greenspan's view does leave room for non-retributive attitudes to be communicative in a sense, though not in the sense intended by Benn. For Greenspan, 'incorrigible' agents, including psychopaths, are not members of the 'moral community', and so retributive attitudes, which have the function of bringing about change in the object, are not appropriate. However, Greenspan describes attitudes such as contempt and disgust as 'sentiments of personal exclusion or dismissal from

---

[15] Greenspan (2003), pp. 421–2.   [16] Ibid., p. 417.

the moral community'.[17] Incorrigible agents merit these reactions precisely because they are impervious to the 'communicative' aspects of attitudes such as anger and indignation. We can still see these non-retributive attitudes as essentially communicative: by holding them towards incorrigible agents, we are communicating to them, and perhaps just as importantly to others, that they are to be excluded from the moral community. Because there is no assumption inherent in this act of communication that it will have any effect on the attitudes or behaviour of their object, incorrigible agents, including psychopaths, can be apt targets for these reactive attitudes. Thus, in Strawsonian terms, they are at least partly responsible.

This plausible suggestion shows, I think, that the implications of a Strawsonian picture for psychopaths' responsibility are not as simple as Benn suggests. Psychopaths cannot be shown not to be responsible in a Strawsonian sense simply in virtue of their problems with holding reactive attitudes themselves. However, while I agree with Greenspan that Benn's argument is not enough to demonstrate that psychopaths are not morally responsible, I also do not think that Greenspan's argument is enough to show that psychopaths *are* morally responsible. The key point is that it is not clear that Greenspan's description of the attitudes, which it is intuitively appropriate to hold towards psychopaths, is more accurate than Benn's.

We can see the problem by recalling a point from Chapter 1 which applies to the link between ill will or indifferent disregard and the reactive attitudes, which Greenspan, drawing on Strawson, assumes. Psychopaths are indeed capable of ill will and indifferent disregard towards other people, but what if it could be shown that they are not capable of understanding that other people are *due anything other than* ill will and indifferent disregard? As I noted in Chapter 1, it is not clear as a matter of intuition that someone like this is morally responsible, and it is similarly unclear that they are apt targets of the reactive attitudes in which judgements of responsibility are expressed. Contempt and disgust are not obviously appropriate attitudes towards agents in this kind of predicament. We might be more inclined to feel sorrow at the hopelessness of the situation, or simply fear at what someone with this kind of psychology would be capable of doing. These are not Strawsonian reactive attitudes at all, and Greenspan could not use them as the basis for a case for moral responsibility, even of a limited kind.

---

[17] Ibid., p. 427. Presumably Greenspan has in mind a particularly moral kind of disgust here. People often feel disgust at non-human animals, including rats, snakes and so on, but the emotion in these cases is not communicative in the way Greenspan has in mind.

The trouble is that the question of what it is *natural to do* – what attitudes we naturally hold towards people or groups of people – is central to the Strawsonian justification for the practices and attitudes involved in holding people morally responsible. Strawson's justification is a justification of those attitudes which we do, as a matter of fact, naturally hold towards people. It is because holding any other set of attitudes, if it became a general policy, would cause mental strain and the impoverishment of human relationships, that we should continue holding the attitudes we do. Quite a lot therefore rests on Greenspan's claim that the attitudes of exclusion – disgust, contempt and so on – are the natural attitudes to hold towards psychopaths.

3.3   Psychopaths and Reasons

What about the reasons-responsiveness model of moral responsibility? Can psychopaths be said to lack responsiveness to reasons in a way that is relevant to moral responsibility? One way in which an agent can lack (local) responsiveness to the reasons that bear on an act is if they are reasons of which they are not aware, and cannot reasonably be expected to be aware. So, imagine A gives a glass of wine to B, unaware that B is a recovering alcoholic. The two were not previously acquainted, and A had no way of knowing this fact about B. In the event, the temptation is too much for B, who drinks the wine and then several more. We might say that A has helped to set B back on the road to addiction, but we should not think of A as being morally responsible for this act. A was non-culpably ignorant of the circumstances in which they acted, and specifically of the facts about B's history, which gave A a reason for refraining from offering wine to B.

We can formulate a similar case in which the ignorance is the result of a fact about the psychological state of the person performing the act, rather than of a special fact about the circumstances in which they act. So, to return to an example which I have used previously, C suffers from paranoid schizophrenia and, because of her condition, thinks that D is out to get her. C harms D in what C wrongly believes to be self-defence. Now, assuming that C is not morally responsible for D's condition or for the delusions that arise from it, it seems clear that, again, C is not morally responsible for the act of harming D. Owing to a confusion which is not her fault, she believes she has a reason to harm D, when in fact she does not, and she has all the usual reasons for refraining from harming D.

Is it possible that a psychopath's condition can cause them to be ignorant, or irrational, in a similarly responsibility-negating way? In his

brief discussion of psychopaths in *Responsibility and the Moral Sentiments*,
R. Jay Wallace focuses on the possibility that psychopaths might have
a diminished capacity to 'engage in intelligent critical reflection'[18] which, if
true, may provide support for the claim that they have diminished moral
responsibility:

> It has been suggested that psychopaths lack the qualities of imagination and
> practical understanding required to bring common moral principles to bear
> in new cases; for instance, they often have great difficulty distinguishing
> between trivial and important moral concerns, and so lack the capacity to
> engage in intelligent critical reflection on moral issues. This severe impair-
> ment of the capacity for reflective self-control would set the psychopath
> apart from an 'ordinary' evil person . . . providing us with a reason for not
> treating the psychopath as a morally accountable agent.[19]

For Wallace, this impairment in moral reasoning puts psychopaths outside
the class of beings that have the kind of rational ability that is required for
moral responsibility:

> The understanding required is a kind of participant understanding that goes
> well beyond the ability to parrot the moral principle in situations in which it
> has some relevance. What is needed, rather, is the ability to bring the
> principle to bear in the full variety of situations to which it applies,
> anticipating the demands it makes of us in those situations, and knowing
> when its demands might require adjustment in the light of the claims of
> other moral principles.[20]

It certainly appears to be the case, from the reports of clinicians and
scientists, that psychopaths often have trouble engaging with moral principles in anything more than a very superficial way. Take, for example, the
following remarks by three psychopathic inmates, reported by Robert
Hare:

> When asked if he had any regrets about stabbing a robbery victim who
> subsequently spent three months in the hospital as a result of his wounds,
> one of our subjects replied, 'Get real! He spends a few months in a hospital
> and I rot here. I cut him up a bit, but if I wanted to kill him I would have slit
> his throat. That's the kind of guy I am; I gave him a break' . . . .
>   I was once dumbfounded by the logic of an inmate who described his
> murder victim as having benefitted from the crime by learning 'a hard lesson
> about life.'
>   'The guy only had himself to blame,' another inmate said of a man he'd
> murdered in an argument about paying a bar tab. 'Anybody could have seen

<hr>

[18] Wallace (1994), p. 158.   [19] Ibid., p. 157.   [20] Ibid.

I was in a rotten mood that night. What did he want to go and bother me for?' He continued, 'Anyway, the guy never suffered. Knife wounds to an artery are the easiest way to go.'[21]

If taken at face value, these three remarks reveal individuals who profoundly misunderstand the moral principles which they are ostensibly employing. They appeal to considerations which any non-psychopathic person would immediately recognise as irrelevant, and entirely miss considerations that appear to the reader as glaringly important. The impression is of people who are doing an impersonation of someone engaging in 'moral talk'. The impersonation is so poor, however, that it only reveals a profound and startling lack of understanding of how morality works even on a very basic level. Nor would there apparently be any motivation for these interviewees to exaggerate their misunderstanding. On the contrary, as prison inmates it would presumably be in their interest to convince officials that they understood what they had done and were remorseful. Remarks such as those listed earlier are only likely to reduce any chance of parole.

If these remarks are taken to be representative of psychopaths generally, it is easy to see how psychopaths might be thought to 'lack the capacity to engage in intelligent critical reflection on moral issues' to the extent that they might be excluded from moral responsibility. If moral responsibility consists in being able to respond consistently to the reasons that bear on one's actions, then it would presumably require some kind of minimal ability to recognise and apply moral principles, an ability apparently lacked by the psychopaths quoted earlier. Someone who can, apparently sincerely, justify having killed someone by claiming that it taught them 'a hard lesson about life' appears to have a deeply flawed understanding of what reasons they have and ought to respond to. If it could be shown that this flawed understanding was itself not something for which the person was responsible, then this might count as exempting them from moral responsibility.

On the other hand, it is not clear that such remarks are indeed representative of psychopaths as a whole, as opposed to a small group of psychopaths who have not taken the time to gain a basic understanding of the moral principles that most people take to be important. Elsewhere, Hare quotes another psychopath, a man 'with the highest possible score on the psychopathy checklist':

> I've wasted a lot of my life. You can't get back the time . . . . I intend to live a much more slowed-down life, and give a lot to people that I never had

myself. Put some enjoyment in their lives. I don't mean thrills, I mean some substance into somebody else's life. It will probably be a woman, but it doesn't necessarily have to be a woman. Maybe a woman's kids, or maybe someone in an old folks' home. I think ... no, I don't think ... I *know*, it would give me a good deal of pleasure, make me feel a whole lot better about my life.[22]

This man, who according to Hare had 'a horrendous criminal record' and 'had brutalized his wife and abandoned his children', clearly had enough understanding of moral principles and concepts to put together a fairly convincing speech on the themes of regret and the pleasure to be derived from being a positive influence on someone else's life. This perhaps bespeaks some understanding of what most people would take to be the reasons that other people's rights, interests and concerns present to them. Furthermore, both this psychopath and the others quoted earlier, as prison inmates, would fall into the category of 'unsuccessful psychopaths'. They might perhaps be expected to have a lower level of moral intelligence than those psychopaths who have avoided incarceration, people whose success may be partly attributable to them having convincingly assumed the mantle of ordinary, morally concerned agents. It might be that some psychopaths will have a diminished facility with moral principles to the extent that they will be excused to some degree from moral responsibility. However, the evidence that this is really a widespread feature among psychopaths is somewhat mixed. It would of course be preferable to base an argument on robust, quantitative evidence if such evidence were available.

3.4   The 'Moral/Conventional Distinction'

Some evidence that has been taken by many to be of this kind comes from experiments into psychopaths' ability to understand the 'moral/conventional distinction'. In this research, carried out in the 1990s by James Blair,[23] which has been much discussed by philosophers, psychopaths and controls are judged on their ability to distinguish between two different kinds of judgement: 'moral' and 'conventional'. Ordinary subjects judge 'moral' and 'conventional' transgressions to be different from each other on three dimensions: (1) whether or not they are *permissible*, (2) how *serious* they are and (3) whether or not they depend for their force on the word of some *authority*. 'Conventional' transgressions are typically more

[22] Ibid.   [23] Blair (1995), Blair (1997).

often thought to be permissible, are thought to be less serious and are thought to be authority dependent. In addition, when asked to explain *why* a given transgression is impermissible, subjects are more likely to adduce reasons relating to a *victim's welfare* if the transgression is 'moral' rather than 'conventional'.

A scenario which is supposed to exemplify a 'moral' transgression might involve a child hitting another child, and a scenario which is supposed to exemplify a 'conventional' transgression might involve a child talking in class. Typically, subjects are more likely to judge that the 'moral' scenarios involve impermissible action (it is impermissible to hit another child). They also tend to believe that it makes a difference in the 'conventional' scenarios whether a relevant authority has given their assent to the act described (e.g. 'it's okay to talk in class if the teacher says you can'). In the 'moral' scenarios, however, they do not judge that the assent of authority makes any difference to the permissibility of the act (e.g. 'it doesn't matter whether the teacher says you can hit a child – it's still wrong'). They also judge the supposedly conventional transgressions to be less serious than the moral ones (hitting a child is a more serious transgression than talking in class). Finally, they tend to believe that the 'moral' scenarios are impermissible not so much for reasons having to do with a victim's welfare (hitting a child harms the child) compared to other reasons (e.g. it's not fair if one child talks in class when the others can't).

Blair's experiments involved presenting these scenarios to a set of psychopaths (diagnosed using PCL-R) and non-psychopathic controls. Psychopaths, in comparison to controls, were found to be significantly less likely to be able to distinguish between the two types of case on all three dimensions listed (permissibility, seriousness and authority dependence). Psychopaths were also less likely than controls, when asked why 'moral' transgressions were impermissible, to produce explanations that appealed to the victim's welfare.

In evaluating these experiments, it is worth noting that the traction they have had with philosophers probably has more to do with the philosophically interesting nature of their conclusions than with the robustness of their empirical base. The original 1995 study involved ten psychopaths and ten non-psychopathic controls. In 1997, there was a follow-up study with children with psychopathic tendencies, which involved sixteen such children and sixteen controls. Only in the second study were the results completely as Blair predicted, i.e. the children investigated interpreted supposedly moral transgressions how non-psychopaths judged 'conventional' transgressions. In the 1995 study the results were the other way around: the subjects interpreted all transgressions, both 'moral' and 'conventional', as 'moral'. Blair explained the discrepancy by hypothesising that the imprisoned psychopaths would be motivated to appear 'virtuous' in the hope of securing improved treatment, and would therefore tend to overstate the perceived severity and universality of transgressions in the experiment. He therefore took the latter results to be more trustworthy, and concluded that psychopaths think that all transgressions are 'conventional', rather than that they are all 'moral'. This may be correct, but it is interesting to note the slim empirical foundations on which this auxiliary hypothesis was built.

It is also worth noting that, as Vargas and Nichols point out, Blair's experiments did not show that psychopaths consistently 'miss every case of the moral/conventional task'.[24] Rather, the psychopaths in the studies tended to make the relevant distinction less consistently than non-psychopathic controls. It is not clear, therefore, how we ought to apply the conclusions of any arguments built on these empirical foundations. Given that even most of the psychopathic subjects appeared able to make the distinction in some cases, should we be looking for differences among the cases used, and only excuse psychopaths in scenarios that are relevantly similar to those in which they have proved themselves unable to recognise a moral/conventional distinction? In Vargas and Nichols' words, 'experiments on psychopathologies usually produce data that is less ordered than we might hope for', and therefore, 'it is misleading to say that . . . psychopaths *cannot draw* the moral/conventional distinction'.[25] In particular, while psychopathic subjects were indeed less likely than controls to appeal to reasons relating to a victim's welfare when asked to explain why moral transgressions were impermissible, several of them did in fact make appeals of this kind (five psychopaths in the original study, compared to nine non-psychopathic controls).[26] It should be noted too that studies showing any difference in actual verdicts given to moral dilemmas are quite difficult to find. As we saw in the 'neuroscience' section in Chapter 2, psychopaths have been shown to give broadly the same types of answer in response to a range of moral dilemmas as non-psychopathic controls.

Moreover, the emphasis on authority-dependence in the 'moral/conventional distinction' as tested in the experiments is problematic in at least two ways. First, authority-dependence cannot be the basis for a distinction between moral and conventional transgressions, at least on any ordinary understanding of the word 'conventional', because many conventions

---

[24] Vargas and Nichols (2007), p. 158.   [25] Ibid., pp. 157–8.   [26] Blair (1995), p. 18.

simply have nothing to do with authority. For example, it is a useful convention that people who want to get onto a train wait for all passengers to get off first. This convention is not supported by any authority. Conventions frequently (perhaps even usually) come to exist as a kind of mutual understanding between peers, and are sustained by their usefulness in, say, avoiding inconvenience or social awkwardness, and not by the efforts of an authority.

Second, if psychopaths fail to recognise that some transgressions are not authority dependent, there is evidence to suggest that they may not be unusual in this respect. In Kohlberg's famous experiments on moral development, most subjects were found to reside in his 'Stage 4', in which morality is understood largely as authority-based.[27]

However, while Blair's exact interpretation of his experimental results can be legitimately questioned, it is nonetheless quite likely that something interesting is going on here. There is a genuine distinction between different types of transgression which was somewhat reliably picked up by the normal subjects, but less reliably picked up by the psychopaths. Some transgressions are such that most people would take them to rely on the strictures of an authority figure for their normative force, while other transgressions are generally taken not immediately to depend on a specific authority in the same way, though it may be that, pressed for an 'ultimate' explanation of their provenance, the best most people can offer is an appeal to authority of some kind, which would explain Kohlberg's finding. This distinction, exemplified by the two classroom situations described earlier, is real enough, though no doubt 'moral/conventional' is not the best label to apply to it. If some psychopaths experience some difficulty with moral judgements in the way described, then it is perhaps reasonable to suppose that these psychopaths' responsiveness to reasons might be compromised to some extent.

Walter Glannon has attempted to use Blair's studies, as well as other clinical studies involving psychopaths, to ground an argument for the view that psychopaths have limited, but not complete, moral responsibility, focusing on their capacity to be motivated by different kinds of reason. Glannon notes that psychopaths have been shown in studies to be adept at using aggression in instrumental as well as in reactive ways. (Instrumental aggression is defined as the controlled use of aggression as a tool to manipulate others, usually through intimidation, whereas reactive aggression is more

---

[27] Kohlberg (1981). See Shoemaker (2011b) for useful criticism of the way the moral/conventional distinction has been applied to responsibility by philosophers.

impulsive, less focused and stems from emotions such as anger.) If psychopaths can use aggression in this way, Glannon argues, this shows that they are capable of recognising and reacting to instrumental reasons. Now, assume for the sake of argument that we think that the message we should take from the moral/conventional distinction experiments is that psychopaths think that morality is a form of convention. Although we have reason to think that psychopaths are not motivated by moral reasons, we know that they can be motivated by instrumental reasons, and we know that they can recognise conventional reasons. Furthermore, the evidence from Blair's experiments does not give us reason to think that they could not be motivated by conventional reasons. If they can be so motivated, they could therefore presumably be motivated by those reasons that they take to be conventional, but which are in fact moral. This, argues Glannon, would be 'normatively equivalent' to being motivated by moral reasons *as* moral reasons since in either case the subject is following rules which are 'designed to inhibit moral wrongdoing and enable an individual to refrain from performing actions that harm others'.[28] Moreover, in Glannon's phrase, 'the content of the subject's mental states'[29] would be the same in either case. If responsibility is assigned on the basis of motivational states, and of the practical aspects of one's actions, then whether one recognises the rules that one violates as moral or conventional cannot make any difference to whether one is morally responsible. Therefore, psychopaths, insofar as the aforementioned description applies to them, are morally responsible.

Even if we were to accept the notion of 'conventional' reasons that is implicit in Blair's experiments, and that psychopaths can recognise, and be motivated by, moral reasons that they take to be conventional in this sense, it is difficult to see why Glannon thinks this would be 'normatively equivalent' to recognising and being motivated by moral reasons as moral reasons. To bolster this claim, Glannon emphasises both the motivational capacities of psychopaths and the content of their beliefs, arguing that both of these are similar enough to their equivalents in non-psychopaths to ground moral responsibility. Taking motivational capacities first, one might think that the psychopath (as described by Glannon) has motivational capacities that are equivalent to those of non-psychopaths in the sense that both are capable of being motivated by reasons stemming from transgressions, although one takes those transgressions to be moral and the other 'conventional'. But this seems too weak to ground *moral* responsibility. It is not clear why someone who can be motivated by what

---

[28] Glannon (2008), p. 163.   [29] Ibid.

they take to be *conventional* and not *moral* transgressions is nonetheless *morally* responsible.

Turning to the content of psychopaths' beliefs, Glannon claims that 'their capacity to recognise moral reasons provides them with enough reflective self-control to realise that they *should not* perform actions that are harmful to others and to refrain from performing them'. However, there is a potential equivocation here. If I believe that an action is outlawed by some authority, in what sense do I believe that I *should not* perform it? Imagine, for example, I am told by a police community support officer not to walk on the grass in the park. In what sense do I believe that I should not walk on the grass? It is quite possible that I believe that I *morally* should not walk on the grass. However, for this to be the case, I would presumably need to take the authority of the police community support officer to have moral legitimacy. That is, I must think that I have moral reasons to follow the instructions of a person with this kind of authority. Without this, we are left with a sense of 'should' that is prudential, rather than moral. I should not walk on the grass because the police community support officer might punish me in some way, or perhaps simply because they would think ill of me, and I do not like people thinking ill of me.

There are also situations in which even this prudential 'should' would not apply. What if the police community support officer sees someone else walking on the grass, and tells me to punch that person? In these circumstances, there is no sense in which I should perform the action. Indeed, it seems clear that I *should not* perform the action, morally.

Now, assuming that the psychopath has no way of recognising the moral legitimacy or otherwise of an authority – and it is hard to see how they would recognise this if we take the conclusions of the moral/conventional experiments at face value, i.e. if we accept that they cannot tell the difference between moral and conventional considerations – then they are left in the position of being unable to distinguish between situations like the one aforementioned and situations in which they should, morally, comply with the authority's dictum. It seems, then, that while the psychopath might believe that they should (prudentially) comply, we have no reason to think that they can *know* that they should (morally) comply, in any sense that is strong enough to ground moral responsibility.

In the latter of his two papers on this subject, Glannon offers an alternative description of the content of the psychopath's mental state, which he takes to be enough to ground moral responsibility. The psychopath, claims Glannon, 'could be capable of recognizing that the actions could not be justified by any normative reason, and on this basis he could be capable of recognizing that the actions were wrong'.[30] Again, however, there is reason to doubt Glannon's conclusion, at least if we take 'wrong', as I assume we must, to mean '*morally* wrong'. To recognise that an action is morally wrong, we might think, requires not only the recognition that it is not morally justified, but also the recognition that for it not to be morally wrong would *require* it to be morally justified. If the psychopath is not capable of taking moral reasons to apply to their own choices, they may not be capable of recognising this. If they are only capable of recognising *conventional* reasons as applying to their choices, then they may be capable of recognising actions which contravene those reasons as being *unconventional*. If they are capable of recognising only reasons stemming from the word of some *authority*, then they are capable of recognising that the actions are *outlawed*. Neither of these things amounts to the same as recognising that they are wrong.

Neil Levy is another philosopher who has used the results of the 'moral/conventional' experiments as the basis for an argument that psychopaths have diminished responsibility. This description is in fact compatible with Glannon's description of psychopaths as having 'partial responsibility'. However, Levy's emphasis is on showing what components of moral responsibility are lacked by psychopaths, rather than what components they supposedly retain.

Levy interprets the moral/conventional experiments as showing that psychopaths believe that 'harms to others [are] wrong *only because* such harms are against the rules'.

> For them, stealing from, or hurting, another is no more wrong than, say, double-parking or line-jumping. But the kind and degree of wrongness, and therefore blame, that attaches to infringements of the rules is very different, and usually much less significant, than the kind and degree attaching to moral wrongs. For psychopaths, all offences are merely conventional, and therefore – from their point of view – none of them are all that serious. Hence, their degree of responsibility is smaller, arguably much smaller, than it would be for a comparable harm committed by a normal agent.[31]

If psychopaths think that all transgressions are wrong only because they are against the rules, thinks Levy, then they cannot, when they transgress, be thereby expressing the kind of ill will towards others that grounds attributions of moral responsibility.

It is plausible to suppose that psychopaths, described in Levy's terms, might lack responsiveness to reasons. The kinds of reason presented by an

[30] Ibid.   [31] Levy (2008).

infraction of 'the rules', while pressing, are much less pressing than the kinds of reason that are salient to normal agents when considering an action that will cause harm to others. If psychopaths can indeed only recognise and respond to these kinds of reason, then they are missing an important piece of the normal agent's psychological repertoire, and their moral responsibility will indeed be diminished.

On the other hand, the moral/conventional experiments do not show that psychopaths *cannot* understand this distinction, only that some of them *do* not, some of the time. The experiments concern a distinction based on the degree of wrongness of certain transgressions, whether they are impermissible, whether they are dependent on authority for their force and what it is that makes them wrong. The problem for any argument that would seek to attribute a degree of moral responsibility to psychopaths based on their misunderstanding of these features is that, while they are certainly fundamental to ordinary moral thought, they are all quite capable of being explained to someone who is rational. What, for example, if you explained to a psychopath that a child hitting another child was wrong, not because it was outlawed by some authority, but directly because it caused harm to the victim? Do we have any reason to suppose that the psychopath would be incapable of understanding this? Not on the basis of Blair's experiments, or of any other evidence of which I am aware. There is no evidence that I know of to show that psychopaths do not understand what harm is, for example, or that harm can be a wrong-making feature of an action. Now, if they are capable of understanding this – and again, the moral/conventional experiments can only show a lack of understanding, not a lack of the capacity for understanding – then why should we think that they lack moral responsibility?

We do not ordinarily think of a lack of understanding as being excusing, if the person concerned is capable of acquiring the relevant understanding. To see this, imagine someone who, somehow, has failed to grasp the idea that ordinary disputes should not be resolved through violence. Perhaps they were brought up in a community in which disagreements routinely led to punch-ups, and this was seen as normal and morally unobjection-able. If this person, now at large in mainstream society, went about punching strangers with whom they had minor disputes, how would we react to this? I think, while we might excuse them the first few times on the basis of their lack of understanding, we would in the long term expect them to acquire an understanding of widely accepted moral norms governing the use of violence. Confusion over the proper use of moral concepts can only be excusing to some extent, as long as the person concerned is capable of overcoming that confusion. Ultimately, we tend to think that people have a duty to acquaint themselves with the way such concepts are used, and as a result we hold them responsible for their actions which are, or ought to be, informed by those concepts. If all we know about psychopaths is that they are confused about the proper use of concepts such as justification or authority-dependence, and we do not know that they are incapable of overcoming this confusion, then they may be in exactly this situation.

The earlier discussion of the moral/conventional experiments, and of Glannon and Levy's ideas, then, leaves us with two general conclusions about psychopaths and moral responsibility, relevant to the aims of this book. First, if some psychopaths can be partially exempted from moral responsibility because they exhibit difficulty in handling moral concepts, then this is unlikely to represent a clean distinction between psychopaths and non-psychopaths. An argument based purely on the moral/conventional experiments could exempt only those psychopaths who suffer from confusion in using the concepts involved in morality – confusion about their degree of force, authority-dependence and so on, and it would only exempt them in situations where this confusion actually affected their judgements. Second, an argument of this kind would only excuse psychopaths who lack not only understanding, but the capacity for understanding, and the moral/conventional experiments cannot show that any psychopaths lack the capacity for understanding.

Gwen Adshead notes that the 'rational amoralist', which she describes as 'the typical layperson's psychopath', is 'almost nonexistent in clinical samples'.[32] However, she does go on to speculate that the more rationally unimpaired type of psychopath might be more common in the general population than in the prison and psychiatric populations, which form the basis of clinical samples. (Here, perhaps, we see again the distinction between 'successful' and 'unsuccessful' psychopaths.) In any case, we must accept that in psychopaths we are dealing with, in Adshead's words, 'a highly heterogeneous group of people'.[33] Even if we conclude that difficulty in making the moral/conventional distinction is fairly widespread among psychopaths, it remains the case that it is a distinction that can be explained, and that presumably could be understood intellectually by someone who did not feel the emotional force of moral transgressions as opposed to 'conventional' ones. It seems unlikely – and the experiments themselves do not show – that psychopaths are congenitally unable to understand that most people take transgressions that involve directly

---

[32] Adshead (1999), p. 43.   [33] Ibid.

harming other people to be wrong *just for that reason*, and not because they are against the rules, or because some authority says they are wrong, or for another extrinsic reason of this kind. If – as I strongly suspect – there is a class of psychopath who is perfectly capable of understanding this, and indeed does understand it, then these psychopaths would at least have the ability (to revisit Wallace's formulation) to 'bring the principle to bear in the full variety of situations to which it applies, anticipating the demands it makes of us in those situations, and knowing when its demands might require adjustment in the light of the claims of other moral principles', but might still not see moral principles as particularly important *for them*. Arguments based on the type of confusion with moral concepts that I have been exploring have nothing to say about these people.

Paul Litton argues, not on the basis of the moral/conventional experiments but on the basis of clinical cases such as those described by Cleckley and Hare, that psychopaths suffer from an impaired capacity for rational self-governance that is not specific to the moral domain. Litton concludes that psychopaths exhibit 'a weakened capacity for possessing any kind of evaluative standards'.[34] Having evaluative standards means we can reflect on our immediate desires as fulfilling, or not fulfilling, something that is genuinely valuable or desirable. 'Treating a consideration as a reason for action involves, at least implicitly, some evaluation about the desirability of the end of that action', and evaluative standards are 'standards according to which we evaluate and assess what we have good reason to do'.[35] Psychopaths lack moral responsibility, for Litton, not because they lack responsiveness to a specific kind of reason, but because their weakened capacity for having evaluative standards renders them weakly responsive to reasons across the board.

It is plausible that many of the psychopaths described by Cleckley and Hare do indeed lack evaluative standards in the way Litton describes. We see many cases of psychopaths failing to recognise what is in their own interests, even given their stated goals, or to follow consistent life plans. For Litton,

> Part of the explanation for this characteristic also supports viewing these individuals as less than adequately rational: they have a diminished capacity for resisting impulses and the urge to satisfy a present desire in favor of long-term plans, both those professed by the individual and which he should have, given his complete set of desires. As such, they appear to have a diminished capacity for appreciating prudential reasons, especially those associated with their long-term interests.[36]

---

[34] Litton (2008), p. 375.   [35] Ibid., p. 364.   [36] Ibid., p. 381.

If this is true, then psychopaths exhibit, not a specific inability to recognise the value of others, but a difficulty in recognising value across the board, which leads them to lack a *general* rational power which is necessary for moral responsibility.

However, it is far from clear that *all* psychopaths lack evaluative standards across the board in this way. If the possible existence of 'successful' psychopaths is enough to cast doubt on their ability to reason effectively about moral matters, it is certainly enough to cast doubt on their ability to have evaluative standards which allow them to reason effectively about their own self-interest. The psychologist Kevin Dutton summarises evidence for the idea that there is a class of person who, despite strongly exhibiting core characteristics of psychopathy such as low empathy, low anxiety and shallow affect, do not appear to have any difficulty acting consistently and apparently rationally in their own interest. According to Dutton, many such people are attracted to high-status professions such as law or medicine (and particularly surgery). Such roles presumably require one to stick consistently to life goals in order to become qualified and then to stay in a job.[37] It is not clear what Litton would say about such individuals, but there is nothing in his argument to suggest that they would lack moral responsibility.

Given the apparent heterogeneity of psychopathic personalities, in order to have something to say about a broader range of psychopaths, we must make assessments of their moral responsibility that rely on characteristics that are more broadly shared among them. I believe it is possible to do this, by focusing on the way they see other people, and the psychological deficits underlying this.

3.5   Imperviousness to Reasons

My overall aim in this book is to show that psychopaths, or at least some psychopaths, lack moral responsibility. Since I understand moral responsibility to be a matter of responsiveness to reasons, I will need to show that there are some reasons to which psychopaths, defined in the way I have defined them, are not responsive. On the other hand, there are clearly a great many reasons to which psychopaths *are* responsive. For example, a psychopath who is hungry will certainly recognise this as a reason to eat (or if they do not, it will not be because they are a psychopath that they do not). A psychopath who steals an object will typically have done so in

---

[37] Dutton (2012), p. 173.

response to some reason, or to what they take to be a reason; the simple fact that the object is desirable in some way would constitute a reason of this kind. But to judge that a person is or is capable of being responsive to one set of reasons is not automatically to judge that the person is or is capable of being responsive to all reasons. As Anthony Duff points out, 'the realm of reasons' has 'internal borders'.[38] It is perfectly coherent, for example, to imagine an incorrigible philistine who altogether lacks responsiveness to aesthetic reasons, while remaining responsive to other reasons – for example, the reason to eat presented by one's being hungry.

There are controversies surrounding how we should think of the reasons that any agent has, but we can surely say with confidence that many of the reasons that apply to non-psychopathic agents will also apply to psychopathic agents, and that psychopaths will be equally responsive to many of these. Nonetheless, I maintain that there is a particular class of reasons to which psychopaths are not responsive. Later in the book, I will present evidence that this is the case, but first it will be necessary to determine what that class of reasons is.

Whatever kinds of reason psychopaths do have trouble with, it is noteworthy that this trouble consists not in their being *oblivious* to such reasons, but in their being in some sense *impervious* to them. Carl Elliott describes the difficulty of characterising this distinction:

> What [the psychopath] does know is what other people think is wrong. He knows what other people feel guilty about, which actions will be punished, which will be rewarded, when to lie and when to tell the truth. In fact, he often knows all these things well enough to be able to manipulate, flatter and bamboozle people with something approaching genius . . . .
>
> On the other hand, the psychopath seems to lack any sort of deep engagement with morality. His knowledge seems limited to morality's most shallow and superficial features. This sort of deficiency can be difficult to describe, a bit like describing a person who is able to say in the most technically correct, clinical terms why Duke Ellington was the greatest jazz composer of the century, yet who is also clearly and unquestionably tone deaf.[39]

Elliott's description, I think, applies to many psychopaths, though perhaps not to all. The discussion around the moral/conventional experiments appears to show that some psychopaths, to adapt Elliott's simile, might be like someone who has a deficient understanding of music theory, as well as a deficient capacity to appreciate music. Nonetheless, I maintain that the

---

[38] Duff (2010), p. 204.   [39] Elliott (1996), pp. 77–8.

most promising strategy for someone looking for exempting conditions is to see if these can be found in the latter deficiency, not the former.

The type of psychopath with whom I am primarily concerned, then, is one who understands the full range of reasons which normal agents take to apply to their choices, at least in the sense that they understand that *these are the reasons that normal agents take to apply to their choices.* They have no trouble understanding that some reasons are taken to be more forceful than others, or that the fact that an action causes harm to another person is taken to constitute a reason against performing that action, or that the reason against performing an action that is constituted by the fact that the action will cause someone physical harm, for example, cannot typically be nullified by the removal of a diktat from authority outlawing that action. What this putative psychopath lacks, rather, is the understanding that these reasons genuinely are reasons that apply *to them.* They might, and typically would, understand that other people take these reasons to apply to themselves and also that other people take these reasons to apply to the psychopath. But, somehow, these psychopaths do not see these reasons as applying to themselves at all. If they claim to see this, it is only as a means of disguising themselves as ordinary people, and their actions and the way they deliberate about those actions reveal the insincerity of the pretence.

Take, for example, the psychopaths who were inmates of the Oak Ridge Social Therapy Unit described in Section 2.6. If the interpretation of that programme offered by Rice et al.[40] is the correct one, then these psychopaths learned a lot about morality through their involvement in the programme. At least, they learned enough to convince the psychiatrists working at the Unit that they were reformed characters. However, this only made them better able to manipulate and deceive others in pursuit of their own ends; it apparently did not, ultimately, change what they saw themselves as having reason to do. The question I am interested in is whether psychopaths such as these could be said to have become any more responsible for their actions through their treatment. Is understanding 'how morality works' enough to make people morally responsible if they do not understand that morality makes genuine demands on them?

The psychologist Martha Stout presents a series of case studies – some real, some fictional – to illustrate the inability to develop 'real' human relationships that she takes to be a central feature of the condition. One of the real cases concerns 'Luke', the husband of one of Stout's patients,

[40] Rice et al. (1992).

'Sydney'. Quoting extensively from interviews with Sydney, Stout tells the story of how, over several years of marriage to Luke, it had gradually become apparent to Sydney that Luke had never felt any genuine love or affection for her, but had married her purely for the easy and comfortable life he was able to lead by taking advantage of her hefty salary and luxurious home. For years he feigned depression and deliberately encouraged Sydney and her friends to pity him in order to avoid difficult questions about why he never worked or helped around the house, and in fact spent most of his time lying by their swimming pool. Even the child they had together was, to Luke, just another means of manipulating Sydney into allowing him to stay:

> For Luke, societal rules and interpersonal expectations existed only to serve his advantage. He told Sydney that he loved her, and then went so far as to marry her, primarily for the opportunity to ensconce himself as a kept man in her honestly earned and comfortable life. He used his wife's dearest and most private dreams to manipulate her, and their son was an aggravation he moodily tolerated only because the baby seemed to seal her acceptance of his presence. Otherwise, he ignored his own child.[41]

Luke's goal was a comfortable and easy life for himself. He viewed other people – even his own child – merely as tools which he could use to attain that goal.

In popular fiction, psychopaths are sometimes depicted as having obscure or deviant motivations. This is perhaps partly due to a conflation of psychopathy with psychosis. Dr Hannibal Lecter, in Thomas Harris's novel *The Silence of the Lambs*, is described as 'a pure psychopath',[42] yet he is drawn to cannibalise his victims, a motivation which suggests that he has some other disorder as well as, or instead of, psychopathy. Lecter is also depicted as a highly intelligent man, who delights in taunting and outwitting the detectives who are sent to hunt him. While this was an original idea at the time of Harris's first Lecter novel, *Red Dragon*, it is by now a well-worn fictional trope: the obsessive detective locked in a fatal game of cat-and-mouse with a vicious and manipulative bogeyman. Stout's case studies, including that of 'Luke', illustrate that both the capacities and the motivations of real psychopaths are much more varied than this. As Stout observes, aside from the core characteristics of psychopathy – the profound emotional absence – psychopaths have the normal range of human motivations and capacities:

---

[41] Stout (2005), p. 115.   [42] Harris (1999), p. 10.

People are not all the same. Even the profoundly unscrupulous are not all the same. Some people – whether they have a conscience or not – favour the ease of inertia, while others are filled with dreams and wild ambitions. Some human beings are brilliant and talented, some are dull-witted, and most, conscience or not, are somewhere in between. There are violent people and nonviolent ones, individuals who are motivated by blood lust and those who have no such appetites.[43]

My interest here is in psychopaths' capacity for practical reasoning. Specifically, what reasons, or types of reason, do psychopaths take seriously when they are deciding how to act? The things that psychopaths might be seeking to gain through their actions include comfort, wealth, power and pleasure. It is clear that psychopaths see the objects of these desires as reason-giving. My task here is to identify that range of objects that psychopaths do *not* see as reason-giving – or at least as not reason-giving *for them*, since it may be that they see them as reason-giving for others.

What links all of the psychopaths described by Stout, despite their varied motivations, is their selfishness – their complete lack of concern for the needs and interests of other people. Other writers agree. In Hervey Cleckley's words, 'the psychopath is always distinguished by egocentricity . . . usually of a degree not seen in ordinary people and often little short of astonishing'.[44] The impression one gets from reading Cleckley's case studies (as well as those presented by Stout and Hare) is that non-egocentric considerations are not merely outweighed in the psychopath's deliberation. Rather, it appears that such considerations simply do not occur to psychopaths as something of which they should take account or by which they should be motivated.

There are several ways in which non-egocentric considerations enter into the practical reasoning of normal agents. One of these is via obligations. If I believe that I have an obligation, whether this is to another person, to a group of people, to some entity or group of entities other than people, or to no entity in particular, I will take this to present a reason for action – a reason that should be taken into account in my practical reasoning. As has been discussed by Joseph Raz, T. M. Scanlon and David Owens among others, reasons stemming from obligations enter into practical reasoning in a distinctive way, and not just as additional reasons to be weighed alongside whatever other reasons are operative in the situation. According to Owens's analysis, there is a sense in which an obligation 'takes the matter out of your hands':

[43] Stout (2005), p. 2.   [44] Cleckley (1941), p. 395.

... it is no longer up to you to judge whether doing the required thing would be best, all things considered. An obligation does not shape practical deliberation solely by constituting a point in favour of fulfilling it ... it also constrains or limits your practical deliberations.[45]

Imagine I make a firm promise to you to sell you my car, and then I receive a higher offer from someone else. In this situation, I have an obligation to you to sell you my car, and because of this I also have a reason to do so. You might think that I also have a reason to sell my car to the person who has made the higher offer – after all, I would end up better off if I did – and what I should do is to weigh up this reason against the reason stemming from my obligation, as well as any other reasons that are relevant to my decision. I should then act on whichever reasons prove to be more import-ant. However, this would not be true to what Owens calls 'the phenomen-ology of demand'.[46] There is something wrong about the idea that I should even take into account the larger offer made by the second person. To take this into account would be to fail to take seriously the fact that I have, not just a reason to sell you my car, but an obligation to do so.

Exactly what constraints having an obligation should place on one's practical reasoning (or, alternatively, what constraints it places on one's practical reasons) is a matter of disagreement. For Scanlon,[47] an obligation excludes certain apparent reasons entirely from the set of applicable reasons. For Owens, building on Raz's analysis, an obligation does not constrain the set of reasons that apply, but it does provide a second-order reason to exclude certain first-order reasons from our deliberations about how to act. Owens's position has the advantage of being able to explain the fact that the reasons in question continue to apply to other things, such as, for example, my attitude to the decision I have made, or the circumstances surrounding it. For example, the reason stemming from my receipt of a higher offer for the car might cause me to regret having made you a promise in the first place, and it might be perfectly appropriate for me to have this attitude – the importance of the reason is not in this instance nullified by the fact that I have an obligation.

Whatever the correct way to analyse the role of reasons stemming from obligations in the practical deliberation of normal agents, it is reasonable to suppose, I think, that the 'phenomenology of demand' which is appealed to in this discussion would be alien to a psychopath. Psychopaths as described by clinicians and psychologists seem to be impervious to the force of obligations. While this is not a claim for which, to my knowledge,

---

[45] Owens (2008), p. 404.   [46] Ibid.   [47] Scanlon (1998), pp. 156–7.

quantitative evidence exists, the evidence from case studies is compelling. For example, many if not all of the psychiatric patients described by Cleckley were admitted to his hospital after squandering the trust of those close to them. Cleckley's book is full of descriptions of patients whose family and friends had repeatedly lent them money, bailed them out of debt, secured employment for them or vouched for them in situations in which they had got into trouble with the law. Most non-psychopaths, we can surely assume, would have felt the force of deep obligations to these people who had, at considerable expense or risk to their reputation, offered valuable help. Cleckley's psychopaths, however, appeared entirely impervious to any sense of obligation, happily squandering money lent without seemingly having any intention of ever paying it back, throwing away jobs in spectacular fashion and so on. These psychopaths appear to be the opposite of normal agents as described by Owens: instead of the reasons generated by obligations causing other reasons to be excluded from their practical deliberations, it appears rather that reasons stemming from obligations are themselves entirely excluded.

I have introduced reasons stemming from obligations as a kind of non-egocentric consideration. However, it is also possible to have an obligation to oneself, and the reasons stemming from an obligation of this kind would presumably be egocentric ones in a sense. Would psychopaths be likely to recognise obligations to themselves? This is a difficult question to answer. Perhaps an example will help. Imagine an overworked mother who spends her time juggling competing demands from her grown-up children, while also holding down a difficult full-time job. One of her children calls and asks if she would be able to give him a lift to the airport on Sunday night at midnight, so that he can go on holiday. She has an extremely difficult week ahead, starting with a very important meeting at 8.30 on Monday morning. It is part of her character to want to make sacrifices to help her children, and she really wants to say 'yes', but she recalls some advice from a friend who suggested that she had an obligation to put her own interests first in situations like these, because otherwise she would be acting unfairly towards herself. Now, we can imagine the overworked mother feeling the force of this obligation, and that the reason stemming from it would weigh on her decision regarding whether to agree to give a lift to her son.

To remain true to 'the phenomenology of demand', this scenario must be distinguished from, first, the scenario in which the mother simply ignores the son's wishes and thinks only of herself and, second, the scenario in which she weighs her son's potentially stressful trip to the airport against her own busy week and job interview and decides that her own need is greater. The (believed) reason that is relevant to the current discussion is that arising from her (believed) obligation to herself. We might imagine that she begins the process of weighing competing reasons and then, remembering her friend's advice, decides that what she sees as her obligation to herself trumps any competing reasons in the case.

Now, it is hard to imagine a psychopath deliberating in anything resembling this fashion, simply because, as I have been arguing, the non-egocentric reasons constituted by the needs and interests of other people, such as the son in the aforementioned case, do not weigh on the deliberations of psychopaths in the first place, and therefore there would be no need for them to be trumped by reasons arising from obligations in the way described. This, however, is not evidence that psychopaths do not recognise obligations to themselves. It may be that psychopaths do recognise such obligations, such that, if there were competing reasons that presented themselves to the psychopath as compelling, they would be trumped by the obligation-derived reasons in the way recognised by Raz, Scanlon and Owens. It is just that, being impervious to non-egocentric reasons, there are never any other reasons to trump.

A more effective test case, therefore, would be one in which a psychopath must weigh reasons derived from an obligation to themself against competing *egocentric* reasons. If the obligation-derived reasons appear to trump the competing reasons in this case, then we have evidence that psychopaths can recognise some forms of obligation at least. Cases of this kind can be difficult to formulate, let alone to test empirically. Perhaps the most easily imagined type of case would be one in which a person has some long-term goal in mind, and must sacrifice immediate gratification to attain that goal. Perhaps we do sometimes regulate our decision-making in this type of case through the formulation of obligations. Imagine I am a student who has resolved to study every Thursday night, because I attend a lecture on Thursdays which I find particularly difficult to understand. I am worried that if I do not spend time reviewing the contents of the lecture on Thursday night, I will not, over the course of the module, absorb sufficient knowledge about the subject. I come to see this Thursday night study as an obligation; as something that presents a particularly compelling reason, one which should in the normal run of things trump any competing egocentric reason which might come into conflict with it, for example the reason presented by a particularly good band playing this Thursday in the student union.

It is much more difficult to state, especially based on a mere thought experiment, whether a psychopath would be capable of feeling the force of an obligation of this kind. As discussed in Chapter 2, there is some disagreement over the extent to which psychopaths are capable of subordinating their short-term desires in the pursuit of long-term goals. For Robert Hare, the inability to do this is one of psychopathy's central features. As I have already noted, for Kevin Dutton,[48] on the contrary, many psychopaths are attracted to, and can be extremely successful at, careers such as surgery and law which require dedication and self-sacrifice. Even if the latter characterisation is the correct one, it would be impossible to know whether this self-sacrifice is mediated by the formation of obligations; it could just as easily be the case that the reasons stemming from long-term goals are weighed against the reasons stemming from short-term goals, and simply found to be more compelling. The question of whether psychopaths are capable of recognising obligations to themselves, therefore, is one on which we must remain agnostic.

Aside from through obligations, there are of course other ways that reasons stemming from other people – from their rights, interests and concerns – enter into the practical reasoning of ordinary agents. We could designate this broader class of reasons the class of supererogatory altruistic reasons – reasons that are not egocentric, but which do not arise because of any obligations the agent has. For example, while walking in the town centre you see someone who is obviously new in town and having trouble finding their way around. You stop and ask if you can help. You clearly need not have believed yourself to have an obligation to help, but nonetheless, the fact that they were lost and in need of help gave you, so you believed, a reason to help them. I think we can say with some confidence that psychopaths do not recognise reasons of this kind. The behaviour of psychopaths as they are described in the literature is always, ultimately, directed at their own egocentric ends.

The word 'ultimately' is important here, however, because it should be acknowledged that psychopaths are apparently capable of recognising other people as presenting a certain kind of reason for them, namely instrumental reasons. Psychopaths are perfectly capable of acting in another person's interests in order to fulfil their own desires. For example, a psychopath in a work situation might be helpful towards someone in a position of power in order to attain influence with that person and thereby increase their own access to power. In the Martha Stout case study, the psychopath Luke began his relationship with Sydney by treating her extremely well, and being highly attentive to her needs and interests. In both of these cases, the reasons to which the psychopath is responding are

[48] Dutton (2012).

purely instrumental. The other person is valuable to the psychopath as a means of attaining their own goals, and the attentiveness is, ultimately, merely a form of manipulation. If the psychopath could achieve the same outcome more easily by using force or violence, we may suppose, they would be equally willing to take this approach.

As well as reasons derived from other people, the conclusion that psychopaths are impervious to non-egocentric reasons applies equally to other types of reason that are not egocentric in the way I have been discussing, but which also do not derive from any particular person or group of people, or even from people at all. One such type of reason would be the type presented by non-human animals. It should be noted that the idea that animals present us with reasons which guide our behaviour need not be derived from any potentially controversial thesis, such as that animals have rights, or are persons and so on. Presumably any philosopher on any side of the various debates in animal ethics would at least agree that, presented with a kitten, and in a situation in which my actions would never be known to anyone else and in which I could never suffer any negative consequences in respect of my actions towards the kitten, I nonetheless would at least have a reason not to torture the kitten to death. A true psychopath would apparently not recognise such a reason as applying to them.

There are also, of course, a great number and variety of reasons that are neither egocentric nor arising directly out of consideration for other people or animals. This set of reasons would include reasons stemming from abstract ideas such as justice or from more concrete entities which are still neither human nor animal, such as the environment. Again, it seems unlikely that psychopaths, impervious as they are to reasons stemming directly from the rights, interests and concerns of others, will be any less impervious to these more abstract moral considerations. A clue that this might be the case comes from accounts of psychopaths misusing such concepts. Earlier in this chapter, I quoted Robert Hare's descriptions of psychopaths opining that their murder victim had 'learned a hard lesson about life', or that the three months spent in hospital by their stabbing victim was light compared to their own prison sentence. Underlying these statements appears to be a concept of fairness or justice, or at least a caricature of such a concept. While it appears that at least some psychopaths can learn to use such concepts more competently, the fact that many psychopaths see no problem with using them in such a nakedly self-serving way suggests that this competence would not be based upon a firm foundation of care and respect for other people, and therefore that the concepts, once learned, would not be deeply motivating for them.

A final category of reasons which deserves attention is that of aesthetic reasons. Reasons can be derived from a number of different aesthetic considerations. For example, the fact that something is aesthetically valuable – a painting or sculpture, say, or a musical performance, or something with natural beauty such as a tree or an unusual rock formation – would normally be taken as constituting a reason not to destroy or deface that thing. But this same fact might also constitute a reason to look at, listen to, or otherwise experience it. Often people can take these reasons to be quite powerful, as when someone expends considerable time, money and effort to travel to the city where a particular artwork is kept. Artists, of course, are also driven to create by aesthetic reasons: the fact that the artwork an artist intends to create promises to have aesthetic value presents itself to the artist as a reason for the artist to work at creating it. It might also be taken by those close to the artist to constitute a reason for them to indulge the artist's difficult personality and behaviour, or to provide an environment in which the artist can create without the distractions of everyday life. More prosaically, aesthetic reasons are prominent among the reasons people are responsive to when choosing what clothes to wear, or what house to live in, or where to go on holiday. There are, in short, countless ways in which aesthetic considerations affect our choices and behaviour.

Are psychopaths impervious to aesthetic reasons? This is a fascinating question to which the answer is unfortunately unclear. Several fictional characters who are either supposed psychopaths or have psychopathic traits spring to mind here, including Thomas Harris's murderous aesthete, Hannibal Lector, and the Beethoven-loving narrator of Anthony Burgess's *A Clockwork Orange*, Alex. However, while the aesthetic appreciation exhibited by these characters serves a literary function, it may not constitute a realistic depiction of actual psychopaths. The clinical and scientific literature offers no clues here and so, again, it is necessary to remain agnostic.

3.6   The Role of Value

What is it that unites the various categories of reasons presented earlier? It seems to me the best answer to this question can be derived from considering the relation of reasons to value.

It is, I take it, a commonly accepted claim that, if something is of value, then we have reasons to act in certain ways with respect to it, and to have certain attitudes with respect to it. The particular acts that we have reason to perform, and attitudes that we have reason to have, will depend on the nature of the thing in question. They might include, for example, reasons to refrain from defacing a work of art, to respect a person's dignity or to protect an area of natural beauty that is under threat. It is important to note that subscribing to this innocuous claim does not commit one to the more controversial claim that *all* reasons depend on value in this way – it is at least *prima facie* possible that some reasons depend on value, but that other reasons are generated in other ways.

Now, a further claim which I also take to be uncontroversial is that if someone truly understands the value of something, they will also understand the reasons that they and others have with respect to that thing. If someone claimed to understand the value of a work of art, but then defaced that work of art; the value of a person, but then harmed or humiliated that person for no reason; or the value of an area of natural beauty, but were happy to see it levelled and built on, then we would have reason to doubt that they could really understand these things. While it may be possible to question this point about the relation between understanding value and understanding reasons, I am not aware of philosophers who have tried to do so, and it appears to be quite broadly accepted. I will therefore not attempt to defend it here.

Now, to take this thought about value a step further, it also seems to me that what unites the various categories of reason to which I have argued that psychopaths are impervious is that these are all reasons which depend in some way upon the value *of entities other than oneself.* The pathological selfishness of psychopaths (or at least 'hard-core' psychopaths), I contend, extends to their being unable to see value of this kind, to *ascribe* it to others, and they are therefore unable to understand that they have reasons to act, which depend on this value.

Each of the types of reason to which I have described psychopaths as 'impervious' can be understood as depending on the value of entities other than oneself. To begin with the case of people, if someone understands the value of people, they will presumably believe that they have reason at least to respect their rights, their interests, perhaps to some extent their goals and projects (assuming those goals and projects are not immoral). They are also likely to believe that they have reason to support those goals and projects, though facts about the relationship between the valuer and the valued are likely to affect what one has a reason to do in support of these (such reasons are far more demanding, for example, in relationships between a parent and child than they are between work colleagues). All of these are reasons which, if someone did not take themselves to have with respect to a given person or group of people, we would have reason to doubt that they truly understood the value of that person or those people. All of these are reasons which, in fact, psychopaths do not appear to take themselves to have.

The case of animals is also explicable in terms of value and the reasons that depend on value. There are controversies over exactly what reasons we have with respect to animals, and exactly which animals we have them with respect to, but it seems very plausible that whatever reasons of this kind we do have depend on animals having value.

Reasons stemming from ideas such as justice or the environment can also, I think, be explained as stemming from those ideas having value. In the case of many of these reasons, it may be that the value of some more concrete entity or group of entities – either people, animals or some other valued object – lies behind the reasons which we perceive as bearing on our choices and actions. The idea of justice, for example, makes little sense in the absence of some entity – generally people but perhaps also some animals – which has a kind of value which implies that it must be treated justly. In other cases, it may be less clear whether such a valuable entity must exist in order to make sense of the reasons in question. In environmental ethics, there is controversy over whether the value of the environment can be reduced to its extrinsic value in serving the needs of humans, whether currently living or yet to be born, or animals or other entities, or whether it also has irreducible intrinsic value of its own.[49] In any case, it seems clear at least that the ordinary way in which we value the environment implies that we value *something*, other than ourselves, whether this is simply the environment itself, or whether it is the people, animals or other entities whose important rights, interests and concerns are served by the environment.

Aesthetic reasons of the kind discussed earlier, too, presumably depend on aesthetic value. T. M. Scanlon gives the example of Beethoven's late string quartets – if we understand 'the value of music of this kind', then we will understand that a recording of them should not be 'played in the elevators, hallways, and restrooms of an office building'.[50] Now, it might be thought that aesthetic reasons present a potential counterexample to the claim that the reasons to which psychopaths are impervious are those which depend on the value of entities other than themselves. If psychopaths can be shown to ascribe aesthetic value to objects, then they must be able to ascribe value to entities other than themselves. I have two answers to this point. First, it remains to be shown that psychopaths actually can ascribe aesthetic value in this way. Second, if psychopaths can ascribe value of a kind to aesthetic objects, this may merely be the kind of extrinsic value that those objects have as potential sources of pleasure for the observer.

[49] Routley (1973).   [50] Scanlon (1998).

Since the observer is in this case the psychopath, it may be that the ultimate source of value here is the psychopath themself, whose value I am not claiming they are unable to understand.

Indeed, it seems clear to me that psychopaths are able to ascribe value in other ways, where that value is not intrinsic to the entity being directly valued, but is derived from other considerations, ultimately amounting to the value of the psychopath themself. Thus, as noted earlier, psychopaths may value other people instrumentally, as a means to the satisfaction of their own goals or desires; so too for animals, or other entities such as the environment. Since the ultimate source of value does not reside outside of the psychopath themself, I take it that this type of valuing does not constitute a counterexample to my overall claim here.

I also take it that I need not be committed to the claim that the entities I have been discussing have *intrinsic* value themselves, at least if the alternative is something like utilitarianism, according to which only some ultimate good such as preference-satisfaction has intrinsic value, and any value possessed by people, animals and so on is derived from the value of this ultimate good. Whatever the ultimate good may be, it must be an entity other than oneself.

The idea that psychopaths are incapable of ascribing value to entities other than themselves (unless that value is derived from the value they ascribe to themselves) is a natural conclusion to draw from reading the various books and studies that have been written about them. It also explains the various types of reason to which they are impervious. But it also explains why they are *impervious* to these reasons rather than *oblivious* to them. If I do not ascribe value to a particular entity, this in no way precludes me from recognising that others may do so, or that in doing so they may take the value of that entity to present various compelling reasons for them. Examples to show this can be easily formulated involving any of the types of value explored earlier, as well as others. In the aesthetic sphere, imagine we have radically different views of a particular artwork: I think it has no aesthetic value at all, whereas you think it has tremendous aesthetic value. The fact that I do not see the artwork in the same way that you do has no effect on my ability to understand that you see it in the way you do, and that as a result you take yourself to have various reasons arising from what you perceive as its aesthetic value (reasons to contemplate it, to tell your friends about it and so on). It is just that I don't see myself as having the same set of reasons. I might further find it difficult to understand *why* you see it as having value in the way you do, but this does not imply any lack of understanding of the fact that you do.

3.7   The Implications for Responsibility

The next question we must ask is, of course, what this means for moral responsibility. If someone is impervious to a certain set of reasons in the way described, but not oblivious to them, can they be said to be morally responsible for their particular actions and choices that involve those reasons? It is not difficult to think of cases in which someone is oblivious to certain reasons (i.e. they are not aware of the facts constituting those reasons), and as a result they are not morally responsible. Earlier in this chapter, I discussed a case in which, unaware of the fact that B is a recovering alcoholic, A offers B a drink. Let us say A harms B by doing this, because perhaps B is having a difficult time maintaining sobriety and A's offer is the temptation that puts B back on the slippery slope to full addiction. It is surely not the case that A is morally responsible for this harm, however, since A did not know about B's predicament, indeed had no reason to suspect it, and thus was blamelessly oblivious to an important reason that counted against her action of offering B a drink, an action which in the absence of that reason would be perfectly harmless.

However, this type of case does not help us with the present question. In this type of case, the agent is blamelessly unaware of – oblivious to – an important member of the set of facts which provide a reason against performing the act in question. If A knew that B was a recovering alcoholic, A would know that they had a compelling reason not to offer B a drink, and A would therefore be morally responsible for acting against that reason and offering the drink. Now, if A is a psychopath, then they might know that B is a recovering alcoholic, might even know that other people would take this to constitute a compelling reason against offering B a drink, but still they would not, according to my view, be capable of knowing that this fact constituted a reason *for them*, A, not to offer B a drink. If I am to provide support for the position I am defending, that someone in this predicament would not be morally responsible, I need to find a case in which someone is aware of the facts constituting the reason in question, but does not know *that those facts constitute a reason for them*, and as a result is not morally responsible for the act. Specifically, the type of case I am interested in is one in which the protagonist fails to ascribe value to someone or something else, and as a result does not perceive them as providing a reason for action.

I have three cases which appear to me plausibly to fall into this category. None of these cases is without controversy. However, I believe that for each case, the correct reading is the one I have outlined earlier. Together, then, these cases provide support for the idea that to be morally responsible for an action depends not only on knowing the facts that constitute a reason, but also knowing that those facts constitute a reason for oneself.

The first case is one that has been discussed in a slightly different context by Neil Levy.[51] It is the idea of an anthropologist living amongst an alien civilisation. This anthropologist, in the course of his work, becomes aware of a number of moral practices and beliefs of the civilisation they are studying. In order to further his project, they transgress moral strictures which the aliens take to be binding. Let us imagine, specifically, that the anthropologist takes a number of plant samples in the course of his visit, despite knowing that the aliens believe that plants have value of the kind that a normal human would take another human to have, in the way that I have been exploring. For the sake of argument, let us suppose that the anthropologist knows enough about the plants to know that they are not essentially different from plants on earth, in a way that would give him reason to refrain from cutting them – they are not sentient, don't have a nervous system and so on. Nonetheless, in cutting away parts of the plants, the anthropologist is committing a great moral wrong, in the eyes of the aliens. Now, three questions present themselves. First, does the value supposedly possessed by the plants present reasons which ought to bear on the actions of the anthropologist? Second, is the anthropologist responsive to those reasons? Third, is the anthropologist morally responsible for the moral wrong which the aliens take him to be committing?

Note first of all that the putative reasons with which we are concerned here are those which might be presented directly by the plants as valuable entities. These reasons are distinct from reasons arising ultimately from the aliens rather than the plants. It is very likely that the anthropologist would be concerned about the feelings of the aliens, so that the anthropologist would want to avoid 'harming' the plants out of respect for the feelings of the aliens. In this situation, the anthropologist would not see the plants as having the kind of value that they have according to the aliens, but would nevertheless treat them as though they did out of respect for another entity which they did take to have the right kind of value, namely the aliens. It is important to discount reasons that are generated in this way because they have no equivalent in the case of psychopaths. Psychopaths, I have argued, see no entities other than themselves as possessing value. Therefore, there would be no situation in which, not seeing one entity as having a particular kind of value, they might nevertheless treat it as though it had that kind of

---

[51] Levy (2014), p. 358.

value out of concern for some other entity which they did see as having value in the right kind of way.

Now it seems clear to me, to respond to the second of the three questions aforementioned, that the anthropologist cannot be responsive to any reasons directly arising from the value of the plants in this way, as distinct from reasons relating to the aliens and the importance of respecting their beliefs, and so on. The anthropologist knows that such reasons exist, at least in the eyes of the aliens, but they cannot take them as applying to them, because they do not share the aliens' views about the value of the plants. To the anthropologist they are just plants. What is not so clear, however, is how we should answer the first question, in other words whether the anthropologist actually *has* reasons of this kind – whether in fact such reasons can be taken to apply to them. This really depends on whether the plants in question do have the right kind of value or not. If they do, then the anthropologist is mistaken, and the reasons in question do indeed apply to them as to everyone, but they are not (locally) responsive to them. If they do not, then the aliens are mistaken, the reasons in question do not exist and the anthropologist cannot be responsive to reasons that do not exist. Since in either case the anthropologist is not responsive to any relevant reasons directly arising from the plants as possessors of value, they cannot be morally responsible for committing the wrong that the aliens stand to accuse them of, though of course the anthropologist might be morally responsible for being insensitive towards the feelings of the aliens and for not treating them or their beliefs with adequate respect.[52]

While this first case is based on the fact that the kind of value attached to particular entities can differ between cultures separated spatially, the second and third cases that I have in mind both rely on the possibility of different practices of valuing occurring over time. In the second case, a time-traveller from an ancient culture vastly different from ours arrives in our time with, as one would expect, their set of values and beliefs intact. Now let us say that in this ancient culture, people of a certain ethnicity were considered not to have rights or interests that needed to be respected,

[52] The dilemma I have presented here – either the plants have this kind of value or they do not – depends on realism about value. It is of course possible to hold an anti-realist position on value, in effect to believe that value is 'in the eye of the beholder'. One would then have to conclude that no putative reasons stemming from the plants' value would apply to the anthropologist, who does not value the plants. It might be possible to claim that the anthropologist has the kind of reasons in question – most pertinently reasons not to take cuttings from the plants – based on considerations which do not include their having value, but it is not clear how one might go about this.

were routinely owned as slaves and could be used for whatever purposes people of the dominant ethnicity saw fit. Observing our own practices, the ancient traveller comes to understand that we see things differently, but thinks this is no more than a weird quirk on our part and born of a misunderstanding of the proper status of the different races. As a result, they behave appallingly towards a number of people of the ethnicity in question.

In the final case, a traveller from our own time is transported in a time machine to a point in the future, and finds themself in the midst of a civilisation in which vegetarianism has become a universally accepted norm, and in which the idea of eating animals is looked on with universal horror and revulsion. Not a vegetarian themself, the traveller brought with them a packed lunch, which includes some chicken sandwiches. Upon arriving in the future, they soon become aware of the different norms surrounding food compared to their own time, and hide the sandwiches, not wanting to incur the wrath of the people of the future. However, later, the traveller finds themself alone and peckish and, not seeing the point of wasting the sandwiches, they eat them, all the time fully aware that they are committing what would be seen by the vast majority of people in the world at the current time as an abomination.

We can ask the same three questions relating to these two cases as we did with the first one, namely: (1) are there any reasons arising from (a) people of the relevant ethnicity or (b) animals, as possessors of value, which apply to the time-travellers and which ought to count against their (a) treating people badly and (b) eating the chicken sandwiches, (2) are the time travellers responsive to those reasons and (3) are they morally responsible for the wrong the locals would take them to be committing? The correct way to respond to these questions is also likely to be similar, in that it is going to depend on whether the people or animals do indeed possess the kind of value in question. If so, then reasons against their actions will apply to the time travellers, but they will be blamelessly unresponsive to them, and hence not morally responsible for committing a wrong. If not, then the reasons in question do not apply to them and they clearly cannot be responsive to them. In either case, the time travellers are not morally responsible for committing a wrong.

In each of the aforementioned examples, the agent is impervious, though not oblivious, to a set of reasons arising from particular entities as possessors of value, and is not morally responsible for acting or failing to act on those reasons. The general conclusion we can draw from the cases is

that responsiveness to reasons depends not only on the ability to understand the reasons in question, but also on the ability to take them as
constituting reasons for oneself. The cases, along with the description of
psychopaths which I developed earlier in the chapter, also suggest that the
ability to take another entity as presenting one with reasons for action
depends on having the ability to see that entity as a possessor of value.

According to the hypothesis under discussion, psychopaths are in an
equivalent position, but they are incapable of seeing *anything* other than
themselves as having value, unless that value is derived from their own
value. If this is right, then the range of reasons to which they are responsive,
and hence the range of acts (and attitudes, states of affairs, etc.) for which
they are morally responsible will be much more restricted.

Now, there are two objections which might be made to my use of the
aforementioned examples and the claim that they are analogous to the case
of psychopaths, and these objections will point to gaps in the argument
which will need to be filled.

The first objection is that it is perhaps somewhat unclear that the
protagonists in the cases actually have reasons to be responsive to. That
is, they may actually be correct in the assumption that the reasons of which
they are aware do not apply to them. This would be true if in each case it
was the locals, and not the anthropologist or the time travellers, who were
mistaken about the reasons that apply. It would also be true if some form of
moral relativism were true, such that the reasons that apply to the travellers,
in virtue of their origins, might be different from those that apply to the
locals.

It should be noted first of all that, as I have already observed, the
outcome of this would not be that the travellers are morally responsible
for the actions in question, considered as a harmful or a wrong act. Rather,
they would be in a situation akin to that of an animal that attacks another
animal. While a human performing the same act might have committed
a wrong, such considerations simply do not apply to animals. They are not
morally responsible for the act, not because there are reasons to which they
are unresponsive, but because the relevant reasons relating to the act do not
apply to them.

Also, while it might be plausible to suppose that the aliens might be
mistaken about the plants' possessing value, or that the people of the future
might be mistaken about animals, it is less plausible, one would hope, to
suppose this about our attitudes to people of other ethnicities. To make the
equivalent supposition about the case of psychopaths would involve believing that people do not possess value and that we are wrong to believe that

we have reasons to refrain from harming them, for example. I will not argue against this view, which amounts to moral nihilism.[53]

The second possible objection is that, while it might be plausible in all three cases to claim that the protagonist lacks moral responsibility *at first*, it is far less plausible to claim that they would continue to lack moral responsibility if they remained in the situation and failed to adjust to it. This is particularly true if we suppose that the locals in each case are correct. In this case, we might expect the protagonist in the case to come to see the force of the relevant reasons eventually, at which point they would become responsive to them. If psychopaths are going to be truly and permanently lacking in moral responsibility for their acts, it must be the case not only that they do not see the relevant reasons as applying to them, because they do not see other entities as valuable, but that they *cannot* do these things. The next two chapters will be dedicated to showing that this is the case.

Before embarking on this project, however, I need to make a final clarification and refinement of the position I have arrived at in this chapter. This is to make clear exactly what I mean when I talk about psychopaths (and others) 'seeing others as valuable', or 'ascribing value' to others. What I am describing here is, I think, a belief, but there are several different beliefs which could be described in this way, and I need to make clear exactly what kind of belief I have in mind. The kind of belief which I want to make clear I do *not* have in mind here is a kind of abstract, philosophical belief that entities other than oneself have value. One can imagine a philosophical person (even a philosophical psychopath) becoming convinced through argument that other people have value. This would be a belief held at a theoretical level. It cannot be, however, that a belief of this kind is a necessary condition for moral responsibility, since the majority of people are apparently fully morally responsible without having this kind of belief. But can it be a sufficient condition?

---

[53] It should be noted that there is a philosophically respectable position, internalism about reasons, which holds that people cannot have a reason unless they are somewhat motivated to comply with that reason, and I have suggested that psychopaths are not moved by considerations arising from other entities as possessors of value. An internalist would therefore be forced to conclude that such reasons do not apply to psychopaths. It is certainly an interesting question whether psychopaths are in this predicament – reasons arising from other entities as possessors of value do not apply to them – or in the predicament of someone who has reasons but is not responsive to them. I will not attempt to settle this question, since (1) it does not affect whether we should think of psychopaths as being morally responsible or not, and (2) it is an extremely vexed philosophical question about which a lot has been written, (e.g. Williams (1981), Korsgaard (1986), Smith (1995)). Nonetheless it is a question that has implications for how we should think about psychopaths. Are they people whose appalling acts are, however counter-intuitive this may be, not contrary to any reasons they have? Or are they people who commit acts contrary to reasons but are not morally responsible for doing so?

To believe that someone or something is valuable, in the sense that I have in mind, is to believe something about certain acts, attitudes or beliefs relating to that person or thing. For example, if I believe someone is valuable, then I must believe that their interests are valuable, and this will have implications for the ways I can act towards them, or the reasons for which I can act in certain ways towards them. Ordinarily, for example, believing someone's interests are valuable would discount acting or deliberating in a way that does not take proper account of those interests. If you are blocking my way on the pavement, I cannot simply barge you into the road; to do so would be to ignore the fact that your interests would be harmed by my action, and my own interest in getting to my destination more quickly is not enough to outweigh this consideration. Believing that someone's interests are valuable also makes them a candidate to be the object of supererogatory action. If I give money to a homeless charity, it is presumably because I think the interests of homeless people are of value – it is worthwhile to act in their interests.

Our believing that someone or something has value, then, is a basic condition which must be fulfilled before various evaluative beliefs can be entertained about various acts, attitudes and so on relating to them: that it is worthwhile helping them; that harming them without some overriding reason is impermissible; that (in the case of persons at least) they have rights which must be respected and so on. Now, it is possible to imagine someone coming to believe that someone or something has value in this sense purely through having come to adopt a general, theoretical belief in the value of people and things. Say I am persuaded to the theoretical conviction that all people have value in this sense. Then I must, rationally, believe that you, a person, have value. Would this be enough to make me morally responsible for my actions towards you? Perhaps it would. In such a hypothetical case, I would understand not only that your interests, rights and concerns provide reasons, but also that those reasons apply to me. However, because the belief that someone is valuable is the basis for other beliefs such as that helping these people is worthwhile, that harming them is impermissible and so on, in order to show that I genuinely have this founding belief, I would need also to have the accompanying beliefs. And these accompanying beliefs are intimately connected to how I act, and to how I deliberate about my actions. If I were to find myself seriously considering punching you in the face for my own amusement, for example, this would demonstrate that my theoretical belief in your value did not amount to a genuine belief of the kind that can ground a proper appreciation of the reasons generated by your value.

Applying this to the case of psychopaths, it seems unlikely that a 'hard-core' psychopath who came to believe that others are valuable as a matter of theoretical conviction, would as a result develop the full set of evaluative beliefs and attitudes which I have alluded to here. On the other side of the divide, it seems highly unlikely that this kind of general theoretical conviction has anything to do with the way non-psychopaths come to see others as valuable. This, in my view, is more likely to be the result of patterns of value-ascription being formed through a developmental process, employing emotions and empathy, in which others are represented as valuable. In Chapters 4 and 5, I will set out how I think this works.

3.8 Conclusions

In Chapter 2, I gathered evidence of the emotional deficiencies characteristic of psychopathy. In this chapter, I have considered various interpretations of these deficiencies in terms of moral responsibility, offering as the best interpretation that psychopaths do not recognise reasons stemming from the rights, interests and concerns of other people, due to their inability to recognise sources of value other than themselves.

So far, my conclusion that psychopaths are indeed incapable of recognising others as sources of value, and thus the reasons based on that value, is based on a plausible reading of the scientific literature describing psychopaths' behaviour and attitudes. The task of the next two chapters is to trace a line to that conclusion from the conclusions of Chapter 2, relating to the peculiar emotional deficiencies which make up the psychopathic personality. I will begin this task in Chapter 4 by examining the tendency for general emotional deficiencies to interfere with one's ability to make evaluative judgements.

CHAPTER 4

Emotions and Value

4.1 Introduction

In the second part of Chapter 3, I presented psychopaths as impervious to certain kinds of reason, namely reasons that depend on seeing entities other than oneself as sources of value. I argued that this leads psychopaths to lack moral responsibility in cases in which such reasons bear on their choices. However, the claim that psychopaths cannot see anything other than themselves as a source of value was based only on a plausible reading of descriptions of cases in the scientific and clinical literature. It would help to bolster this claim if it could be shown that more firmly established facts about psychopaths' psychological makeup would be likely to result in such a radically unusual outlook at the level of value. The best-established facts, as I have explained, relate to their deficient, 'shallow' emotional experience. In this chapter, I will explore this and examine its implications, arguing that it begins to explain the unusual pattern of value ascription, and hence responsiveness to reasons, that I described psychopaths as exhibiting at the end of Chapter 3.

To get to this point, it will be necessary to engage with the extremely vexed question of what emotions are. If psychopaths have emotional deficits, what exactly is it that they thereby lack, and what implications does this lack have for the ability of psychopaths to ascribe value? I will argue that a general shallowness of emotional experience interferes profoundly with the psychopath's experience of value. To see why this is so requires understanding what emotional experience *is*: in my view, a complex of embodied feelings and evaluative judgements. This takes us into difficult philosophical territory, and disentangling the various conflicting views in order to arrive at a settled position will take the majority of the chapter. Having done this, I will be able, at the end of the chapter, to turn to the implications of the view I favour for psychopaths and the way they ascribe value to the world, connecting this to the conclusions of Chapter 3.

4.2 Theories of the Emotions

The debate between competing 'theories of the emotions' is a highly contested area in philosophy. In order to begin to negotiate this territory, it is useful to consider what it is that we know, or apparently know, about emotions – the data which theories of the emotions must try to explain. Peter Goldie[1] has a list of these, which includes: diversity in duration, focus, complexity, physical manifestation, degree of development and degree of action-connectedness; the fact that many (if not all) emotions appear to be evolutionarily adaptive; the fact that animals and babies, without language, appear to be capable of at least some emotions; and the fact that emotions stand in rational relation to other psychological states (for example, they can be justified by the same reasons which justify beliefs). I will consider each of these in some depth later in the chapter, so will leave them unexplained for now.

Two further properties of emotions listed by Goldie are particularly important for my purposes here. First, emotions are about what matters, what is important and what is of value to us. If something makes you sad and you cry, it is because whatever has made you sad is something that is important to you. Second, emotions seem to provide motivation in some way. So, for example, it would be strange to claim that one is angry about something and yet to have no motivation at all to do anything about it. Whether that motivation will translate into action is of course another question altogether. However, if one professed absolutely no motivation, this would bespeak a kind of indifference that seems to be incompatible with genuine anger.

Another feature of emotions which is generally agreed upon is that they are, or are capable of being, intentional. The word is used here in the phenomenological sense indicating *directedness*, or '*aboutness*'. Emotions are, at least typically, *about* something.

There is a common practice here of drawing a distinction between emotions, which are always about something, and moods, which may be about nothing. If we were to follow this practice, we might also want to try to analyse the connection between moods and emotions. Moods, we might say, involve a disposition to experience emotions in response to certain stimuli. For example, I might go around in a sad mood all day, without that sadness being directed at anything in particular, but one result of my being in that mood will be that when a subject of conversation, say, is presented

---

[1] Goldie (2007a).

to me, I will be more likely to feel sad about that particular thing, as a result of my generally sad mood. This is a general claim about the probability of my being sad about any given thing; it does not imply that I will exhibit increased sadness about every single thing that is presented to me. There may well be things about which I will continue to feel happy when I think of them, regardless of how sad my mood is. Nonetheless, if there were not a general increase in my propensity to be sad about things, it would seem inaccurate to describe me as being in a sad mood. However, while there is some intuitive appeal in this distinction between emotions and moods, it seems to me to be, to a large degree, stipulative. There seems nothing unnatural, as a matter of ordinary language, in describing the kind of general mood of sadness described earlier as being an *emotion*. It might therefore be more helpful to describe emotions as usually, but not always, intentional. At least, they clearly *can* be intentional. Furthermore, their intentional objects can be things external to the subject. For example, if I am afraid of a bear, my fear is *about* the bear. This fact will turn out to be important when we consider what kind of thing an emotion might be.

Theories of the emotions are usually divided into three general types: non-cognitive, 'feeling' theories, cognitive theories and perceptual theories. 'Feeling theories' have their roots in the work of William James,[2] who claims that emotions are perceptions of bodily changes brought on by stimuli. Modern feeling theorists, including Jesse Prinz[3] and Jenefer Robinson[4] are indebted to James to varying extents. Cognitive theories, by contrast, hold that thoughts are in some way essential to emotions. Cognitive theories are to be found in the work of Martha Nussbaum[5] and Robert Solomon,[6] both of whom hold that emotions are essentially a species of evaluative judgement. According to perceptual theories, emotions either are, or are closely analogous to (can be modelled on) perceptions, usually of value. Ronald De Sousa[7] is a prominent defender of a perceptual theory of the emotions.

As noted by Goldie, there is a high degree of variability, in respect of a number of qualities, between the phenomena that are usually called, as a matter of ordinary language, emotions. This variability has led some, including Paul E Griffiths[8] and Amélie Oksenberg Rorty,[9] to call for the

---

[2] James (1884).
[3] Prinz (2004a). Prinz's theory is a sophisticated one which contains elements of perceptualism, but it is a feeling theory in the sense that it identifies emotions with internal perceptions of physiological states and changes.
[4] Robinson (2004).   [5] Nussbaum (2004).   [6] Solomon (2004).
[7] De Sousa (1987), De Sousa (2002).   [8] Griffiths (2004).   [9] Oksenberg Rorty (2004).

abandonment of the idea that there can be a single unifying 'theory of the emotions'. Griffiths argues that emotions are not a natural kind – that 'the psychological, neuroscientific, and biological theories that best explain any particular subset of human emotions will not adequately explain all human emotions'.[10] The alleged distinction between mood and emotion discussed earlier is one example where the limits of the vernacular category of the emotions may not coincide with boundaries that can be drawn at a theoretical level. Another such distinction has been suggested based on the work of Ekman and Friesen,[11] which identifies six 'basic' human emotions: anger, disgust, fear, joy, sadness and surprise. It may be that some instances of some of these basic emotions do not have enough in common with more complex emotions such as indignation or resentment for it to be plausible that what explains one group at a theoretical level will also (completely) explain the other. In any case, those who do wish to pursue a project of theorising about 'the emotions' must be careful to be clear about which phenomena are to be included in the category and which are not.

The question of what we think emotions are, then, is relevant to the question of how we would expect someone's emotional capacity (or lack of it) to affect the way they experience value. Crudely, if emotions are evaluative judgements, then they are central to our ability to access value through judgement; if they are perceptions of value, then they are central to our ability to access value through perception; if they are feelings, then it is not clear whether they would be *central* to our ability to access value, but they would still be likely to affect the extent to which we value some things, and the kind of value we attach to them. This much is true even of other, non-emotional, feelings: for example, my feeling cold and wet when out for a walk is likely to affect my evaluative judgements about the weather.

It is important to understand, however, that even if a cognitive or a perceptual theory is the correct one, in neither case can it be true that emotions are the *only* available means of accessing value.

First, considering cognitive theories, it seems clear that some evaluative judgements, which look equivalent or at least similar to the kind of evaluative judgements that a cognitivist would identify with emotions, can be made in an apparently non-emotional way. Imagine a very experienced judge who is used to making complex evaluative judgements about the accused in criminal cases. They have presided over thousands of such cases, and in each one they have been required to make a number of

---

[10] Griffiths (2004).   [11] Ekman and Friesen (1971), Levenson et al. (1990).

judgements about the character of the accused and, ultimately, whether and to what degree each person *deserves* to be subjected to criminal sanctions. It certainly does not seem incoherent to suppose that this judge, with the benefit of their great experience, could make such judgements without becoming emotionally involved in each case. In fact, it might even be thought concerning if the judge was bringing their emotions to bear on cases; handing out a more severe sentence, for example, when the case made them angry. Clearly, the operation of emotions is not a necessary condition of evaluative judgement. Furthermore, it appears that – at least in some cases – alternative routes to value might be at least as reliable as emotional routes. It might be that these routes are available even to people with emotional deficits.

Considering perceptual theories, even if emotions are evaluative perceptions, it might be that we have other ways of accessing value than direct perception – for example through judgement. Seen in this way, the case of the psychopath might be somewhat analogous to the case of a driver who suffers red/green colour-blindness. Even though such a person would not be able directly to perceive a traffic light as red, they would nonetheless be able to infer that it is red, from its position on the traffic light, for example. The colour-blind driver would have cognitive access to a fact that others would be able to access directly through perception. Similarly, it might be that a psychopath, though unable to access the value of other people through direct perception, might be able to infer such value cognitively. Of course, it would need to be established that value can be inferred in this way.

In the following sections, I will argue that emotional experience involves both cognitive elements and elements of 'feeling'. There are, I think, strong arguments in favour of each element being part of what we experience when we experience an emotion. Rather than to isolate a single element and call that the emotion, we reach a better explanation by accepting that both are present in and essential to emotional experience. To show why I think this is, I will first examine arguments in favour of, and against, the three broad types of emotion theory, taken in turn. I will then try to show why we should accept a hybrid theory which combines elements of cognitive and feeling theories.

4.3   Feeling Theories

Why might someone be attracted to the position that emotions are essentially feelings? To answer this question, we must first understand what is meant by 'feelings'. The Jamesian view equates feelings with internal perceptions of physiological reactions. One simple reason to favour this view, then, is that emotions very often do appear to involve physiological reactions of one kind or another. The hairs on the backs of our necks stand up when we are afraid. We get 'butterflies in our stomachs' when we are nervous. When we are angry, we become physically agitated and our faces go red. To identify emotions with the perceptions of these physical reactions would have the virtue of explanatory economy: we know they exist, and we know they tend to happen in cases when emotional experiences occur. An explanation which identifies one with the other is at least a simple one.

Another apparent reason to favour this view might come from the thought that it does justice to the phenomenology of emotional experience. This point has been made forcefully by Peter Goldie. As Goldie points out, the presence of such feelings in emotional experience is 'utterly familiar to us',[12] and an explanation that leaves them out, or tries to explain them away as something other than feelings, fails to do justice to this experience. This is an argument from introspection: examining one's own emotional experience, according to Goldie, reveals it to have a phenomenal character closer to that of feelings than to that of beliefs or judgements. This phenomenal character is more readily explained by the idea that emotions actually *are* feelings.

It is worth considering what emotions are being compared to on this view. Other, non-emotional, feelings include the feeling of being cold, or hungry, or in (physical) pain. These feelings are psychological, rather than physiological, yet they are reactive to physiological phenomena in a way that means it is natural to think of them as perceptions of those phenomena, though they would need to be a unique kind of perception, and not the only kind of perception available, at least in many cases. For example, hearing my stomach rumbling is an alternative means of perceiving some of the physiological activity of which hunger would be a feeling-perception.

One thing we know about perceptions is that they can sometimes go awry. The usual example is a stick held in water: I perceive it as bent but I know that it is in fact straight. Can feelings go awry in a similar way? It is possible for me to be sitting in a room with the heating turned up to full, so that the vast majority of people in that situation would feel hot, and yet still feel cold, perhaps because I am ill. In these circumstances, it is perhaps natural to say that I only *feel* cold; I am not *really* cold. On the other hand,

[12] Goldie (2004).

if I have just eaten a large meal and have no need of further food, and yet still feel hungry, it is less obviously natural to say that I am not *really* hungry. To be hungry just is to feel hungry. The difference between these two cases may simply be one of linguistic convention: when we apply the predicate 'hungry' to a person, we are referring to the feeling they are experiencing, whereas when we apply the predicate 'cold', we are referring to an objective fact about them – their body temperature, perhaps. In any case, it does seem that we can have the feeling without the corresponding physiological process or property being present, which is compatible with these feelings being perceptions of physiological processes or properties, which can go awry in a similar way to other perceptions. Of course, it will remain true in these cases that we are experiencing a feeling of hunger, or of cold, or whatever, but this may simply mean that we are experiencing a feeling *as of* our stomach being empty, or our body being cold, or whatever. In a similar way, the person seeing the stick in water is perceiving it *as if it were* bent.

The idea that emotions too are perceptions of physiological reactions has received some empirical support from scientific studies. One series of studies has been particularly influential in philosophy. In the studies of Ekman and Friesen and Levenson et al.,[13] each of six 'basic emotions' – anger, disgust, fear, joy, sadness and surprise – was shown to be accompanied by a unique pattern of physiological response, specifically heart rate, skin conductance, finger temperature and somatic activity. The significance of these results is that they appear to show that the physiological response alone is enough to distinguish between emotions, at least for the six 'basic emotions' that were studied. If this is right, then our experience of each physiological response pattern could plausibly be expected to have a sufficiently different character to be constitutive on its own of the corresponding emotion. There would be no need to bring in other mental phenomena in order to explain how we can tell one emotion from another.

One objection that could be made here is that it is not clear that all of the physiological states listed earlier are really the kind of thing that we would typically perceive. Even if we can perceive them, we would certainly not need to be aware of perceiving them when we are experiencing one of the six emotions also listed earlier. When we feel afraid, we need not be aware of an increase in our heart rate or our body temperature. There is a potential difference here between emotions and feelings such as hunger: the feeling of having an empty stomach is at least part of the way we

---

[13] Ekman and Friesen (1971), Levenson et al. (1990).

experience hunger, and this can be established just by examining the kind of feeling we have when we are hungry. By contrast, it is not clear that the perception of any of the physiological states listed earlier is part of the way we typically experience fear, and examining the experience closely does not make this any clearer. On the other hand, the claim under consideration is not that the four physiological states identified in the experiments are specifically central to emotional experience – they are simply states for which relatively simple, accurate measuring techniques exist. If emotional experience really is a matter of perceiving physiological states, then the states involved must presumably be quite complex, and individuating them through introspection might be expected to be very difficult indeed. The claim made on behalf of the data is that distinguishing unique patterns of response across these four factors is enough to establish that the basic emotions can be individuated through physical processes alone. The existence of further processes only strengthens this conclusion. Perhaps it is plausible that a more complex pattern of physiological response might be processed by the brain in such a way that it is experienced as a single emotion, without the complex underlying structure of the emotion being transparent to the person experiencing it. In an analogous way, the experience of recognising my friend emerging from a shop further up the street is made possible by the processing and interpreting of a huge amount of complex visual data, but my subjective experience is simple: I see my friend, over there.

An objection that has been made to feeling theories is based on the apparent fact that many emotions are extremely long in duration. Robert Solomon uses the example of love:[14] one can be in love for a long time – decades – and it is not plausible to think that one's body is in a continual state of perturbation for the entirety of this time. If not, then the emotion must, for some of the time at least, exist without any physiological correlate. The long duration of some emotions is supposed to be better explained by a cognitive model: we are used to accepting that someone can hold certain beliefs, for example, for a long time, and without those beliefs being present in that person's consciousness at any given moment. It seems extremely strange to suppose that perceptions of physiological reactions can operate in the same way.

Jesse J. Prinz has given an answer to this objection on behalf of feeling theories, which is to draw a distinction between *occurrent* and *dispositional* emotions.[15] No doubt this distinction is a real one: being in love for a long

---

[14] Solomon (1976).   [15] Prinz (2004a).

time does not imply that one constantly *feels* in love. Rather, one is disposed to feel in a certain way in certain circumstances – when seeing or thinking about one's beloved, for example. The feeling theorist can say that the long-term lover has a long-standing disposition to experience the relevant embodied reaction in those circumstances. To ascribe an emotion to someone is therefore sometimes a matter of describing them as having such a disposition, rather than as (currently) experiencing the relevant embodied reaction. Thus, the feeling theorist is able to explain both the dispositional and the occurrent emotion in terms of embodied feelings, without being committed to the implausible position implied in Solomon's objection.

One problem with this answer is that, if emotions are supposed to be feelings, then we might expect a similar distinction to exist between 'occurrent' and 'dispositional' in the case of other feelings, but in fact we do not find this distinction. I can be disposed over a long period of time to feel hungry in certain circumstances, i.e. when I have not eaten – in fact, perhaps barring certain pathological conditions, *everyone* is thus disposed – but this does not imply that I am permanently hungry, in any sense. Why should emotions be different, if they are just feelings?

The feeling theorist can reply that a disposition to feel hungry when one has not eaten is not analogous to the lover's disposition to experience loving feelings when thinking about the beloved. Rather, it is analogous to a disposition to experience loving feelings when one falls in love. Anyone might have this disposition without this implying that they are already in love. However, there is a closer analogy available which does seem prob-lematic for the feeling theorist. Imagine I really like donuts. This might imply a disposition to feel hungry when thinking about donuts, seeing a sign advertising donuts and so on. Clearly, it would not imply that I am always hungry. Why then should the disposition to experience loving feelings when thinking about (seeing) the beloved, imply that one is actually in love over the entire time that the disposition exists?

However, this analogy points to a major problem with the use of the example of love to make this point. The problem is that, just as a preference for donuts is not a feeling, it is not clear that love (or at least the kind of love that exists over long periods of time without a corresponding occurrent emotion) should be called an emotion at all. Indeed, the very wide range of unique emotional reactions that can be precipitated by love – including euphoria, anger, jealousy, pride, yearning, self-disgust, resentment and so on, as well as what we might think of as the occurrent emotion of love – suggests that it should rather be thought of as a very complex state of being that manifests in dispositions to experience an array of possible emotional reactions according to circumstance.[16]

Love, then, is perhaps an unusual case and therefore a difficult one with which to illustrate the point. Do we think differently about other phenomena? Take patriotic pride as another example. There is apparently a *feeling* called pride, and yet it does not appear to be a condition of one's being proud that one is actually experiencing that feeling at any given moment. It might be thought that a simple dispositional model applies here: patriotic pride as a dispositional emotion is a disposition to experience pride as an occurrent emotion when thinking about one's country, perhaps. However, as with love, the occurrent emotion which is the offshoot of dispositional patriotic pride may not always be pride itself. It may rather be fear or anger if the country is perceived to be under threat, or even shame if the country is perceived to have disgraced itself.

We might be inclined to ask, however, where this disposition comes from. Why would the patriot have a disposition to feel emotions in a certain pattern in connection to their country? The most obvious answers involve beliefs or evaluative judgements: the patriot believes their country is great, or judges it to be important, or some combination of the two or of other related beliefs and judgements. But these are cognitive phenomena and therefore are supposed to be unavailable to the feeling theorist as constituents of emotions. The feeling theorist would therefore have to accept that these cognitive phenomena exist and play a causal role in producing long-term emotions, but deny that the cognitive phenomena are part of the emotion, identifying this instead purely with the disposition which results from them. This seems implausible – surely it is more natural to think that the patriot is disposed to feel (occurrent) pride when thinking of their country *because* they are proud of their country, rather than that they are disposed to feel occurrent pride and this disposition is itself pride. By contrast, a cognitive theorist who believes that emotions are (something like) evaluative beliefs can perhaps more readily explain how a belief about something held over a long period of time can result in a particular set of beliefs held about that thing in different situations. We are used to the idea

---

[16] Indeed it is far from clear to me that there is an 'occurrent emotion of love'. I was struck recently when reading the precisely expressed autobiographical writing of the Norwegian writer Karl Ove Knausgaard (2013) that he does not use the word 'love' to describe the emotion he feels when seeing and empathising with his daughter, preferring a word which the English translator had rendered as 'tenderness'. Words such as 'tenderness', it seems to me, tell us much more about the phenomenology of emotional experience than the word 'love' could. Love, then, might be a fact about the individual that explains a range of different emotions, and not at all an emotion itself.

that believing one thing can dispose us to believe another when faced with a particular set of circumstances.

The feeling theorist, then, must hold that long-term emotions are non-cognitive, but also that these emotions are intricately, causally related to cognitive phenomena to the point where a more plausible explanation might have the cognitive phenomena as at least partly constitutive of the emotions. It seems to me that this is a problem that arises not only for long-term emotions but for short-term emotions too. Again, there is a potential disanalogy with other kinds of feeling here. I can feel hungry without having any particular beliefs or making any particular judgements, not only about what I am feeling, but also about any of the circumstances which are producing that feeling, for example that I have not eaten for a while, that my stomach is empty and so on. By contrast, it is not clear that emotions can be experienced in the same cognitively unmediated way. Can they?

It may be useful to return to the supposed distinction between 'basic' and 'complex' emotions here. Leaving aside the 'basic' emotions for the moment, in the case of 'complex' emotions at least, I would suggest it is rather implausible to suppose that they can be experienced without cognitive mediation. For example, how could I experience jealousy without having some kind of belief or judgement that precipitates my jealousy (the belief that the girl I like is flirting with the handsome stranger at the party, for example). How would the jealousy originate if there were no relevant belief or judgement? The same could be said of indignation, pride or resentment.

However, even in the case of the 'basic' emotions, it is far from clear that cognitively unmediated emotional experience is possible. First, the emotions that are included in the list can have objects which are not accessible to direct perception, either in principle or just as a matter of fact, and hence that require cognitive or imaginative activity to bring them to mind and thereby prompt the emotion. I cannot experience fear of a global environmental catastrophe, or disgust at the cynicism of a government's foreign policy, or anger at the lout who I infer must have dropped that fast food wrapper in the street, without calling those things to mind and, presumably, having some beliefs about them. Second, even in the case where I experience a 'basic' emotion towards an object that can be directly perceived, it is still far from clear that cognitive mediation is not required. Imagine I am walking through the woods when a bear emerges from behind a tree. I instantly feel afraid. Is there cognitive mediation involved in this emotional reaction? Not if by cognitive mediation we mean deliberation. I am unlikely to have time to think about whether I should be frightened of the bear: I simply see it and am frightened. However, cognitive mediation need not involve deliberation; it could consist in the application of a concept to the object I am perceiving, for example the concept of fearfulness or even just of being a bear. As another example, imagine there is a mouldy loaf of bread in my breadbin. Wandering into the kitchen, I smell the bread and am disgusted. I need not know that what I am smelling is mouldy bread in order to be disgusted by it. However, it may not be possible for me to be disgusted without applying a concept such as disgustingness to my experience.[17]

It would appear, then, that at least some emotional experience requires cognitive mediation, and it is quite possible that all emotional experience (or at least all emotional experience on the part of mature humans) requires it. The position the feeling theorist needs to defend, then, is that while cognition may be present in some if not all emotional experience, this cognition is not essential to the emotion itself. The cognition, for the feeling theorist, would not be what comprises the emotion, but what causes it. Thus, it might be that some emotions can be triggered by direct perceptual experience, while others will always require the intervention of thought, but that thought is what causes the emotion, and is not the emotion itself. Perhaps a person cannot experience righteous indignation without believing that they or someone else has been wronged in an important way. Still, this belief is not part of the emotion itself, but merely its cause, by being the cause of the physiological reactions, the experience of which comprises the emotion.

If these physiological reactions are supposed to play this role in emotional experience, one would presumably expect them each to have a unique and distinctive structure. If jealousy and indignation really are different emotions – as they surely are – and there is nothing to them but the experience of different physiological reactions, one would expect the physiological reactions to be distinguishable from each other at the level of physical description. The experiments I have already mentioned suggest that this is possible for the 'basic' emotions. In fact, however, there is also

---

[17] There may be some room to doubt whether disgust is always really an emotion. The purely visceral reaction that I experience immediately upon smelling the mouldy bread might be something more akin to non-emotional embodied reactions such as physical pain, with truly emotional disgust only entering the picture with some degree of awareness of and reflection on that feeling and its object. For this reason, the fact that infants and animals can apparently experience disgust in some form may not be a counterexample to the position expressed above. One might want to call these reactions only 'proto-emotional' or simply to accept that in these unusual cases emotions like disgust can indeed be unmediated by cognition, while maintaining that nonetheless, in mature human emotion, cognitive mediation is essential.

some evidence for the contrary position: that even basic emotions are not distinguishable from each other in this way. Schachter and Singer[18] present evidence to this effect, described here by Jesse Prinz:

> [Schachter and Singer] argue that bodily changes qualify as emotions only when coupled with judgments that attribute those changes to emotionally relevant objects or events. To show this, they injected subjects with adrenaline, which causes autonomic arousal. All subjects were told that they had been given a drug that was designed to improve vision. While waiting for a vision test, some subjects were seated in a room with a stooge who engaged in silly behaviour, such as playing with hula hoops and making paper aeroplanes. Other subjects were given an offensive questionnaire to fill out and seated with a stooge who feigned being irate about the questions contained therein. All subjects were secretly observed as they interacted with the stooges, and all were given a questionnaire about their physical and psychological states after waiting in the room. Schachter and Singer observed that subjects with the silly stooge behaved as if they were happy, and subjects with the irate stooge behaved as if they were angry. There were also control subjects who had been given a placebo and subjects who were forewarned about the effects of the drug. Both showed less response to the stooges. The experimenters concluded that bodily change is indeed necessary for emotion, but cognitive interpretation is needed to determine what emotion a bodily change amounts to.[19]

The supposed implication of Schachter and Singer's experiment is that bodily change alone cannot account for emotion, since the bodily change produced by the drug was identical in each case. Only when coupled with the subjects' judgements about the events around them do these physiological changes count as distinct emotions.

While this is a conclusion I endorse, I do not think Schachter and Singer's experiments offer strong support for it. As Prinz observes, there are alternative interpretations of the experimental data:

> The experiment does not actually establish that the subjects in the two conditions have different emotional states. While their behaviour is different, subjects in both groups report being relatively happy when they filled out the questionnaire about their current emotional state in the final part of the experiment. Schachter and Singer dismiss this, saying the subjects may have been trying not to offend the experimenters, but the same logic could be used to explain their behaviour while interacting with the stooges. Perhaps they were just playing along with the stooges to be sociable. On the face of it, this would not explain why the control subjects were less

---

[18] Schachter and Singer (1962).   [19] Prinz (2004a).

responsive to the stooges, but there is an explanation for this as well. If the adrenaline made the subjects happy, they may have become more sociable, and thus more likely to mimic the stooge. Subjects without the drug were simply less sociable. Subjects who were informed about the effects of the drug may have recognised that their expected states of arousal felt pretty good. They would have concluded that their happiness was caused by the drug, and knowing that it wasn't caused by being in the presence of another person, they may have been reluctant to act in the sociable way that happiness otherwise promotes.[20]

These interpretations are indeed plausible, but there is another issue with the experiment, which seems to me to be even more problematic. Even if it is conceded that the subjects in the different groups did indeed experience different emotions, the experiment as described does not sufficiently isolate the physiological from the cognitive elements of the subjects' experience, because it does not guarantee that the physiological reaction of the subjects is identical in each case. This assumption appears to be based on the supposition that the only physiological reaction present is that caused by the adrenaline. However, by introducing the different stooges, the experimenters have introduced an additional potential cause of physiological reactions in the subjects. It may be that, having been made happy or angry by the presence of the stooges, the subjects experience the unique pattern of physiological reactions which the feeling theorist would expect to be present in such cases. To assume that the only effect that the stooges have on the subjects is to provoke judgements on their part is to beg the question against the feeling theorist, who would expect the stooges to provoke emotional reactions which they (the feeling theorists) would identify as physiological, not cognitive. Nor, again, are the two control groups sufficient to contradict this interpretation of the results. Feeling theorists are committed to nothing that would imply that the adrenaline should not increase the force of the emotion. Two emotions that have unique accompanying patterns of physiological response might nonetheless be such that the addition of a drug such as adrenaline has an intensifying effect on them both. If so, one would naturally expect the subjects who had been given a placebo to feel less anger, or less happiness, than those who had been given adrenaline. Those who had been forewarned about the effects of the drug, on the other hand, might be expected to 'tone down' the behaviour that results from their anger or happiness, even if they felt that anger or happiness to a similar degree. Aware that some of the intensity of

[20] Ibid.

their experience was attributable to the drug, they might be wary of acting inappropriately, and modify their behaviour accordingly. Even if the subjects in this last group had an emotional experience, as opposed to merely exhibiting behaviour, that was weaker or less intense as a result of their being forewarned, this does not contradict the feeling theorist's position either. The feeling theorist's claim is not that emotions never *respond* to cognitive processes – this claim is indeed obviously false. The claim is rather that the cognitive processes are not themselves *part* of the experience that is properly described as the emotion. This is compatible with the idea that the subjects who were forewarned about the drug had a less intense emotional experience as a result.

So, at least for the basic emotions, the idea that each emotion is accompanied by a unique pattern of physiological response, so that the inner perception of that response might be expected also to be unique and might therefore account for the experience of the emotion, has some empirical support and is not falsified by the experiments described earlier. Nonetheless, this kind of account starts to look less plausible when applied to the more complex emotions. To borrow a useful list, again from Jesse Prinz, the states of mind that are normally described as emotions include such things as 'guilt, shame, jealousy, love, indignation, amusement, resentment, nostalgia, schadenfreude, and existential dread'.[21] Are we really to believe that each of these complex emotions has a unique pattern of bodily response associated with it? There is (to my knowledge) no experimental data to draw on here, but common sense would seem to suggest that, for example, shame and guilt are very closely associated in what it *feels* like to experience them. Similarly, it seems unlikely that anger and indignation could be distinguished according to their bodily correlates alone. These emotions, it would seem, require cognitive elements to provide the context which is necessary to distinguish one from the other. Indignation is only indignation, and not anger, if accompanied by a judgement that some injustice, or some slight, has taken place. Yet anger and indignation are clearly distinct emotions. If this is right, one might think, then these emotions cannot be 'pure feeling' but must include cognitive elements too.

Prinz's reply to this objection is brief but interesting. He draws on an analogy made by Gordon[22] between emotions and the phenomena of windburn and sunburn. Windburn and sunburn are physically identical reactions of the skin. They cannot be distinguished from each other in respect of their physical manifestations, but only in respect of their cause:

---

[21] Ibid, p. 53.   [22] Gordon (1987).

one is caused by wind and the other by sun. Yet we have no trouble accepting that windburn and sunburn are distinct conditions, or that they consist in their physical manifestations. The burn on the skin just *is* the windburn, or the sunburn, even though we would need to know how a particular burn was caused in order to identify it correctly as one or the other. Similarly, the thought goes, emotions such as indignation and anger can only be distinguished from each other by their eliciting conditions. If the emotional reaction is elicited by some perceived injustice, or slight, then it counts as indignation. If not, call it anger. Assuming the physiological correlates of indignation and anger are identical, there must be some cognitive phenomenon – some judgement, perhaps, that an injustice or a slight has occurred – if we are to tell indignation from anger. But this need not imply that this cognitive phenomenon is *part of* the indignation, any more than the wind or sun is part of the windburn or sunburn.

This explanation has a certain plausibility, partly because it fits commonsense definitions of the emotions concerned. *Anger at an injustice or slight* is a pretty good working definition of what indignation is. This point also applies to several of the other complex emotions aforementioned. Schadenfreude is joy at another's misfortune – that is, in fact, precisely what schadenfreude *means*. So, the feeling theorist might say, one would expect it to be distinguishable from other forms of joy through its eliciting condition: it is schadenfreude because it is joy specifically at someone's misfortune, and not joy at some other object. Still, it might still be that the *feeling* of joy – the perception of an embodied reaction – is what we should identify as the schadenfreude, and not our judgement that someone has suffered a misfortune, or a judgement that this misfortune is enjoyable, or any other cognitive phenomenon.

However, this point reveals an ambiguity in the notion of an 'eliciting condition' that I have been using earlier, which points to another important feature of emotions. Windburn is windburn because it is *caused* by the wind, but schadenfreude is joy *at* another's misfortune, and the language of causation does not capture this quality of *directedness* that emotions have. The fact of the other person's misfortune – or my awareness of that fact – is not just part of the causal explanation for my experiencing schadenfreude; it is also what the emotion is *about*. In philosophical jargon, it is the *intentional object* of the emotion. This fact about emotions is more readily explained if they are cognitive phenomena such as beliefs or judgements, or if they are perceptions, than if they are embodied feelings. It is generally accepted that beliefs, including evaluative beliefs, are *about* things: If I believe the bear is frightening, my belief is about the bear – the bear is its intentional object. This is also true of perceptions: when I see the bear, the bear is the intentional object of my visual perception. However, if a feeling – an internal perception of a physiological change – has an intentional object, then that object is surely the physiological change itself, and not some additional thing outside my body.

The intentionality of emotions is one of the most difficult aspects for feeling theorists to explain, and their attempts to do so are sometimes elaborate and complex. For example, Jesse Prinz's theory holds that emotions are about external objects in the sense that the embodied feelings that constitute emotions represent external objects as part of an evolved mechanism. I do not intend to evaluate this or any other specific feeling theory in detail here, or indeed any other specific theory of the emotions. I think it is fair to say, however, that the apparent intentionality of emotions sits very uneasily with the claim that they are pure embodied feelings. This can be further brought out by noting a related problem for feeling theorists, which is the difficulty of explaining what separates emotions from other feelings. As Prinz acknowledges:

> If the essence of being an emotion is being a perception of a (relatively global) bodily change, then fatigue and starvation should qualify. This suggests that emotions must have some other essence. The [feeling] theory leaves the most fundamental question unanswered: What is it to be an emotion?[23]

This problem exacerbates the intentionality problem, because intentionality seems as though it must be part of what separates emotions from 'other' feelings. 'Fatigue and starvation' are not about anything but the bodily states they represent. By contrast, fear is about whatever I am afraid of. The feeling in my stomach after I have eaten some bad food is about nothing other than whatever is going on in my stomach. My disgust at the corrupt politician, however, is about the politician. This intentionality of the emotions seems as though it must be part of what demarcates them from embodied feelings, because it is so hard to explain how embodied feelings could be intentional in this way. Now, it may be that the feeling theorist can use intentionality as part of an explanation of what separates emotions from other members of the set of embodied feelings of which they are one sub-type. Indeed, this is Peter Goldie's approach in the development of his idea of emotions as 'feelings-toward'. However, such an explanation would run counter to the common-sense intuition which says that emotions have distinct intentional objects whereas embodied feelings do not.

Another apparent feature of emotions which is difficult for feeling theories to explain is the fact that emotions appear to be open to justification in the same way that judgements and beliefs are open to justification. Imagine I am annoyed with you because you said you would meet me for dinner and then you failed to turn up without providing an explanation. If your failing to turn up was simply a result of your being careless and forgetting the appointment (and let us say this is simply the latest incident in a long line of similar lapses on your part) then my annoyance might be justified. It would be justified, then, in the same way that a number of evaluative and non-evaluative beliefs on my part would be justified: for example, my belief that you are careless, or just my belief that you have forgotten the appointment. If it turns out that your failure to turn up is due to a medical emergency, then this fact would render my anger unjustified, in the same way that it would render the aforementioned beliefs unjustified. The status of the emotion as justified or unjustified is responsive to a number of facts about you and your behaviour in the same way that beliefs and judgements are responsive to such facts. This is a further bolster to the case for emotions themselves being, or being akin to, beliefs and judgements. If not, and they are simply 'brute' feelings, it is hard to see how they can be the kind of thing that can be subject to justification at all. It would be as though someone who had sunburned skin despite not having been in the sun was described as having an 'unjustified' reaction. Such a reaction would be unusual, to be sure, but the language of justification is simply inappropriate in such cases. How might a feeling theorist respond to this argument?

I think the most plausible response would be similar to the one I sketched earlier in relation to the question of whether emotions can be experienced without cognitive mediation. That is, the feeling theorist would need to hold that people experiencing emotional reactions do have beliefs and judgements that are part of the cause of those reactions, but that the beliefs and judgements are not the reactions themselves. Othello becomes convinced that Desdemona has been unfaithful to him and experiences jealousy as a result. Someone who was aware of the facts of the situation would be entitled to infer a set of beliefs on Othello's part – that Desdemona is unfaithful, that she is treating him with contempt, and so on – beliefs which would not be justified by the facts. When we say that Othello's jealousy is unjustified, therefore, we might really mean that the beliefs which cause him to be jealous are unjustified. This would make the idea that Othello's emotion of jealousy is unjustified by the facts – or that in the alternative case where Desdemona really has been unfaithful, it is justified – an intelligible description of the case in ordinary language, though it may not be precisely correct at the level of philosophical analysis.

As in the previous discussion, however, it seems as though the feeling theorist has conceded quite a lot with this response. Cognition, it is suggested, is closely bound up with emotional experience, to the point where it may not be possible to experience an emotion without accompanying beliefs or judgements. If there is indeed pure feeling involved, it must be so intricately connected to those beliefs or judgements, so embedded in the experience of having an emotion, that they are naturally described as a single entity, so that we think of our emotions as being subject to justification, and not just the beliefs and judgements on which they are based. (It is worth noting again, by the way, that this would apply as much to 'basic' as to 'complex' emotions, since we think of these too as being subject to justification.) Still, the feeling theorist must claim, only *that bit there*, the embodied feeling is the emotion itself. The rest is incidental. But why should we believe this? Why not instead believe that emotions involve both cognitive and feeling elements? In fact, I think this is the most plausible description of emotions.

4.4   Cognitive Theories

I have given some reasons to reject the idea that emotions are pure feeling, but there are at least two further possibilities on the table: first, that they are pure cognition, and second, that they are perceptions, or something akin to perceptions. Let us consider the cognitivist view next.

The considerations that speak in favour of cognitivism are essentially those I have adduced earlier in arguing against pure feeling theories. The idea that emotions are (or are akin to) beliefs or judgements can make better sense of a range of apparent attributes of emotions than can the idea that they are pure feeling. These attributes are their intentionality, their justifiability and the fact that cognition appears to be present in most if not all emotional experience, at least as a causal factor, and is probably needed to distinguish between different emotions, again in most if not all cases.

Nonetheless, there are a number of reasons to doubt that emotions can be accounted for purely in cognitivist terms. One of these is that, quite simply, the experience of having an emotion is not like that of having a thought. A major reason why feeling theories have any traction in the first place is presumably just that the view of emotions as being at least partly embodied accords with the subjective experience of having an emotion. Strong emotions can manifest in powerful bodily reactions, including shaking, paralysis, increased body temperature, restlessness and so on. Here we see the mirror image of an argument against feeling theories I presented earlier: clearly when we experience emotions we do undergo physiological changes, and our experience at the time is partly constituted by our internal perceptions of these changes. Why then deny that this is part of the emotion we are experiencing? The pure cognitivist would need some reason why we should think of only the beliefs or judgements as being the emotion, and not the embodied reactions we are experiencing at the same time.

In arguing against pure feeling theories, I suggested that these theories have difficulty explaining why some feelings are emotions and others are not. Again, there is a parallel worry for cognitivists. If emotions are evaluative beliefs or judgements, then why are some evaluative beliefs or judgements apparently not emotional? More specifically worrying for cognitivists is the fact that many of the particular evaluative beliefs or judgements that might be thought to constitute emotions in one case can in another case apparently be experienced in an entirely non-emotional way. I used the example earlier of a judge who makes careful evaluative judgements about their cases without becoming emotionally engaged. In an alternative case, they *might* become emotionally engaged, empathising with the defendant or the victim, feeling angry or disgusted about the crime itself and so on. In the two cases, their evaluative beliefs and judgements might apparently be exactly the same. How then can the cognitivist explain the difference between the two cases? It seems to me that the difference is more readily explained by an absence of feeling in the former case than by an absence of any beliefs or judgements.

Another aspect of emotional experience which cognitivists find difficult to explain is the fact that emotions can sometimes persist after the judgements or beliefs which caused them, and which the cognitivist would identify with them, have changed. Imagine I am alone in the house late at night, when I suddenly see what appears to be a human face looking in through the kitchen window, which naturally terrifies me. Now imagine upon closer inspection it becomes clear that the 'face' is actually some trick of the light. Nonetheless, it had looked so real at first that I still feel afraid after realising this. Perhaps I have to switch the lights on and sit down to compose myself. Why am I still afraid? If my emotion of fear is purely a set of evaluative judgements about the terrifying face at the window, then one would expect that emotion to disappear as soon as it becomes apparent that no such face exists. If, on the other hand, my fear is partly my experience of the physiological reactions which result from my experience, then it is natural to think that at least that part of the emotion will persist, to a gradually decreasing extent, while my body reverts to its normal equilibrium.

One answer the cognitivist might have to this challenge would be to say that, although I may not be aware of them, some evaluative judgements do persist in cases like this. Indeed, there may be some cases in which we tend to think of the lingering emotion as betraying a certain judgement on the part of the person experiencing it. Imagine David is annoyed with his wife for losing his keys, and then he realises that she did not lose them, but his annoyance persists. Beyond a certain point, an observer might start to suspect that it was not really the keys that David was annoyed about. There is some other judgement he is secretly, or perhaps not fully consciously, making about his wife, some other belief he secretly holds about her, that is the real, deeper cause of his annoyance. In fact, the cognitivist might say, it may be more difficult for feeling theories to account for cases like this than it is for cognitivist theories. After a certain point, it becomes unlikely that David's residual annoyance is attributable to his body gradually regaining equilibrium, and the observer becomes entitled to infer a second belief, or set of beliefs, that is sustaining his emotional state. However, a cognitivist would need to explain *all* cases of emotional persistence as betraying the presence of some hidden belief or set of beliefs. This seems less plausible. Sometimes, as with the 'face at the window' case aforementioned, emotions persist in a manner that apparently puts them in conflict with *all* of the relevant judgements and beliefs that we hold.

4.5   Perceptual Theories

The difficulty both cognitivist and feeling theories have in explaining how emotions can persist apparently in the absence of relevant evaluative judgements is frequently cited as a consideration in favour of theories which either identify emotions with perceptions, or 'model' them on perceptions in some way, i.e. suggest that they share some key attributes with perceptions, rather than with thoughts or feelings. The perceptualist can observe that we have no trouble accepting that perceptions can exist in conflict with beliefs or judgements. For example, I can perceive a stick held in water as if it is bent. It *looks* bent. Nonetheless, I do not believe it is bent, because I am aware that my perception is unreliable. In the same way, the example of David and his wife discussed earlier does not seem problematic if his annoyance is neither an evaluative judgement nor an embodied feeling, but a perception of his wife as having certain evaluative attributes (thus, a perception of value). David does not hold any particular evaluative beliefs about his wife that constitute his emotion, so the explanation goes, but he continues to see his wife as annoying. In the 'face at the window' case, I have ceased to believe that there is a face at the window, but nonetheless perhaps whatever it is that looks like a face is so uncannily face-like that it is still frightening to me. In each of these cases, the perception involved is in conflict with the beliefs and judgements entertained, but there is nonetheless no logical contradiction involved in experiencing the perception while entertaining the belief or judgement. This conflict without contradiction is used by Döring[24] as the basis for an argument in favour of perceptualism and against cognitivism. If emotions were judgements or beliefs, we would expect them to be susceptible to change in the light of alterations in the other beliefs that we hold, but in fact they are recalcitrant to such change. Because perceptions are also recalcitrant to change in the same way, as illustrated by the stick example, we ought to think of emotions as being, or being akin to, perceptions.

However, as Salmela points out in a reply to Döring,[25] this argument mischaracterises the particular kind of conflict that can exist between emotions and beliefs. This relates to the fact about emotions that I noted earlier – that they are subject to rational justification. To put this another way, in the emotion cases, there is a norm of rationality governing our emotional reactions which is violated by the persisting emotion, whereas in the straight perception case, there is no such norm of rationality governing the perceptions. It is not the case that I ought to see the stick as straight. I am not irrational if I continue to perceive it as bent despite believing it to be straight. However, my continuing fear after realising that the 'face' at my window is not really a face is irrational, and I am irrational in continuing to experience it. Similarly, David's continued annoyance at his wife is irrational, at least insofar as it is supposed to be justified by his wife's losing his keys. Unless there is some other good reason for David to be annoyed with his wife, he ought to stop being annoyed with her. If he is concerned about his own rationality, and wants to be reasonable, David will try to stop being annoyed with his wife, in a way that does not work in the stick case – despite knowing that the stick is straight, I am under no normative pressure to try to see it as straight. As Salmela observes:

> The fact that we regard many recalcitrant emotions as well as pathological emotions as irrational rather than *arational*, and try to get rid of them, implies that the problem with recalcitrant emotions is not so much whether they *need* to be revised in the light of better knowledge, but rather whether they *can* be so revised.[26]

This highlights a fundamental disanalogy between emotions and perceptions, as between emotions and embodied feelings (there is no norm of

---

[24] Döring (2004).   [25] Salmela (2011).   [26] Ibid, p. 15.

rationality or 'rational ought' governing these either – if I feel cold despite not being cold, I am not thereby irrational and it is not the case that I, rationally, ought not to feel cold).[27] Despite the claims made by Döring and other perceptualists, the rational relations which apparently hold between emotions and beliefs are in fact better explained by the cognitivist view. It is not impossible for someone to feel afraid of something while also knowing it not to be worthy of fear – to experience an emotion and to hold a belief that are in conflict with each other – but they are irrational in doing so. In the same way, it is not impossible for someone to hold two contradictory beliefs, but they are irrational in doing so.

Another issue with perceptualist theories is that, in order to provide a clear alternative to cognitivist accounts of emotional experience, perceptions would need not to be cognitive themselves. As Salmela notes, however, cognitive activity is bound up intimately with perceptions, or at least with the perceptions of non-infants. Most, if not all, of our perceptual experiences are experiences of 'perceiving as'. In the case where I am afraid of a bear, it seems unlikely that I can see the bear without seeing it *as* something, whether as a bear, or a big hairy brown thing, or a threat, or something else. While I may not be aware of this, I am nonetheless applying a concept to my perceptual experience, which involves thought. As Salmela puts it, '*recognition*' is 'a kind of cognition'.[28] Certainly, this appears to be the case in those instances where my perception is emotionally 'coloured': in order to be afraid of the bear, I must see it as a threat, or as something fearsome, or whatever. But then this means that, again, cognition is in the frame as a possible explanation for the emotional aspect of the experience. As in the discussion of feeling theories, it appears to be impossible to isolate perceptions in an account of a specific emotional experience, so that we can say, 'here is the emotion, and here is the perception, and there is no cognition, therefore the emotion must be a species of perception and not of cognition'.

4.6 Reconciling Theories of the Emotions

In this chapter, I have set out considerations in favour of, and against, the three main families of theories of the emotions. With only a limited space

---

[27] There are, perhaps, applicable norms here. We might say that someone 'should not be feeling cold' with the implication that there is something either physiologically or psychologically awry which is interfering with the feeling and its relation to external conditions. Whatever kind of norm this is, however, it is not a norm of rationality.

[28] Salmela (2011), p. 10.

in which to do so, I have had to confine myself to reasoning at quite a high level, not seeking to engage with the detail of specific theories, but rather looking at the general considerations that are either friendly or unfriendly to each family of theories. Of course, it is entirely possible that an answer can be found to each of the criticisms I have raised against each family of theories, but these answers will in each case need to convince us of a somewhat counterintuitive conclusion.

For clarity's sake, it will probably be a good idea to summarise here the considerations I have looked at so far. I have argued that feeling theories are attractive partly because they do justice to the phenomenology of emotion. There is something that it *feels* like to experience an emotion, and embodied feelings are a plausible model for this. It is also apparently the case that, at least in many cases, emotions are accompanied by physiological changes, and we do experience an internal perception of those changes. Why not then think that this internal perception is itself a part of the emotional experience? I also noted some empirical support for feeling theories which comes from experiments which have apparently shown that at least the 'basic emotions' can be distinguished from each other based on their physiological correlates alone. On the other hand, I argued that the prospects for distinguishing emotions on the basis of their physiological correlates alone were much shakier when considering the 'complex emotions' (i.e. those other than anger, disgust, fear, joy, sadness and surprise) for which it is likely (and this is acknowledged by feeling theorists such as Prinz) that their eliciting conditions, which will probably include cognitions, will be necessary to distinguish between them. Against feeling theories, I noted the difficulty they have in explaining why some feelings are considered emotions while others are not. I also noted their difficulty in explaining how emotions can apparently persist over long periods of time – and that the most plausible available solutions to this problem appear to push the feeling theorist into cognitivist territory.

In favour of cognitivist theories, I argued that judgements or beliefs are present in, and apparently integral to, the vast majority of emotional experiences, to the point that a good reason would be needed to exclude these cognitions from what constitutes emotions (and again, this is particularly well brought out by considering the phenomenon of emotions persisting over a long period of time). I also noted the intentionality of emotions, a feature of emotional experience which feeling theories have difficulty explaining but which is much more readily explained by cognitivist theories. I also pointed out that emotions are apparently subject to justification in a way that is characteristic of beliefs and judgements but not of embodied feelings. Against cognitivism I noted that cognitivist theories, too, have difficulty explaining what is distinctive about emotions, given that it is apparently possible to entertain the evaluative judgements and beliefs which the cognitivist would hold to be constitutive of emotions, in an entirely non-emotional way.

Finally, I considered the perceptualist alternative, which is attractive because it purports to account for the phenomenological character of emotions while also accounting for the rational relations which hold between emotions and beliefs (as well as other emotions). However, I argued that perceptual theories in fact mischaracterise these relations in a way that makes them poorly suited as a model for emotions. I also argued that, as with feeling theories, cognitive elements appear to be present in cases of emotional experience which are candidates for explanation along perceptualist lines, so that, again, we need a special reason to exclude those elements from the set of what constitutes the emotion.

So where does this leave us? If each of the prevailing families of theories has problems which they have great difficulty addressing, what should we conclude about the nature of emotions? I believe this very difficulty of fitting emotions into an existing category points us towards the most plausible answer, which is that emotions are complex entities with elements of both feeling and cognition. When we experience an emotion, we make judgements, or entertain beliefs, with evaluative content, but we also experience the embodied feelings that those judgements or beliefs cause in us. My suggestion is that it is our combined experience of these thoughts and feelings that we call the emotion. When I see the girl I like apparently flirting with the handsome stranger at the party, I believe that she is flirting with him. Perhaps I judge this situation to be threatening to my plans, projects or desires: perhaps I was planning to flirt with her myself, or would like to. Perhaps I thought she was interested in me, and this flirtation – when she knows I am right here, after all – is an indication that this belief is mistaken. This storm of cognitive activity also sets off a visceral response in me, and I experience this from the inside in combination with these various cognitions. My combined physiological upheaval together with cognitive upheaval, I experience as jealousy. Crucially, the elements of thought and feeling involved in this experience are intimately connected with each other and act on each other in subtle and complex ways. Not only does the complex of beliefs and judgements I am experiencing precipitate my embodied feelings, but the embodied element of the experience sustains and intensifies its cognitive elements. As I watch her flirting with *him*, it is the churning in my guts, and the hot feeling in my skin, that signifies to me how *bad* this situation is, and perhaps also makes me aware in a way that I had not previously been aware, of what *she means to me*.

It seems to me that this combined view makes better sense of what it is like to experience an emotion than either feeling or cognitivist theories alone. The fact that my experience includes elements of belief and judgement explains its intentionality: it is directed at the scene I am watching because many of the beliefs and judgements involved are beliefs and judgements about that scene, or about the people involved in it. On the other hand, there is something that it *feels* like to witness this scene, and I am viscerally engaged in it in a way that I would not be if I were merely making a set of judgements, or entertaining a set of beliefs. It would be conceivable for me to make all of the same judgements in a completely non-emotional way; the fact that there are embodied feelings involved in my experience explains why it is an emotional experience at all.

There is an immediately apparent difficulty with this kind of combined account, which might be put as follows. While it may be true that the experience of having an emotion has elements that are best explained as cognitive, and others that are best explained as embodied feelings, it is apparently not the case that we experience these things as separate entities. When I experience jealousy, I just experience *jealousy* – I experience it as a single thing, perhaps one with elements of cognition and feeling, but not as a bunch of separate feelings and cognitions. Why would I mentally combine all of these disparate elements into a single experience and call it 'jealousy'?

There may be a way to explain this while also explaining two apparent facts about emotion which I noted at the beginning of the chapter, and which I stated would turn out to be important for my overall thesis: the fact that emotions are about what is important to us, and the fact that emotions are motivating. The explanation is that emotions serve an evolutionary purpose which would not be served if they were experienced simply as their disparate elements. Fear needs to be motivating, so that we will consistently take steps to avoid the things we are afraid of, which in typical cases will be dangerous. Disgust needs to motivate us to avoid its object, because the things we are naturally disgusted at – at a very basic level – are things that are likely to make us ill. Anger, perhaps, in its basic form, motivates us to take action on behalf of ourselves or our family or community when they are threatened. Each of these emotions has a physical manifestation which also serves a parallel evolutionary purpose. When afraid, we enter a state of high alertness, our muscles tense and we prepare physically for 'fight or flight'. When disgusted, our stomach churns, motivating us to avoid eating or drinking, and to remove ourselves from the vicinity of the object of disgust because of the unpleasant sensation it evinces in us. When angry, blood flows to our muscles, our fists clench, we instinctively make threatening gestures, all of which can be seen as preparations for aggressive and fighting behaviour. What I am suggesting is that we have evolved to experience these physical changes in combination with related beliefs and judgements in a way which motivates and readies us, at a psychological level, to take the form of action appropriate to the stimulus which has prompted them. This experience is what we call an emotion. That we experience these sets of phenomena as coherent, apparently unified mental phenomena called emotions can perhaps be explained by the fact that the experience needs to motivate us to respond quickly to cues from our environment.

Another problem that the combined view I am proposing faces is similar to one I noted in connection to feeling theories before: if an emotion is a combined experience of physiological reactions with relevant beliefs and judgements, why do only some such combined experiences count as emotions? For example, I can feel that my stomach is empty, and I have a set of evaluative beliefs and judgements directed at the cake in the shop window, concerning how delicious it looks and so on. The feeling of hunger will intensify the judgements I make about the cake in a way which looks quite similar to what I have described in the case of emotions. Why then is the hunger I experience merely a feeling, and not an emotion?

One difference between this and seemingly analogous cases of emotional experience is related to intentionality. It might be said that I am 'hungry for' the cake, and in this sense the hunger has the cake as its intentional object. All the same, the intentionality of this experience is not essential to it in the same way that the intentionality of emotional experiences is essential to them. I would still be hungry if no cake existed, and I can be hungry without thinking about or perceiving any food. While my hunger might motivate me to take action – to find food for example – it does not need to have any object other than my own internal physiological state. It has served its purpose by alerting me to the fact that my stomach is empty and I have not eaten recently. It is not clear that it is possible to be angry, or fearful, in the same way. Even if I am stomping around being angry at nothing in particular, my anger will still find objects, whether trivial or important, and which may include myself.

A related difference is that it is apparently not essential to feelings other than those involved in emotions that they depend on beliefs or judgements, whereas the preceding discussion suggests that this is the case for emotions. When we experience jealousy or indignation, our jealousy or indignation is precipitated by events and states of affairs in the world, but the link between those events and states of affairs and the emotional reaction is indirect – there is a cognitive link in the chain between these two things. I have to believe that the girl I like is flirting with the handsome stranger before I can feel jealous about this fact. Non-emotional feelings such as hunger and fatigue, on the other hand, are not, or at least not typically, like this. We do not have to believe that we have expended a lot of energy, or spent a long time without sleep, in order to be tired. We just *are* tired, as a direct result of our having expended a lot of energy, or spent a long time without sleep. The relationship between emotional feelings and emotional thoughts is thus more intimate, more interactive, than the relationship between non-emotional feelings and thoughts. This difference might be enough to explain our practice of putting emotions and non-emotional feelings and cognitions into two distinct categories.

Against this, it might be pointed out that it is not the case that non-emotional feelings are never cognitively mediated, that they never depend on beliefs and judgements. It is a well-recognised phenomenon that feelings such as pain, or the feeling of being hot or cold, or fatigue, can be greatly influenced by the judgements and beliefs of the person doing the feeling. Imagine you have been running around trying to get things done all day, having had a bad night's sleep last night. You don't feel tired because you haven't had time to think about being tired. Sometime in the evening, you are telling a friend about the kind of day you have had, when they interject, 'you must be really tired'. Suddenly, you realise that you *are* tired, and immediately feel an overwhelming sense of fatigue. In this case, it might be that the belief that you are tired has precipitated the feeling of tiredness.[29] This seems like a case of a non-emotional feeling being cognitively mediated in a way that I have suggested is characteristic of emotional feelings. So now we have arrived at a position where both emotional and non-emotional feelings can sometimes be cognitively mediated. How then can this characteristic be the basis of a distinction between the two?

One slightly weak answer to this objection is that, despite the cases I have just described, in most typical cases the difference in character which I have ascribed to emotions and non-emotional feelings holds true. Moreover, this is how we typically think about the two different kinds of feeling. There is something weird, and surprising, about cases like the tiredness case. We expect to feel tired just because we are tired. The idea that we sometimes have to first believe that we are tired, though it may be true, seems to undermine our common-sense beliefs about how these things work. In contrast, it is

---

[29] It could be asserted that it is not the belief that you are tired that precipitates your tiredness in this case. Rather it is the fact that you have allowed yourself to relax while talking to your friend. But it need not be the case that you have allowed yourself to relax – in fact you might still have things to do

essential to emotional experiences that, while they involve embodied feelings, they also involve evaluative beliefs.

Another difference between emotional cognition/feeling complexes and non-emotional ones is that the beliefs involved in the emotional cases are, essentially, evaluative beliefs about things that are important to us. It is quite possible, if perhaps unusual, for someone to feel hungry without this fact being particularly important to them. In contrast, I cannot imagine being angry but not caring about whatever I am angry about.

The clearest difference, though – and hence the strongest answer to the objection aforementioned – points to a truly distinguishing feature of emotions on the account I have been developing. In the case in which my feeling of tiredness is precipitated by my coming to believe that I am tired, the relation between the belief and feeling in question is causal and contingent. The tiredness is the embodied feeling that I am experiencing. In this case, the tiredness has been caused (partly) by my coming to believe that I am tired; in another case, some other cause might bring about exactly the same feeling and there is no question that this feeling would still constitute tiredness. In the jealousy case, however, not only is the embodied feeling I am experiencing partly caused by a certain kind of belief or judgement having to do with the scene I am witnessing and my relation to it, but the experience I am having would not even count as jealousy unless something like that set of beliefs or judgements were present, bound up with the embodied feeling. The cognitive element of the experience is not just causal but also constitutive of the emotion in a way that the cognitive element of the experience in the tiredness case is not constitutive of the feeling of tiredness in that case. Moreover, it is a constitutive *condition* of the emotion, without which (or without something of the same general kind) it would not count as that specific emotion.

The complexes of thought and feeling that comprise emotions, then, are distinguished by the complex interactivity which exists between their two components. Emotions essentially involve – are partly constituted by – evaluative beliefs and judgements about things we care about, and the feelings involved in emotions depend on these beliefs and judgements. In turn, the feelings involved in emotional experience give that experience its characteristic phenomenal intensity. Although these feelings are separate entities from the beliefs and judgements involved, because we experience them as coherent wholes, the phenomenal character of the feelings affects the

and might be anxious to get away from your friend so that you can get them done. Still, her observation, and your recognition of its truth, makes you feel tired.

character of our evaluative beliefs and judgements. When observing the girl I like at the party, I do not simply draw a set of conclusions about her behaviour and its effect on me, I *feel* the importance of these implications of what I am observing. The intensity of my perceptions is affected too because I am not simply perceiving a scene taking place, I am seeing this scene *as* something disastrous for me personally. My powerfully held evaluative beliefs are giving my perceptions emotional colour and force.

I have argued that it is possible to make evaluative judgements, and to hold evaluative beliefs, either emotionally or non-emotionally, with the difference between the two cases explained by the presence or absence of an embodied feeling within the experience. I have also described such feelings as both motivating and concerned with things that we care about. Does this then mean that it is not possible to hold a belief or make a judgement that is (a) motivating and (b) about something I care about, without this belief or judgement being part of an emotional complex, that is without my experiencing it as part of a whole which includes elements of embodied feelings?

When it comes to motivation, presumably this *is* possible; it is not the case that we always need to be emotionally engaged in order to be motivated to act. Furthermore, we can sometimes be motivated to act in a way that is opposed to the motivation provided by our emotional state, as in situations where 'the head rules the heart'. In the case of the emotionally unengaged judge, the judge is certainly motivated to make judgements, and to act on them, but they are apparently not motivated by emotions. Philosophical accounts of motivation reflect this possibility. According to Humean moral psychology, for example, motivation requires the presence of beliefs and desires. Neither of these things is the same as an emotion, or implies the presence of an emotion. The link between emotions and motivation appears to be a contingent and a defeasible one. Desires can arise from various sources, which would include emotional experience: we might foster a desire to right a wrong, for example, as a result of being angry about that wrong. We might foster a desire to avoid something as a result of being afraid of it. But it is quite possible to imagine both of these desires arising in the absence of the relevant emotional reaction. The tendency for desires to arise in this way is perhaps enough to explain our tendency to think of emotions and motivation as closely linked, but we need not invoke a necessary connection to make sense of this, nor, I think, is it plausible to do so.

Then we have the apparent connection between emotions and value. At the beginning of the chapter, I suggested that emotions are about what is important to us. I then went on to argue that emotions are a combination of evaluative beliefs and judgements, together with embodied feelings, where the embodied feelings play the role of intensifying the evaluative judgements. This, of course, is highly pertinent to the question of whether (or to what extent) psychopaths are morally responsible for their actions. Psychopaths, as we have seen, experience general attenuation of the emotions, and particular deficits of anxiety and empathy. I have also suggested that they appear to lack the ability to see entities other than themselves as possessing the kind of value that would imply that their rights, interests and concerns provide reasons for action. If emotions are partly a matter of evaluative judgements and beliefs, then psychopaths' emotional deficits promise to provide an explanation for their deficit in seeing value.

However, the link between emotions and value turns out to be far from straightforward. First, in the account I have presented, there is nothing special about the evaluative judgements and beliefs involved in emotion that confines them to the realm of emotion. Any of these judgements and beliefs can, theoretically, be made and held without embodied feeling, and therefore without emotion. In that case, it should be possible for someone to judge something to be valuable without emotional engagement. Nor, when we examine cases, do we find that emotional engagement appears to be a necessary condition for a thing to be seen as valuable. Again, it is perfectly possible that all aspects of the cases with which the judge is concerned are important to them: the decisions they have to make, their outcomes and consequences. It seems clear, then, that at least actual, in-the-moment emotional engagement is not a necessary condition of seeing something as important.

On the other hand, there would be something unusual about a judge who *never* engaged emotionally with cases, or with the issues raised by them, to the point where we would perhaps suspect their ability to make certain kinds of judgements – genuinely moral judgements, perhaps – as opposed to mechanistically applying laws and legal precedents to cases. Still more worrying would be a judge who had been genuinely unable, since childhood and perhaps for their whole life, to feel empathy, or deep emotional engagement with the world around them.

4.7   Psychopaths' Emotions

In Chapter 3, I argued that psychopaths are incapable of seeing entities other than themselves as possessing value. We have also seen that psychopaths have an unusual, 'shallow' emotional experience, apparently lacking emotional engagement with the world around them. In this chapter, I have argued that emotional experience essentially involves both cognitive and feeling elements. A natural question to ask at this point, then, is, how should we characterise the 'shallowness' of psychopaths' emotional reactions in terms of the cognitive and feeling components of emotional experience? Are psychopaths missing the cognitive elements, the feeling elements or both?

Robert Hare's descriptions of psychopaths are highly suggestive in this regard. Discussing fear, Hare makes the following remarks:

> For most of us, fear and apprehension are associated with a variety of unpleasant bodily sensations, such as sweating of the hands, a 'pounding' heart, dry mouth, muscle tenseness or weakness, trembles, and 'butterflies' in the stomach. Indeed, we often describe fear in terms of the bodily sensations that accompany it: 'I was so terrified my heart leapt into my throat'; 'I tried to speak but my mouth went dry'; and so forth.

He goes on:

> These bodily sensations do not form part of what psychopaths experience as fear. For them, fear – like most other emotions – lacks the physiological turmoil or 'colouring' that most of us find distinctly unpleasant and wish to avoid or reduce.[30]

Earlier in the same chapter, Hare describes an individual whose reports of his own emotional experience illustrate this point:

> Another psychopath in our research said that he did not really understand what others meant by 'fear.' However, 'When I rob a bank,' he said, 'I notice that the teller shakes or becomes tongue-tied. One barfed all over the money. She must have been pretty messed up inside, but I don't know why. If someone pointed a gun at me, I guess I'd be afraid, but I wouldn't throw up.' When asked to describe how he *would* feel in such a situation, his reply contained no reference to bodily sensations. He said things such as, 'I'd give you the money'; 'I'd think of ways to get the drop on you'; 'I'd try and get my ass out of there.' When asked how he would *feel*, not what he would think or do, he seemed perplexed. Asked if he ever felt his heart pound or his stomach churn, he replied, 'Of course! I'm not a robot. I really get pumped up when I have sex or when I get into a fight.'[31]

Hare's descriptions suggest, not that psychopaths are incapable of bodily feeling, or have reduced capacity to experience bodily feeling in general (they 'really get pumped up' when the situation calls for it), but for whom the interplay of cognitive activity and bodily feeling which is

---

[30] Hare (1995), pp. 55–6.   [31] Ibid, pp. 53–4.

characteristic of emotional experience is missing, or greatly reduced. The suggestion is also that the missing element is primarily on the feeling side, not on the cognitive side. Psychopaths, it would seem, are capable of the beliefs and judgements involved in emotional experience, but in them the tendency for these cognitive elements to provoke physiological reactions is greatly reduced. In turn, the feeling element of emotional experience which intensifies it – in Hare's word the 'colouring' – is also greatly reduced. This explains the tendency – remarked upon consistently not only by Hare but also by other writers including Stout and Cleckley – for psychopaths' emotions to be 'bloodless', short-lived and not deeply felt.

The feeling component of emotions intensifies emotional experience, and affects the depth of our commitment to the evaluative judgements which are the other component of emotion. I can appreciate a piece of music which does not move me, but if I experience emotional upheaval while listening to a piece of music, my evaluative judgements about that piece are likely to be more deeply held, and to mean more to me. Psychopaths, lacking the intensity of full-blooded emotional experience, are likely to experience less depth of commitment to evaluative judgements they make. If their interactions with others are lacking in feeling, any evaluative judgements they make about others are likely to be less deeply held.

Finally, it is worth noting that this is unlikely to be something that is under psychopaths' volitional control. The empirical literature that I surveyed in Chapter 2 suggested that psychopaths, to a greater or lesser extent, lack the neurological hardware necessary to process and experience emotions in the normal way. If this is right, then psychopaths will not have the ability to *will* themselves to a deeper form of emotional experience. This suggests, perhaps, that the general ability to ascribe value to others may also be outside psychopaths' volitional control. This would be important for the central enquiry of this book, since a lack of moral responsibility implies an absence of relevant psychological *capacities*, and not just psychological tendencies. If psychopaths are not morally responsible, it must be because they *cannot* value others, not because they *do not*. However, it may be that other routes to value ascription do not require the emotional capacities in question, and therefore are within psychopaths' volitional control. To draw a firmer conclusion about psychopaths' lack of moral responsibility, we will need more persuasive evidence that this is not the case.

4.8 Conclusions

Psychopaths' emotional deficiencies, then, lead to evaluative judgements which lack depth of commitment. This provides something of an explanation for psychopaths' tendency not to see value in others. Whereas non-psychopaths come to see others as having value in a way which is relatively deeply felt, psychopaths might only come to see this value in a way that is shallow and unmotivating. In turn, this might interfere with their ability to recognise reasons stemming from that value, including reasons relating to the interests, rights and concerns of other people.

However, my conclusion in Chapter 3 went further than this by suggesting that psychopaths are actually *incapable* of seeing others as sources of value. The mere possession of attenuated emotions and the effect of this attenuation on psychopaths' evaluative judgements are not in themselves enough to fully explain this unusual pattern of valuing. Again, the judge example shows us this. The judge does not engage emotionally with the cases they preside over, and yet they are capable of making a series of complex and incisive evaluative judgements about those cases. They ascribe value to the people involved in the cases perfectly competently. (We can imagine a judge who, as a result of weary repetition and habituation, begins to forget the value of the people in their cases, but this *need not* happen, and the mere absence of direct emotional engagement in a case would not be enough to make it happen in respect of that case.) Therefore, people can make evaluative judgements that imply the possession of value by other people (and, by extension, non-human entities) without those evaluative judgements being *emotional* evaluative judgements.

Nonetheless, again, it is less obvious that a judge who had *never* made emotional evaluative judgements about other people would be able to make reliable non-emotional evaluative judgements about other people. That would be a strange kind of person indeed, and one whose capacity to ascribe value to others we might reasonably question.

But why would we question this, and would we be right to do so? This is the topic of Chapter 5. In it, I will present an account of the developmental role played by empathy in the practice of ascribing value to entities other than oneself, which builds on the account of emotional experience I have developed in this chapter. I will argue that psychopaths' inability to empathise, either because of a genetic predisposition or because of a traumatic childhood or both, accounts for their unusual pattern of value ascription.

CHAPTER 5

Empathy and Moral Development

5.1 Introduction

There is an old controversy over whether or not empathy has a central role to play in morality. The controversy partly stems from the wider dispute around broad ethical and meta-ethical positions. Rationalists about morality are inevitably opposed to allowing a central role for something as apparently emotional as empathy. Those following in the Humean tradition are more likely to do so; Hume's own notion of 'sympathy' is similar in many ways to what we might now call empathy. Certainly, it would be odd if empathy turned out to have *nothing* to do with morality. After all, we are surely often motivated to do good, or to refrain from doing harm, by our feelings of empathy for other people. People I know whom I would think of as being particularly moral people – not moral fetishists or those who are very morally punctilious, just *good* people – are invariably people whom I also think of as having a large capacity for empathy.

That empathy can have a motivating role is self-evident. The more interesting question is whether empathy is in any way *necessary* for morality. This is particularly interesting in the context of psychopathy research, because as we have seen, psychopaths suffer from emotional deficits and from a deficit of empathy specifically. In a way, psychopathy constitutes at least weak empirical support for the proposition that empathy is necessary for morality. At least there is a correlation here: psychopaths are not good at empathy, and they are also not good at morality. One possible explanation for this correlation is that the former capacity is a necessary condition of the latter, though of course, this is not the only possible explanation.

If there is going to be a plausible version of the proposition that empathy is necessary for morality, it cannot imply that, for every given instance of acting morally, or of making a moral judgement, there must be a corresponding event of empathising. This is clearly not plausible. We very often act for the benefit of other people without actively empathising

132

with them. Many acts are broadly 'moral' without being aimed at any particular person or group of people. Recycling one's plastic is (or can be) a moral act, but no one goes around empathising with future generations while taking the bins out.

In fact, one might think that it would not be desirable for people to be empathising all the time while making moral judgements, because empathy might even interfere with their ability to make those judgements effectively. We know that empathy is subject to a number of biases – we tend to empathise more effectively with people from a social background similar to our own, for instance – so too much reliance on empathy might lead us to make judgements with a partiality that is inconsistent with the demands of morality; even with what we ourselves conceive of as the demands of morality. Another way in which our tendency to empathise can introduce bias is simply that we are more likely to empathise with those directly in front of us than with others who are further away from our immediate attention, but whose rights and interests might be equally or more important.[1]

In Chapter 4, I introduced the case of a judge who considers cases in court. I suggested that, for such a judge, too much direct emotional engagement with each case is likely to be a barrier to effective moral judgement. It seems to me that this point holds for empathy as a specific emotional process. We might imagine the judge lurching from one witness to the next, empathising strongly with each in turn. When it came time for them to make their judgement, the real or imagined emotional condition of those involved in the case would be so powerfully salient that it would be impossible for them to think clearly about the other important aspects of the case, including legal statutes and precedents, the interests of the wider public, the principle of deterrence and so on. The idea that empathy could be a reliable *basis* for judgements in this type of case seems particularly hopeless. Where someone is convicted of a crime with a clear victim, and the maximum sentence is very long, what does empathy require of the judge? Empathising with the victim might lead them to hand out a higher sentence; empathising with the perpetrator might make them want to show restraint.

In fact, it seems quite likely that the deliberations of effective legal judges are affected by empathy at most only intermittently. On the other hand,

---

[1] Bloom (2016) gives a provocative account of the various ways in which empathy can interfere with morality.

would we want a judge's pronouncements *never* to be tempered by empathy for the people they affected? This seems equally undesirable.

We therefore have a puzzle. Sometimes, morality requires that we raise our attention from the immediate situation in order to apply principles and values at a more abstract level. It seems likely that this kind of activity would be rendered much less effective if we were to try to empathise actively with all of the relevant people or groups of people when making moral judgements about them. Doing this would seem to be unnecessary, unrealistic and also potentially counterproductive. On the other hand, a person who *never* managed to empathise would surely be less effective in making and acting on, or perhaps just less *inclined* to make and act on, moral judgements. So what exactly is the role that empathy plays in morality?

In this chapter, I will argue, based on empirical evidence, that empathy plays a developmental role in furnishing us with a capacity to ascribe value to entities other than ourselves. I will argue that the fact that this capacity is missing in psychopaths is a function of their lack of empathy, either because they lack the neurological hardware to empathise from the beginning, or because any natural capacity for empathy they may have withers away in childhood, and fails to manifest in normal patterns of value ascription. In this way, I hope to build on the work of Chapter 4 by explaining why psychopaths' emotional deficiencies interfere not only with their *tendency* to ascribe value to entities other than themselves, but with their *ability* to do so. In turn, this leads to an inability to recognise reasons which depend on the value of others, including reasons relating to the rights, interests and concerns of other people, as reasons, and hence bolsters my overall conclusion that psychopaths are not morally responsible for failing to act on these reasons.

5.2   What Is Empathy?

In order to get to the bottom of what role empathy might have to play in morality, we might think a good starting point would be to get clear on what we mean by 'empathy'. It turns out that this is not a simple task, and there have been disagreements both among scientists and among philosophers on this question.[2] In this section, I will begin by drawing some

---

[2] A good starting point for readers who would like to engage with a range of material on empathy is Coplan and Goldie (2011). The introductory chapter provides a thorough and scholarly review of work on empathy from several disciplines: philosophy (including philosophy of mind, ethics and

central conceptual distinctions which are prominent in the literature on empathy, beginning with the more psychologically 'basic' processes and progressing to the more psychologically sophisticated. While the question of what processes or states should be called 'empathy' is an interesting one, it is for my purposes not so important as the question of which processes have a role in moral development, and which processes, lacking in psychopaths, explain their unusual patterns of valuing others. I will therefore remain agnostic on what exactly empathy is, and instead gloss a number of different processes, all of which I think have some claim to be considered for inclusion in the category of empathy, as 'empathy-like processes'. For simplicity's sake, and because I want it to be an open question whether any empathy is taking place, I will refer in example cases to the putative empathiser as 'the subject' and the person putatively empathised with as 'the target'. In the following section, I will then consider how these processes might contribute to moral development.

Empathy perhaps consists in a kind of transfer of emotion between people. However, not all forms of emotional transfer are effected in the same way, and it is not clear which should be called empathy. At the simpler end of the spectrum, there is a basic psychological phenomenon usually referred to as 'emotional contagion'.[3] This has been observed in very young children, including some only a few days old,[4] and happens when a child observes the outward signs of a particular emotion in another child, and experiences that emotion herself. Child A and Child B are playing happily together. Child A drops a toy and starts crying, upon which Child B also starts crying, not because they has dropped their toy or has any other personal reason to feel upset, but simply because Child A is crying. This phenomenon does not involve the second child in any way 'taking the perspective' of the first. We know this because it occurs in children who are too young to have the cognitive resources to adopt the perspective of another child, or even to recognise that other children have identities separate from their own.

This simple emotional contagion is not unique to children but also occurs in adults. Imagine, for example, that you are sitting on a train working on a laptop while, in the seat behind you, a woman is speaking on the phone. She is audibly upset – perhaps she is talking to her friend about her recent breakup from a long-term boyfriend. Although focused on your

aesthetics), psychology (including clinical, developmental and social psychology), neuroscience and ethology.
[3] Eisenberg and Strayer (1987), Wispé (1987), Hatfield et al. (1992, 1994), Davies (2011).
[4] Field, et al. (1982), Haviland and Lelwica (1987), Waters, et al. (2014), Fawcett, et al. (2016).

task, and at no point taking the time to engage imaginatively with the woman's situation, it is possible that, over time, the woman's sad tone of voice would cause you to become sad yourself. In contrast, if she was laughing and joking and talking with enthusiasm about an imminent holiday, your own mood might become upbeat, again without actually giving any conscious thought to the woman's situation. These simple transfers of emotion, unmediated by imaginative perspective-taking, are examples of emotional contagion.

Contrasted with this are more sophisticated processes in which the imagination does come into play in adopting the point of view of others, and experiencing an emotional reaction, in some sense, either as if one were another person, or as if one were in that person's situation. An important distinction here is between what Amy Coplan calls 'self-oriented perspective-taking' and 'other-oriented perspective-taking'.[5] Self-oriented perspective-taking (or to use Peter Goldie's phrase, 'in-his-shoes perspective-shifting'[6]) describes cases in which the subject imagines themself in the target's situation, but does not imagine themself to *be* the target; they do not imaginatively take on the psychological characteristics, dispositions and preferences of the target, only aspects of their situation such as, for example, the choice with which they are faced. By contrast, in other-oriented perspective-taking, the subject has to imagine actually *being* the target. This is a much greater imaginative feat: in order successfully to achieve other-oriented perspective-taking, the subject must imaginatively take on what they infer to be the target's psychological characteristics as well as their situation. Note in particular that this is distinct from merely logically inferring the other person's emotional state. It is not, as it were, saying to oneself, 'the target has a short fuse, therefore I imagine they would feel angry in this situation.' Other-oriented perspective-taking would involve the subject understanding the target to have a short fuse, among other psychological facts about the target, and allowing that understanding to influence their thought processes in a subjective, imaginative engagement with the target's situation in which they imagine themself to be the target. As Peter Goldie has pointed out,[7] however, such an imaginative engagement has at least one important limitation, since the subject would still need to have in mind some conception of the kind of person the target is, and such a conception of their own personality and character is only rarely a feature of the target's internal experience. This, argues Goldie, is a distorting factor in other-oriented perspective-taking.

[5] Coplan (2011).   [6] Goldie (2011), p. 309.   [7] Ibid.

Other-oriented perspective-taking is, without doubt, a very challenging imaginative process, but it is one which promises to yield results which one might suspect are not available through self-oriented perspective-taking, in cases where the person being empathised with is significantly different from the person doing the empathising. In Amy Coplan's example, she (hypothetically an introvert) attempts to empathise with her extrovert sister Bettie. Bettie has been spending a lot of time alone recently, and Coplan, imagining herself in this situation, feels happiness and contentment. She fails to feel what Betty feels (anxious and upset) because she does not imagine *being* Bettie, she merely imagines herself in Bettie's situation. Self-oriented perspective-taking has led her to fail to accurately model her sister's emotional state when other-oriented perspective-taking would have been a more successful strategy, and the result is confusion and miscommunication between the sisters.

However, there are a number of ways in which the hypothetical Coplan – let's call her Amy to distinguish her from her hypothetical sister – might seek to improve matters, which stop short of other-oriented perspective-taking. One very simple approach would be to infer Betty's emotional experience logically and then simply to imagine experiencing the relevant emotion. Knowing that Betty is an extrovert, and knowing that she has been spending time alone, she might simply infer that this would be likely to cause Betty upset, and then imagine feeling upset herself. This would be enough to give Amy some kind of simulacrum of Betty's emotional experience. Another slightly more complex approach would be to manipulate features of her own imagined situation in a way which would be likely to reproduce an imagined scenario which is somewhat analogous to Betty's real situation, and which would be likely to produce a similar emotional reaction. Perhaps there is a threshold of time spent alone above which Amy herself would start to feel upset – months rather than weeks, say. Amy simply imagines having been alone for months, and successfully achieves an imagined emotional state similar to Betty's real state.

I think I probably engage in both of the processes described earlier from time to time, in an effort to empathise with people. Both more common and more intense, however, are episodes of empathy that are much more direct than this, but which do not obviously fall into the category of other-oriented perspective-taking either. In fact it is not clear that there is any perspective-taking, or imaginative reconstruction of another's emotional state, happening at all.

Parents, I suspect, tend to empathise particularly strongly with their children. My own experience of interacting with my young son is shot through with episodes of what I would think would be properly called empathy, but which do not feel like *imaginative* processes. Elijah is refusing to eat a bowl of pasta. Despite the fact that he regularly eats and enjoys pasta, there is something about *this* bowl of pasta that is very unappealing to him. As I try various methods – encouraging, cajoling, bargaining – to get him to eat it, he just digs his heels in further. He is feeling frustrated, upset and angry with me for trying to make him do something he doesn't want to do. Though I'm obviously annoyed that he's behaving like this and the pasta I cooked is going to go to waste, as I watch his face contort and the tears start to flow, I'm also feeling upset *for* him. Now, this seems to me to fit neatly into neither the category of self-oriented perspective-taking nor that of other-oriented perspective-taking. I'm clearly not simply imaginatively putting *myself* into his situation and reacting accordingly, because if I was presented with a bowl of pasta I'd eat it happily or, if not, I would politely refuse, not cry and throw my spoon. But neither am I really imagining what it is like to be him. It's possible that I might get somewhere with trying to imagine what it is like to be a three-year-old who doesn't want to eat his dinner. It's true that I was a fussy eater as a child myself, which probably gives me some residual *sense* of what it is like to have that kind of reaction to food. But it has been so long since I experienced the world as a three-year-old does that I think it is a stretch to say that I am capable of imagining accurately what it is like to be one now. I do not think what I am doing here is imagining. Rather, it seems to me that I *perceive* his emotional state through his behaviour. I know him well enough that I don't need to interpret this behaviour consciously – I just perceive the emotions of which it is a manifestation. And, perceiving them, and being close to him as I am, I feel them, or some version of them, with him. This perceptual process is not imagination, but it is also not the simple emotional contagion I described earlier, since it involves awareness of the existence of another mind, and of its subjective experience, in a way that emotional contagion does not.

So far in setting out distinctions among empathy-like processes, I have been varying what we might call the communicative component of these processes – the process by which emotional communication takes place between the subject and the target. As we have seen, the scope of this component can vary from cases in which there is no role at all for imagination (as in emotional contagion, and the process of non-imaginatively perceiving emotion in others) through cases in which one person imagines themself in another person's situation (self-oriented perspective-taking) to cases in which one person imagines themself *be* another person, imaginatively taking on board what they infer are that person's character traits and long-standing dispositions, and also more short-term aspects of their psychological state (other-oriented perspective-taking). Empathy-like processes, however, also have an emotional component, which can also be varied.

There is a controversy in the literature over whether, in defining empathy, one should insist on an 'affective match' between the subject and the target.[8] On the one hand, it might seem obvious that empathy consists in feeling on behalf of another person, and perhaps to a different degree, *just that emotion* that the other person feels. After all, empathy is often recommended as a way of gaining a better understanding of other people. If the emotion one feels when empathising with a person is not the same emotion that the person feels, then how can one claim to have come to a better understanding of that person through empathising? On the other hand, there are other processes which look similar to this in form and effect but which do not include an affective match, and it seems reasonable to include these at least in the gloss of 'empathy-like processes' that I have been using.

The psychologist Martin Hoffman argues for an inclusive definition of empathy as including all 'psychological processes that make a person have feelings that are more congruent with another's situation than with his own situation'.[9] While this definition is intended to include cases where the emotion felt by the observer is the same emotion as that felt by the observed, it is also intended to include many cases in which the emotion is different. Here are three examples of situations which might fall into this latter category:

1. Your friend has tickets for a new play that you would really like to see. You imagine yourself in their situation and feel excitement, despite the fact that they are uninterested in the play and are only going because they have been invited by another friend and don't want to cause offense.

2. You are watching someone walking on a tightrope high in the air. You imagine yourself in their situation and feel fear on that person's behalf, even though the tightrope-walker is a seasoned performer and feels no fear themself.

3. You observe a situation in which two people – a bully and their victim – are interacting. The victim, it would seem, is used to being bullied, to the extent that they feel no indignation or anger at their plight. They

---

[8] See Davis (1996), Hoffman (2000), Preston and de Waal (2002).   [9] Hoffman (2000), p. 30.

feel instead a kind of bruised acceptance. However, you, as an observer, imagine yourself in the victim's situation and, doing so, feel
yourself becoming angry towards the bully.

All three of these cases are examples of self-oriented perspective-taking.
This, presumably, is an inevitable feature of cases of successful, imaginatively mediated empathy-like processes in which the emotion felt by the
subject does *not* match the emotion felt by the target. In cases of other-
oriented perspective-taking, the subject is imagining themself *being* the
target, taking into account relevant features of the target's psychology. In
such cases, if the subject's emotion does not match that of the target, then
there must have been some failure to accurately model the target's psychology, and so the attempt to empathise has not been successful.

The first case is really just another case of failed self-oriented perspective-
taking ('failed' in the sense that it cannot lead to an accurate reading of the
target's emotional state) similar to the case of Amy Coplan and her
imagined sister. Nonetheless, it is presumably the case that the joy the
subject feels at imagining themself about to see the play is 'more congruent'
with the target's situation than with their own, since the subject is not
actually about to see the play. Therefore, this would seem to count as
empathy according to Hoffmann's definition.

In the second case, the emotion felt by the subject is again more
congruent with the target's situation than with the subject's, because the
subject is safe on *terra firma*. However, it is less clear that the mismatch
between the subject's and the target's emotional state represents a failed
process. This is because the process promises to tell the subject something
useful about the target and their psychological state, as long as the subject
has other means of becoming aware of what the target is really feeling.
Imagining themself in the tightrope walker's situation, she feels fear.
Knowing that the tightrope walker herself does not feel fear, they arrive
at a better appreciation of the tightrope walker's courage, or perhaps of the
power of their skill and experience to render less frightening a situation
which would terrify most people.

The third example is, at first glance at least, perhaps more plausibly an
instance of empathy than either the first or second case. Indeed, it appears
to be this kind of case that Hoffmann has in mind as a case of empathy
without an affective match.[10] In this case, as in the tightrope case, the fact

---

[10] 'The empathy-arousing processes often produce the same feeling in observer and victim but not
necessarily, as when one feels empathic anger on seeing someone attacked even when the victim feels
sad or disappointed rather than angry.' (Ibid).

that there is no affective match between the subject and the target does not automatically suggest that the process is a failed one.

What these three cases suggest, it seems to me, is that the usefulness of empathy-like processes may not lie in their propensity to deliver an accurate depiction of the internal emotional state of the target, so that the subject comes to understand better how the target feels. Rather, the usefulness of these processes might lie in their propensity to lead the subject to engage evaluatively in a number of ways with the witnessed scene. In the tightrope case, the observer experiences certain emotions on behalf of, or directed at the tightrope-walker – excitement, pride, concern – and comes to see them as having certain evaluative qualities – bravery, skill and grace. Moreover, they are justified in seeing them in this way. The observer's *appreciation* of the tightrope walker and their situation is heightened and sharpened by their engaging empathically with the scene. In the bullying case, the observer appreciates the victim's situation more acutely, and their own anger – a justified anger – is sharpened as a result. These are the successful cases. In the unsuccessful 'theatre' case, the subject simply fails to truly appreciate the character of the target's emotional state.

Hoffman's definition of empathy as including 'psychological processes that make a person have feelings that are more congruent with another's situation than with his own situation' has the disadvantage that it includes some instances of what would appear to be *failed* processes – as in the theatre case. Nonetheless, the diversity of ways in which empathy-like processes can be *successful* – which I have briefly and far from exhaustively sketched – supports a broad conception of what types of process should be the object of our attention. At least this is true if the aim of our enquiry is to illuminate the role of empathy-like processes in moral development, and this is indeed the aim of Hoffmann's enquiry as well as my own. Rather than the idea of congruence, however, perhaps a more useful way to talk about what links empathy-like processes is that they are instances of a subject experiencing an emotion *on behalf of* the target. While it may not be possible to find a precise account of what it means to experience an emotion on someone else's behalf, it does seem to me to capture what allows successful empathy-like processes to be successful. In the bully case and the tightrope case, the subject feels an emotion or set of emotions – anger and fear respectively – on behalf of the target, even though the emotion they feel is not the same as that felt by the target. In the theatre case, the subject is really feeling the emotion on their own behalf, rather than that of the target.

In addition to the two imaginative processes discussed, thinking of empathy as feeling something on someone else's behalf allows us to include the kind of non-imaginative process that I identified earlier in observing my own interactions with my son, since in that case I was still feeling the emotion on his behalf, even if I was not doing so through imaginative engagement. (This type of process, of course, would not be excluded by Hoffman's definition, since the emotion in question is more congruent with the target's situation that with the subject's.)

It is now hopefully beginning to become apparent how what I have been exploring here links to the argument of the previous chapters: that psychopaths have an inability to see entities other than themselves as possessing value. The aforementioned examples show a number of the ways in which empathy-like processes can help us to engage evaluatively with other people's points of view. Because emotions have a component of embodied feeling, which gives them an intensity and motivational force that is not present in mere judgements, aspects of the target's point of view become powerfully salient to the subject through the act of empathising. The sense that the target has value is a central feature of this experience. Through the act of empathising, it becomes part of the subject's worldview.

The ability to engage in empathy-like processes, then, is plausibly an important means of achieving normal patterns of value-ascription, and it is plausible to suppose that someone lacking this ability would be significantly disadvantaged in this respect. Still, this does not establish that we need empathy-like processes in order to see people – and still less entities other than people – as possessing value themselves. To show how this might be true requires a focus on the developmental role of empathy. In the next section I will try to elucidate this role.

5.3   Empathy and Moral Development

Hoffman identifies a key role for empathy in the development of morally motivated behaviour in response to the witnessing of harm befalling another individual ('the bystander model') as well as in the inhibition of harm-causing behaviour in oneself ('the transgressor model').[11] For Hoffman, as for many developmental psychologists, empathy is a key factor in the formation of very many forms of moral or 'prosocial' behaviour – for example, avoiding harming others ourselves, alleviating the harm caused to others, preventing harm by perpetrators or taking action against perpetrators.

---

[11] Ibid, Parts I and II.

Hoffman's description of the developmental role played by empathy is complex. The picture is of a developmental process through which the child's parents (or other adults with significant caring responsibilities – I will use 'parents' as shorthand) employ the child's ability to empathise as raw material with which to encourage the development of a concern for other people. Hoffman's description of how this happens involves what he (in common with other psychologists) calls 'inductions'.[12] Inductions occur when the child either commits a moral transgression themself, or witnesses a moral transgression being committed by another person. Inductions are discipline encounters between parents and children through which parents attempt to influence their children's behaviour:

> Inductions, like all discipline attempts, communicate parental disapproval of the child's harmful acts. This makes it clear that the child has done something wrong and arouses a certain amount of concern over parental approval. But unlike other types of discipline, inductions do two additional things: First, they call attention to the victims' distress, and by making the victims' distress salient they exploit an ally within the child, the child's empathic proclivity. That is, inductions activate certain empathy-arousing mechanisms . . . . In this way inductions elicit empathic distress for the victim's pain, hurt feelings, and (if relevant) suffering beyond the situation. Second, inductions are verbal communications that make the child's causal role in the other's distress salient. The child's processing that information under the proper conditions (optimal pressure) results in a self-blame attribution that transforms his or her empathic distress, at least partly, into guilt, that is, transgression guilt, in contrast to bystander guilt over inaction. In short, children's cognitive processing of inductions arouses empathic distress and transforms it into guilt.[13]

Inductions can take a variety of forms, but always contain two key elements: communication of parental disapproval and arousal of empathic emotion. Descriptions of the victim's emotional state, aimed at triggering an empathic reaction in the child, vary in subtlety according to the child's ability to understand and internalise them:

> The earliest inductions point up direct, observable physical consequences of the child's action ('If you push him again, he'll fall down and cry'; 'It's uncomfortable when you walk on me, please let me lie here for a few more minutes'; 'If you have to defend yourself that's all right but you may not

---

[12] I will eschew a discussion of why we should use this particular term and just accept that it is a technical term used by psychologists.
[13] Hoffman (2000), pp. 157–8 (italics author's own).

hit anybody with anything in your hand, you could really hurt them'; 'If you throw snow on their walk they will have to clean it up all over again'). Later, the victim's hurt feelings may be pointed up – at first simple feelings ('He feels bad when you don't share your marbles with him, just as you would feel bad if he didn't share his marbles with you') . . . And still later, more subtle feelings ('He feels bad because he was proud of his tower and you knocked it down').[14]

Also available to parents are a number of ways of bringing attention to the moral implications of the victim's emotional reaction and the child's role in bringing it about:

The harmful effects of the child's action may be mentioned indirectly ('He's afraid of the dark so please turn the light back on'; 'Try to be quiet, if he can sleep a while longer he'll feel better when he wakes up'). The victim's perspective may be implied by stating his intentions or legitim-ate desires in a way that indicates the child's antisocial behaviour was unjustified ('Don't yell at him. He was only trying to help'; 'Couldn't you let him have it for a few minutes just so he can look inside? He wants so much to look inside and I don't think he'll do any harm'; 'He was only taking his turn and he has a right to a turn, just as you do'; 'I won't allow you to hit her when she does something by accident. You must under-stand that it was an accident. She is too young to know what she is doing. She did not mean to hurt you.') And, finally, reparative acts may be suggested ('Would you tell your sister that you are sorry and try to make her feel better about it?'; 'Go over and pat him so he'll feel better'; 'Now I would like you to help him put it [the tower the child knocked down] back together').[15]

The variety of descriptions in the aforementioned quotations shows how empathy can play a role in making salient the perspective of other people in a wide range of different types of encounter involving harm and transgres-sion. Through repetition of these various types of encounter, with their accompanying empathic emotions, according to Hoffman, the child grad-ually begins to see patterns in the behaviour of other children, their own behaviour towards other children, the emotional reaction of those chil-dren, their own emotional states brought on by empathic processes, and parental approval or disapproval. When parental disciplinary efforts are consistent, these patterns form 'scripts' or 'generic event memories',[16] including predictive and explanatory links between the various elements of the pattern, and including the consistent message that other people's concerns, rights and interests are important, and that there are reasons to

[14] Ibid, p. 150.   [15] Ibid, pp. 150–1.   [16] Ibid, p. 156.

treat them in certain ways, for example to help them or to refrain from harming them. When parental disciplinary efforts are guided by moral principles, the child in turn will begin to form moral principles matching those of the parent. In this way, what starts with the use of empathy-arousal in disciplinary encounters ends with the development of fully fledged moral principles in which other people are represented as important and valuable. While Hoffman does not write in terms of value, we can see that the sense that other people have value is a natural product of this form of moral development. When parents point to the upset caused to another child, say, as a reason for refraining from a particular action, this carries the implication that the child's being upset is something that matters. Thus, the value of other people is a feature of the principles that are formed through inductive parenting. The faculties that the parent is trying to encourage the child to develop are therefore a combination of motivational and epistemic. The child acquires the ability to know the effect of actions – primarily their own, but also those of other people – on others, and also the motivation to act in ways that promote some effects and avoid, nullify or mitigate others.

It is notable that the 'inductive' method of parenting described earlier, in common with other forms of parenting, apparently relies for its effectiveness on the child's wanting to please the parent; if the child does not care what the parent thinks, then the parent's efforts to get the child to see things from others' points of view and ultimately to value them will not have much traction. We might wonder, therefore, whether some 'hard-core' psychopaths might be impervious to inductive parenting because they do not have this desire to please the parent in the first place, so that no amount of inductive discipline or encouragement of empathy would have any effect. Presumably this desire comes about in most children through parental bonding, and it may be that empathy-like processes play a role in this bonding, in which case, it is quite plausible that children born with low capacity for empathy might miss out on this crucial stage of development. One can also imagine cases in which children who do have a normal capacity for empathy, who then miss out on parental bonding for some other reason, fail to develop fully fledged empathy or the capacity to value others because any inductive and empathy-based parenting they do receive fails to gain traction because they do not care about pleasing the parent. If this is indeed an accurate description of development in some children, then we have a further way in which circumstances either at or very shortly after birth can lead to the attenuated value-ascription which is characteristic of the adult psychopath.

Hoffman presents an array of empirical evidence in support of his account of empathy's role in moral development.[17] This research essentially supports two separate claims. First, that inductions are effective motivators of pro-social behaviour in the short term, compared with other measures. Second, in Hoffman's words, 'with a high degree of consistency . . . the generalisation that mothers . . . who use induction produce children whose moral orientation is characterised by independence of external sanctions and guilt over harming others'.[18] By implication, this approach is effective in the long-term at producing people who have internalised a worldview in which other people's interests are made salient by emotional reactions, and in which extrinsic motivations such as the threat of punishment are not necessary to motivate moral behaviour. In the terms in which I have been describing normal moral development, other people come to be seen as having value.

In this chapter, I am concerned with the developmental role of empathy in bringing about the capacity to value others in adulthood. The more important of Hoffman's two claims for my purposes, then, is his claim about empathy's long-term role. I will therefore pass over the evidence for the first claim and concentrate on what I think is the strongest example available of a study which supports the second claim. This study, by Krevans and Gibbs,[19] is broad-ranging and subtle in its design, and to my mind constitutes powerful evidence that empathy can have the kind of role described by Hoffman.

Krevans and Gibbs took data through questionnaires from seventy-eight children aged between eleven and fourteen years, their parents and their teachers, relating to (1) the children's tendency to engage in prosocial behaviour, (2) the dominant disciplinary styles in the family home, and (3) their empathic responsiveness and maturity. Several measurement systems were used for each factor in order to avoid the limitations of any one system. Recognising the need for a clear and consistent understanding of prosocial behaviour, Krevans and Gibbs used five separate measures of this, all of which identify prosociality with altruism, and not merely with compliance with a parent or authority figure's wishes. The fifth of these measures consisted of data drawn from an experiment which they carried out themselves:

> Each child was promised a bonus of $1 and received ten dimes [while they were filling out questionnaires]. At the end . . . the child listened to a story

---

[17] For example, Rollins and Thomas (1979), Sawin and Parke (1980), Brody and Shaffer (1982), Kuczynski (1983), Crockenberg and Litman (1990), De Veer (1991), Hart, et al. (1992), Krevans and Gibbs (1996).
[18] Hoffman (2000), p. 165.   [19] Krevans and Gibbs (1996).

about a child from a disadvantaged country . . . . The child was then given an opportunity to donate money to UNICEF, a charity which helps children who, like the one in the story, live in disadvantaged countries. In order to reduce extrinsic motivations for helping, an illusion of anonymity was created. Children were left alone to make their decision and were asked to put a sealed donation envelope in a collection bag whether or not they actually made a contribution . . . . The size of the child's donation served as an index of prosocial behaviour.[20]

By combining this with data from the questionnaires, the experimenters were able to build up a rich and detailed data set through which to measure each child's tendency towards altruistic behaviour. The data on disciplinary styles distinguished between 'other-oriented inductions, that is, discipline which directs the child to attend to his or her victims' perspectives . . . power assertions, that is, discipline which attempts to change the child's behaviour through use of the parent's power over the child . . . and love withdrawals, that is, discipline which withholds parental approval or attention from the child'.[21] Data on this variable were gathered from both the children and their parents, so the data reflected both the parents' and the children's perspective on the dominant disciplinary styles in the home. Finally, the data on empathy measured both the child's level of empathic responsiveness, that is, the strength of the affective reaction felt in response to another's plight, and the sophistication of that response. Sophistication was measured through the 'Empathy Continuum System'[22] which used film clips and questionnaires to gauge the subject's ability to engage in complex acts of empathy with fictional on-screen characters.[23]

The results of the study showed a correlation between empathy scores (all measures) and prosocial behaviour scores, suggesting, perhaps unsurprisingly, that children who are highly and sophisticatedly empathic are more likely to behave morally. The study also showed a correlation between children's empathy scores and the use of inductions (i.e. disciplinary interventions exploiting and seeking to encourage empathy) in the home. There are two ways of interpreting this result: either the use of induction is effective at encouraging a general capacity for, and sophistication in the exercise of, empathy in the child, or parents of relatively highly empathic children are more likely to use induction compared with other disciplinary methods because it is more likely – or they believe it is more

---

[20] Ibid, p. 3268. [21] Ibid, p. 3266. [22] Strayer (1989).
[23] Interestingly, this measure also includes a 'match score' which measures the degree of affective match between the subject and the object.

likely – to be effective as a disciplinary method. It seems plausible to suppose that both of these things are true to some extent.

Finally,[24] the study showed that not only were (1) highly empathic children more likely to engage in prosocial behaviour, and not only were (2) children whose parents used induction more likely to engage in pro-social behaviour, but also (3) highly empathic children were more likely to engage in prosocial behaviour if their parents used induction, and (4) children whose parents used induction were more likely to engage in prosocial behaviour if they were highly empathic. The findings therefore support the proposition that empathy effectively *mediates* inductive parental discipline interventions.

Krevans and Gibbs' study is a powerful example of empirical research supporting the hypothesis that good parenting, mediated by empathy, creates a pattern of behaviour in children motivated by an outlook in which other people are seen as valuable. The fact that this pattern of behaviour survives outside the context of parental discipline encounters, and therefore operates independently of threatened punishment or prom-ised reward, suggests that the outlook encouraged through induction is internalised by children. However, this still leaves open the possibility that alternative routes to the same pattern of valuing are available to those whose childhood is *not* characterised by inductive discipline and/or who are less capable of empathy.

One way to support this claim empirically would be to show that those who lack the neurological resources to empathise effectively, and/or an upbringing characterised by the encouragement of empathy and its enlist-ment in discipline encounters do not, as a matter of fact, develop into adults who value other people. Given that the alternative (non-inductive) disciplinary strategies identified by Hoffman are 'love withdrawal' and 'power assertion', we might expect to find that children whose parents favour these approaches develop a worldview in which the provision and withdrawal of affection, and the exercise of power, are more salient to them as behavioural motivators than the value of other people. I am not aware of evidence either way for the former possibility, but there are some studies[25] supporting the proposition that unqualified power assertion as a parental strategy gives 'children a power-assertive model of how to behave when one wants to change another's behaviour'.[26]

---

[24] The study contains a number of other interesting results, but I am focusing here on the most relevant.
[25] Bandura and Walters (1959), Hoffman (1960).   [26] Hoffman (2000), p. 147.

5.4 When Moral Development Fails

Notably, the aforementioned finding about power assertion also fits with what many psychologists say about the moral outlook of psychopaths. Psychopaths tend to see the world in terms of power relationships, and in those cases where they do succeed in developing a rudimentary moral framework, it tends to be one in which moral authority is identified with the possession and exercise of power. In 2008, the philosopher Jonathan Glover carried out interviews with twenty people diagnosed with anti-social personality disorder in Broadmoor, attempting to piece together their moral outlook. One conclusion he reached was that psychopaths tend to have

> rather retributive, rather harsh moral views, which seem to be rooted not in sympathy for anyone else, [but] . . . often a command morality. 'Why do you think this?' 'It's because my parents told me' or, 'I was brought up to believe it.'[27]

To illustrate this, Glover gives the example of a psychopath who thought capital punishment should be brought back, but specifically for the crime of 'setting fire to the Queen's property'. This description suggests that, in the absence of a moral outlook which includes the value of others, a moral (or perhaps pseudo-moral) outlook based on power assertion and authority might take hold. In this way, the existence of psychopaths can itself be taken as empirical support for Hoffman's theory of moral development.

The psychopathic personality has a complex aetiology almost certainly involving both 'nature' (i.e. genetic) and 'nurture' (i.e. upbringing) components.[28] Among environmental factors, physical abuse and neglect in childhood have been found consistently to contribute to the development of psychopathic traits. The existence of both a genetic factor and of a factor relating to physical abuse and neglect is consistent with Hoffman's theory. Children who are born with a low capacity for empathy might nonetheless increase their capacity for empathy, and build on it to form a mature moral outlook, if they have parents who are highly empathic themselves, encourage empathy in their children and use disciplinary interventions involving empathy. Conversely, children who are born with a capacity for empathy that falls within the normal spectrum, if they then suffer abuse or neglect in childhood, might have that capacity stunted by an experience that is not conducive to the development of fully

---

[27] Glover (2008).
[28] Farrington (2006), Waldman (2006), Farrington et al. (2010), Viding and Larsson (2010).

fledged empathy. We would also expect to find some individuals, at the extreme low end of the spectrum of capacity for empathy, for whom no amount of constructive, empathy-based parenting would be likely to have much effect. These individuals, having extremely little or even no capacity for empathy, would in effect be predestined to become psychopathic adults. In fact, all of these expectations are indeed consistent with what we do find in psychopaths. The two factors: genetic predisposition and abusive or neglectful parenting have been shown to correlate with the development of fully fledged psychopathy, though neither has been shown to be a sufficient condition.[29]

The developmental process described by Hoffmann is a participative, fully engaged process. Empathy-like processes help to form children's moral outlook because they enable them to feel something of other people's emotional condition, or more broadly to feel emotions on other people's behalf. By doing this, they come to see other people as valuable. The wrongness of harming others, and the goodness of helping them, flows from this first realisation of them as valuable beings. Thus empathy acts, negatively, as a check on potentially harmful behaviour, and, positively, as a motivator of behaviour that is likely to benefit another person or increase their well-being in some way. The 'scripts' that one develops through the exercise of empathy and through constructive parental interventions are therefore always scripts in which one appears oneself, not as an actor but as a character. By the time fully fledged moral principles are formed, these too are understood participatively, as principles which apply to one's own conduct. To deny that they apply to one's own conduct would be to deny that other people, whose rights and interests form part of the content of moral principles, have value.

We should not therefore be surprised that psychopaths are often able to piece together an understanding, however imperfect, of the moral principles by which most of us live. By carefully observing the behaviour and reported motivations of others, we would expect someone with a reasonable level of intelligence to be able to develop this kind of understanding. However, without the intervention of empathy, this will never be a truly participative understanding, because it does not contain the value of other people. At most, a psychopath can come to understand that other people think of each other as having value, in the same way that the space-

---

[29] Waldman (2006). It should be noted that the evidence for environmental factors is not conclusive because other factors, including genetic factors but also socioeconomic and other factors, have a confounding effect. For example, parents who themselves have a genetic predisposition towards psychopathic traits are more likely to be neglectful or abusive towards their children.

travelling anthropologist we met in Chapter 3 understands that the aliens think of the plants on their planet as having value. This is far from the same as seeing – or feeling – that value oneself.

It also seems plausible to me that this ability to see value in other people is the basis of a broader ability to see value in entities other than oneself, which includes things other than people, such as animals, or other entities or ideas such as the environment or justice. Once we have fully fledged moral principles, we are then able to reason using them, to refine them and to form new ones. That animals have value of the relevant kind is a reasonable conclusion from the observation that they share many features with humans, including perhaps subjectivity. As it is emotional engagement with another person's subjective experience that enables us to see other humans as having value, the fact that (some) non-human animals, too, have subjectivity means that their value can be inferred, even if it is not made part of our experience through directly empathising with animals (although this is of course also possible). The conviction that other non-human entities such as the environment have value is plausibly the result of further abstraction from principles derived in the way described.

In Chapter 3, I argued that psychopaths are not morally responsible for some of their actions because they are *impervious* to those reasons; that is, they are incapable of understanding something important that is readily available to non-psychopaths. I asked how we should feel about psychopaths if it could be shown that they are not capable of understanding that other people are due anything other than ill will and indifferent disregard. In my discussion of James Blair's experiments using the 'moral/conventional' distinction, I noted that these experiments cannot show that psychopaths are *incapable* of understanding the relevant distinction, and that any argument for the proposition that psychopaths are not morally responsible for some of their actions would need to show a genuine incapacity on their part, rather than simply a tendency to think differently about morality from other people. Later in the chapter, I presented three examples which, I argued, suggest that genuine responsiveness to reasons requires an *ability* to see those reasons as applying to oneself; this argument would fail if all that could be demonstrated was a *tendency* to see reasons as applying to oneself.

The evidence marshalled by Hoffmann presents a compelling case for how non-psychopaths come to see others as having value, and thus, in my view, how they come to be responsive to reasons stemming from the rights, interests and concerns of others. Combined with what we know about the development of psychopaths, we have a plausible account of how psychopaths arrive at a position where they fail to see others as having value.[30] But are we really entitled to infer an *inability* to see others as having value?

Clearly, an important question here is whether, having failed to develop a truly participative understanding of moral principles in this way in childhood, it would be possible for someone to develop one in adulthood. If psychopaths are able to bring themselves to understand that others have value, then they only have a tendency, not an inability to do so. How might psychopaths, having reached adulthood without seeing others as having value, be in a position to bring themselves to do so as adults? One possibility might be that the process, mediated by empathy, through which most people come to see others as having value, or something akin to it, is available to adult psychopaths. Another possibility is that there is some other process, not involving empathy, through which someone can come to see others as having value. I think there is enough evidence for us to reject both of these possibilities on empirical grounds. What I will offer is not a knock-down refutation but an argument to the effect that, given the evidence we have, the most likely explanation is that neither type of process is available to psychopaths. Perhaps more importantly, I think that, even if such a process is available, psychopaths are not morally responsible for failing to take it, because the reasons that count in favour of their taking it are precisely of the kind to which they are unresponsive in the first place.

For the first possibility to be true would require that psychopaths are able to come to develop a capacity for empathy in adulthood, and that this capacity can then allow them to come to value others. While it cannot be established beyond doubt that this is impossible, it does appear that, for the vast majority of individuals at least, such patterns set in childhood are not subsequently reversed. In Chapter 2, I reviewed the evidence for the successful treatment of psychopaths. Many of the treatment studies which were covered in that review involved attempts to encourage empathy in adult psychopaths, with little evidence that such attempts had been successful. Where interventions have been successful, they have not clearly

---

[30] It is worth noting that this picture applies as much to 'successful' psychopaths as it does to 'unsuccessful' ones. Successful psychopaths are supposed to be those in whom we do not find, to the same extent, the various prudential or control-based deficits in Factor 2 of the PCL(R) (e.g. poor behaviour controls, impulsivity, lack of realistic long-term goals), but in whom the interpersonal and affective deficits associated with Factor 1 (e.g. lack of remorse or guilt, shallow affect and, most importantly, lack of empathy) are present. Since they lack empathy, one would expect successful psychopaths to fail to develop the capacity to value others, and this is borne out in the generally accepted view of them as deceitful, manipulative and willing to harm others to get their way, though perhaps not in a criminal way.

demonstrated success in changing the underlying traits of psychopaths, which would include their capacity for empathy, as opposed to simply reducing criminal or violent behaviour. Given this fact, it seems likely that the opportunity to develop a non-psychopathic outlook is lost at some point before adulthood, and that adult psychopaths are therefore incorrigible in terms of their basic personality, and therefore of their responsiveness to reasons.

However, even if it could be shown that some form of therapy is indeed effective in treating psychopaths by helping them to develop empathy, this would still not be enough to show that psychopaths who have not undergone such treatment are morally responsible. First, while this possibility might in theory open the door to psychopaths changing their basic pattern of reasons-responsiveness in adulthood, they could only do so by undergoing a programme of treatment which would presumably be quite intensive. If an easy route to greater empathy were available, then it seems unlikely that more encouraging results would not have been shown in treatment studies. Second, lacking moral understanding in the way that they apparently do, it is hard to see how psychopaths would be able to know *that they should* take whatever means are available to them to develop greater empathy and better moral understanding, even if such means were readily available. They could know, at most, that most people would think that they should do so, or that social norms require that they should do so. But neither of these is the same as knowing that they should do so, and without this knowledge, they cannot be morally responsible for failing to do so. Nor, therefore, are they morally responsible for failing to act on reasons to which they could only become responsive by taking such means.

The second possibility is that alternative routes to value, not involving developing a capacity for empathy, are available to adult psychopaths. The most promising candidate for an alternative faculty which might furnish psychopaths with a route to value is presumably that of reason. There is of course a very popular philosophical position (or set of positions) which emphasises the role of reason in morality, namely rationalism. If some species of rationalism is true, then moral requirements are accessible through reason alone. If psychopaths are rational, then their emotional deficits should presumably not be thought to stand in the way of their coming to have access to the kinds of reason to which I am arguing they are impervious, and so we would presumably have to conclude that they are morally responsible after all.

Short of refuting rationalism – which is clearly beyond the scope of my project here – it is not possible to offer considerations that should conclusively close off this possibility. Nonetheless, there are things that can be said to support my case.

First, let us note that there are several species of view that come under the overall banner of rationalism. To say that rational considerations – some form of the categorical imperative, let's say – form the overall criterion of rightness for morality is not automatically to say that a process of pure reasoning is the way that people do, as a matter of fact, come to understand what is right and wrong. It could be that facts about what is right and what is wrong are ultimately determined by rational considerations, but that the way people come to see what is right and wrong is more akin to the process I have been describing in this chapter, involving emotions and empathy.

However, it can only be true that psychopaths are incapable of responding to reasons in a way that renders them not morally responsible if they *cannot be expected* to become responsive to reasons. That is, any routes to responsiveness which they could reasonably be expected to take must be closed off to them. It does not therefore matter, in determining the responsibility of psychopaths, if they cannot avail themselves of the route to responsiveness that most people do as a matter of fact take. If the faculties they do have – including rational faculties – offer a route that they could reasonably be expected to take, then they are responsible nonetheless.

The description I have set out in this chapter of how people come to see the value of others, and therefore of how they come to take them as presenting reasons for action stemming from that value, if accepted, gives a strong indication that at least the first claim mentioned earlier – that people as a matter of fact tend to come to be responsive to these reasons via a set of processes that essentially involve emotion and empathy – is true. That this set of processes is exhaustive of at least the routes to responsiveness that are typically available to most people is supported by the simple empirical point that psychopaths, lacking these routes, do not as a matter of fact come to see others as valuable and therefore to be responsive to the reasons in question. If there is an easily available route to responsiveness to these reasons that does not involve the faculties that psychopaths lack, then why do psychopaths not avail themselves of them? As we have seen, psychopaths are not (qua psychopaths) lacking rationality. If rationality were enough to see others as valuable, then we would expect psychopaths to see others as valuable, but they do not.

Thus, someone who wanted to claim that reason alone supplies a route to value that is available to psychopaths would need to show what this route is, and give an argument for its existence. But they would also need to give an explanation for why, despite its availability, psychopaths do not in fact take it. More than this, however, they would need to show that psychopaths are capable of knowing that they should take it. Without this, the same point would apply as applied to the argument that psychopaths can develop empathy: if they are not capable of knowing that they should do this, it is hard to see how they are morally responsible for not doing it, and thus are morally responsible for failing to act on the reasons to which they are unresponsive as a result of not developing empathy. In the absence of these explanations, I believe the most plausible conclusion available to us on the basis of the evidence is that psychopaths are not morally responsible for failing to act on reasons stemming from the rights, interests and concerns of others.

5.5 Other Disorders of Low Empathy

At this point, I have hopefully given some good reasons for thinking that psychopaths' deficits in the capacity to empathise, and/or their traumatic childhood experiences, lead to an inability to ascribe value to entities other than themselves, which in turn implies a lack of moral responsibility. However, there is an important objection that could be raised to the account I have been giving, and it is worth pausing to consider this objection before moving on. The objection goes like this: psychopathy is not the only unusual personality type that is characterised by low empathy. If empathy truly plays a key role in moral development, we would expect to find a parallel truncation of moral development in people who are not psychopaths, but who nonetheless experience deficits of empathy, perhaps due to having a different form of mental illness. Indeed, there *are* other forms of mental illness which are characterised by difficulties with empathy, and it is not clear that we do find a truncation of moral development in people with these conditions. So how can it be that the lack of empathy in psychopaths is the cause of their own truncation of moral development?

Two other personality types which are characterised by low empathy are borderline personality disorder (BPD) and autism spectrum disorder. To respond to the objection, let us examine each of these in turn.

Here is a brief description of some of the key elements of borderline personality disorder, focusing on empathy:

> Individuals diagnosed with borderline personality disorder (BPD) are highly sensitive to other people's feeling states, but only as those states affect

them. They possess an anxious egocentricity, which means that any capacity to empathize is severely reduced. There is no wish to understand the other person's mind, only an anxiety about the impact that the other's feelings and behaviour might have on them .... Individuals with BPD present with a complex array of symptoms, such as unstable moods, volatile social relationships and low levels of trust. The lives of people with BPD – around 1 or 2 per cent of the population – seem to be ones of perpetual crisis .... Episodes of depression are common among them .... Those with BPD suffer a pervasive fear of abandonment by *idealized others*. Therefore, although their need for others is high, trust in those others' emotional availability is low. Anxiety reigns and they are particularly sensitive to any hint of rejection. People diagnosed with BPD feel needy, unloved and vulnerable. They generally see themselves as victims and hard done by. Their relationships are characterized by intense feelings, chaos, confrontation and instability. Their behaviour is impulsive, unpredictable and self-destructive.[31]

The type of empathic deficit experienced by people with BPD, then, differs greatly from that experienced by psychopaths. Whereas psychopaths might be able to accurately represent another person's point of view in their imagination, but are unmoved by it, people with BPD care desperately about other people's points of view – albeit only so far as they bear on themselves – but their disorder causes them consistently to misrepresent this point of view in their imagination, creating fantasies of rejection and abandonment in place of whatever attitude the other person actually holds towards them.

Like psychopathy, borderline personality disorder appears to have a combination of genetic and social origins.[32] BPD shows a moderate degree of heritability, suggesting a genetic predisposition in some individuals.[33] However, instances of sexual abuse, neglect and traumatic experiences in childhood are much higher in people diagnosed with borderline personality disorder than in the general population.[34] It is plausible to suppose, therefore, that the problems with empathy associated with BPD may be caused either by an abnormal empathic pattern being present from birth, or by a relatively normal capacity for empathy not reaching full maturity due to traumatic experiences in childhood, or by some combination of these two factors. This would mirror the supposition I made about psychopaths' empathic development, except that whereas psychopaths' attempts to empathise can be accurate (in the sense of

---

[31] Howe (2013), (italics author's own).   [32] Gabbard (2005), Leichsenring et al. (2011).
[33] Skodol et al. (2002), Torgerson et al. (2008).   [34] Yen et al. (2002), Zanarini et al. (2002).

accurately representing others' mental states) but lack emotional colouring, similar attempts by people with BPD would be likely to have lurid emotional colouring but would be unlikely to be accurate. The person with BPD attempt to empathise results only in an imaginative construction of the other person's point of view, which is a product of the subject's disordered psychological state, rather than accurately representing the target's point of view. The affective component of empathy also then goes astray: imagining that the other person holds them in contempt – for example, the person with BPD feels fear, or resentment, or misery in response. In reality, the other person might be feeling concern for them, perhaps combined with exasperation over their behaviour. Given that BPD (in stark contrast to psychopathy) is characterised by high levels of anxiety, this too will further derail empathic processes, crowding out other emotions and making the complex mental states associated with mature empathy all but impossible to achieve.

Working with Hoffman's account of the role of empathy in moral development, what effect on moral development would we expect BPD to have? If inductive parenting techniques are used, we would presumably expect them to be marred by the exaggerated and unrealistic attitudes to oneself imagined in others by the child with tendencies towards BPD. These imagined attitudes, and hence the other's imagined affective state, would also not be responsive to the child's actions in the same way that others' actual affective states are. For example, a child who steals another child's toy and who is asked to imagine how that child feels, only succeeds in imagining an exaggerated version of the other child's attitude to themselves, either positive or negative, which has nothing to do with the stolen toy. They would not, therefore, make a stable connection between actions like toy-stealing and the real affective states of other people. However, they might well form false associations between their actions and the reactions of others, which they have imaginatively misrepresented. We would therefore perhaps expect people with BPD to develop a set of 'scripts' and for these to form into principles of a kind in adulthood. However, we would not expect these scripts and principles to match up with the kinds of scripts and principles developed by people without BPD. We would instead expect to find a moral outlook very much centred on others' supposed (in fact exaggerated or inaccurately represented) attitudes to oneself. We would perhaps expect to find the possibility of moral condemnation of others for negative attitudes towards oneself. We might also expect to find a sense that one ought to behave in ways towards other people that are likely to sustain positive attitudes and reverse negative ones. However, because the imagined attitudes are not responsive to one's actual behaviour, we would expect to find an erratic and inconsistent view of what these ways of behaving should actually be.

Most importantly, we would not expect to find that people with BPD fail to ascribe value to other people. As described, they do feel emotions on behalf of other people and, doing so, they should be able to construct a value-laden sense of the other's point of view. This will be less effective than the other person's in matching the affective and evaluative character of the other person's actual point of view, but it can still convey the value of other people in the way implied by Hoffman's theory. In terms of moral responsibility, it may be that people with BPD will not be morally responsible for some things because of their tendency to be mistaken about other people's motives, beliefs and so on. However, their lack of moral responsibility would not have the same explanation as that of psychopaths – an inability to ascribe value to others – and it is unlikely that they would lack responsibility entirely.

Another personality-type characterised at least partly by low or abnormal empathy is autism spectrum disorder. People with this disorder find social interaction very difficult. They tend to like predictability and are easily made to feel uncomfortable by anything which deviates from their accustomed routine. They often develop narrow obsessions about certain subjects, and they are attracted by order and given to systematising behaviour. They also find empathising with other people very difficult:

> People who interact with autistic children sometimes feel as if they are being treated as no more than objects. Autistic children's empathy and communication skills seem poor. For example, most toddlers react with upset if an experimenter appears to have hit her thumb with a hammer, hurting herself and yelping with pain. In contrast, autistic children generally show little reaction to the experimenter's apparent distress. Children with autism fail to point to objects to achieve joint attention. They also remain uninterested in other people's emotional attitudes towards objects and events in the world. This can lead to social withdrawal.[35]

Unlike psychopaths, people with autism spectrum disorder do not lack emotional experience, although they apparently lack insight into their own and others' emotions. Whereas psychopaths can imagine the world from another's point of view but feel no emotional engagement as a result, people with autism spectrum disorder have trouble imagining the world from another's point of view. They cannot therefore infer others'

---

[35] Howe (2013), p. 79.

motivations and find people's behaviour unpredictable and bewildering as a result.

As the name implies, people with autism spectrum disorder exist on a spectrum from relatively mild to relatively severe symptoms. For example, about half of children with the disorder do not learn to speak.[36] People at the very severe end of the spectrum may even be permanently catatonic. However, among those who do have some degree of interaction with other people, people with autistic spectrum disorder can appear to be highly morally motivated. It is very rare for someone with autistic spectrum disorder ever to hurt another person except through involuntary actions (e.g. lashing out when upset). They 'rarely lie or attempt to deceive'[37] and many will become highly indignant at perceived moral infractions by others. If empathy indeed has a central role in moral development, why would this be so?

David Howe suggests that there may be another route to moral motivation of a particular kind that is available to autistic people that does not involve empathy:

> Their law-abiding behaviour is not solely based on the restraining powers of empathy but on the high value that they give to rules. Laws and rules make the world predictable. Breaching them destabilises conduct and behaviour and is not to be condoned. So although autistic individuals have low empathy, find relationships difficult, sometimes treat others as if they were objects and as often as not ignore those around them, they never behave intentionally cruelly or exploit others.[38]

This idea goes a long way towards explaining why autistic people can seem intensely morally motivated. Their strong negative reaction to moral transgressions by others derives not from an empathically derived concern for anyone who is being harmed, or whose rights are being violated, but from the fact that breaking moral rules is a way (one way among many) of becoming unpredictable, which is highly upsetting to autistic people. Plausibly, then, autistic people are able to understand morality at least as a system of rules – they identify certain forms of behaviour as 'against the rules' based on the reactions and behaviour of others, and internalise these rules as a way of making the world predictable.

An additional reason might derive from the nature of dishonesty, deception or manipulation, behaviours towards which people with autism spectrum disorder are notably not disposed. Such behaviours require the

---

[36] Ibid. [37] Ibid, p. 82. [38] Ibid, pp. 82–3.

very capacities which autistic people lack: not the affective component of empathy, but the imaginative component. In order to try to manipulate someone, I need to have a sophisticated idea of how they will behave if subjected to certain interventions on my part, which in turn involves understanding their motivations. I also need to understand how to avoid detection, which involves understanding which considerations are salient to them and which will escape their attention. Without being able to put myself imaginatively in their situation, attempts to manipulate them will not get off the ground. It may be, then, that this type of behaviour is not so much inhibited in autistic people through moral disapproval, as simply outside the scope of what would be possible for them. In contrast, there is nothing about the condition of psychopathy that prevents a psychopath from understanding how others think, what is salient to them, what they take to be important considerations supplying reasons and so on. Therefore, there is nothing to prevent them from successfully manipulating people, as well as nothing to prevent them from *wanting* to manipulate people.[39]

Perhaps the key difference between people with either borderline personality disorder or autistic spectrum disorder, and people with psychopathy, in terms of moral development, is that people with psychopathy have attenuated affective reactions across the board. Therefore, the salient motivational factors which act on them in childhood, and through which they develop a motivational pattern in adulthood, are more to do with satisfaction of their own desires and appetites. By contrast, people with the other conditions I have discussed are capable of intense affective reactions, with anxiety a central feature of both the disorders I have discussed. As a result, people with these disorders develop a moral outlook (or perhaps we would want to say 'moral or pseudo-moral', since it is an open question whether people with either disorder are genuinely motivated by moral considerations such as the rights and interests of other people) that is skewed towards disapproval of forms of behaviour that would cause them anxiety. In the case of borderline personality disorder, this is directed at the imagined and idealised other. In the case of autism spectrum disorder, it is directed at rule-breaking, and hence unpredictable, behaviour by others. Psychopaths, in contrast, have relatively little or no moral outlook.

There are other conditions associated to a greater or lesser extent with distorted, attenuated or absent empathy, including, 'Attention Deficit

---

[39] This discussion leaves open the possibility that people with autistic spectrum disorder have absent, or reduced, moral responsibility. See Shoemaker (2015) and Richman (2018).

Hyperactivity Disorder (ADHD), Schizophrenia, eating disorders, conduct disorder . . . and Obsessive Compulsive Disorder (OCD)'.[40] There is not room here to investigate the effect on moral development of each of these conditions. By briefly discussing two of them, I have aimed to show at least that what we know about each of these conditions is consistent with Hoffman's theory of the role of empathy in moral development, and that this theory can tell us something about why adults with these conditions behave the way they do. It is reasonable to suppose, however, that any condition characterised by unusual empathy is likely also to be characterised by unusual patterns of responsiveness to reasons. This in turn may have implications for moral responsibility.

5.6 Conclusions

In Chapter 4, I drew a picture of emotional experience as richly combining cognitive and affective elements. In this chapter, we have seen that empathy, or empathy-like processes, fits into this picture. When empathising, through whatever mechanism, we come to feel emotions on other people's behalf. Hoffman's account of empathy's role in moral development gives us a convincing portrayal of how sophisticated principle-based thinking in adulthood, and the recognition of value in others, has at its root the exercise of empathy in childhood.

As I have already noted, it is key to understanding this developmental process that we see it as something that is experienced 'from the inside', so to speak. From our earliest experiences of social interaction, we have the capacity – and when exposed to 'inductive' parenting techniques, we are encouraged – to empathise with other people. The affective reaction we experience as a result of that empathising is recruited by our parents or other parental figures as a means of setting limits on our self-oriented behaviour, and of motivating other-oriented behaviour. In combination, discipline encounters and the experience of empathy show us that others have value, and thus that the rights, interests and concerns of other people present reasons that bear on our choices. Our experiences of interacting empathically with others outside of a discipline context give us further data on others' experiences, and further opportunities to build a library of situation types with accompanying motivational patterns. Gradually we develop 'scripts', which turn into principles, which generate reasons for action. As adults, we can refine our principles through moral reasoning, but also very often through the adult exercise of

---

[40] Gillberg (2007) referenced in Howe (2013), p. 74.

empathy. But because this process makes use of *our* motivations, *our* affective reactions based on others' reactions often to *our* behaviour, it is a process that is only fully experienced from the inside. It is as if we are building a house of morality with many rooms, but we are living in it as we build it.

Without empathy, 'hard-core' psychopaths are denied the opportunity to see others as valuable, and therefore to see the rights, interests and concerns of other people as providing reasons for them. We can see that they *do not* in fact see the rights and interests of other people as providing reasons for them simply by observing case histories of psychopaths, but Hoffman's theory of moral development shows why this is so. And because the process begins in childhood and has reached an advanced stage by adulthood, we would not expect the truncated moral development of psychopaths to be something that can be easily ameliorated in adulthood, a prediction which is consistent with the poor responsiveness of psychopaths to any treatment method that has so far been tried. This suggests that 'hard-core' psychopaths are effectively doomed to be unable to recognise reasons arising from the rights, interests and concerns of other people from a young age, from causes (genetic inheritance and/or disastrous parenting) for which they cannot be held morally responsible. As a result, by adulthood, when the rest of us have constructed and are living inside a complex moral edifice, the best psychopaths can hope to achieve is to build an imperfect copy of such an edifice, which they will never be able to inhabit.

CHAPTER 6

Psychopathy in the Criminal Law

6.1 Introduction

My primary aim in this book has been to elucidate the question of psychopaths' moral responsibility. This, as was already apparent in Chapter 1, is to a great extent a practical question. It is a question concerning what we should *do* about psychopaths. Should we treat them in a way that is not radically different from how we would treat anyone else who behaved towards us as psychopaths often behave? As someone who is troubling, deserving wariness perhaps, but still someone with whom we can remonstrate? Someone at whom it is as appropriate to direct resentment as fear? Or should we treat them with what P. F. Strawson called the 'objective attitude'? As a problem to be dealt with, rather than a peer to engage with?

In this chapter, my aim is to cast some light on the related but distinct question of psychopaths' criminal responsibility. What is the difference between moral responsibility and criminal responsibility? This is a complex question, but we can make some preliminary observations that may at least help us to frame the question in a useful way. Moral responsibility is a feature of interpersonal relationships. If someone is morally responsible for their actions, this allows other individuals to *hold* them responsible for those actions, provided they are otherwise in the correct standing to do so. There are certain attitudes, including praise, blame, resentment, hurt feelings and so on, which we can legitimately have only towards people whom we correctly judge to be morally responsible. There are also some actions which are legitimated by moral responsibility in a similar way. For example, it might sometimes be permissible to remonstrate with someone, or to disassociate ourselves from them, because of certain things that they have done, but only if they are morally responsible for having done those things.

Criminal responsibility, by contrast, is not primarily a feature of interpersonal relationships. It is, instead, a feature of the relationship between an individual and society or the state. The practices that criminal responsibility legitimates, assuming it does legitimate them, such as fines or imprisonment, are practices performed on behalf of the state. They are, of course, still performed by individuals, but only by individuals granted specific powers, and assigned specific duties, by the state, in order to carry out the state's business. For this reason there is, in democratic states at least, a collective, social element to criminal responsibility. The criminally responsible person is confronted by the institutions of society, acting in representation of the collective interests, and perhaps also in some sense the collective will, of the people. This means that questions about criminal responsibility are answerable, in some way, not only to facts about the crime and the person accused of committing it, but also to the purpose of legal institutions and practices, and their role in representing the people. But one must tread a fine line here: thinking about the criminal law must not ignore the people to whom the criminal law is answerable, but on the other hand the criminal law must not become a mere instrument of public opinion. The public as it is actually constituted can be wrong about matters of criminal law, even if the criminal law is answerable to the people as a democratic ideal.

Psychopaths present a difficult practical problem for the criminal law. As I noted in Chapter 2, estimates of the prevalence of PCL-R psychopaths in prison populations vary between 7.7% (male) and 1.9% (female) and 20% overall. Psychopaths have also been estimated to make up some 3% of psychiatric patients.[1] In both settings they are, unsurprisingly, highly disruptive and difficult to deal with. Questions about how we *should* deal with psychopaths – what attitudes we should have to them, and how we should treat them – can be asked on behalf of society as well as of individuals. And, given psychopaths' disproportionate tendency to commit crimes, the question of how we should deal with criminal psychopaths is clearly a pressing one.

The central dispute in the philosophy of criminal law is about the purpose of, and justification for, the punishment of criminals. The justification for punishing a criminal rests either on the consequences of doing so, or on the desert of the criminal, or on some other consideration such as the interest of society in communicating wrongdoing to the criminal, or on some combination of different factors. And while these questions are usually debated in the abstract, the answer one reaches may have implications for the appropriate type or severity of punishment in particular cases,

[1] Douglas et al. (1999).

and perhaps even for the categories of people who should be punished. This comes out very clearly in the case of mentally ill offenders. Empirical questions about, for example, the deterrability of people with particular forms of mental illness, the extent to which they can be rehabilitated or the extent to which incarceration is required to protect the public from them, will have different levels of importance depending on how much weight, if any, one attaches to deterrence or rehabilitation as purposes of punishment.

This dispute is clearly relevant to the case of psychopaths. In Chapter 2, I reviewed the evidence for the effectiveness of treatment of psychopaths, concluding that, despite a few somewhat promising interventions, there is little evidence of consistently effective treatment at present. If carefully designed psychiatric treatment programmes are not effective, it seems unlikely that incarceration in prisons will have a significant rehabilitative effect on psychopaths. This conclusion is borne out by the notoriously high recidivism rate of psychopathic offenders.[2] Deterrence is more complex, partly because it is unclear how susceptible to deterrence by the prospect of criminal punishment psychopaths are, and partly because it is not clear whether we should be concerned only with any deterrent effect that punishing psychopaths might have on only psychopaths themselves, or also the public as a whole. It is clearer that incarcerating at least some psychopaths would have the beneficial effect of protecting the public from them, but it is not clear whether the type or duration of incarceration should be determined by specific crimes that they have committed, rather than by general determinations of their dangerousness.

Whether punishing psychopaths (as opposed to incarcerating them simply on the basis of their dangerousness) does any good, then, is somewhat unclear. But in any case, the view that criminals should be punished purely because of the beneficial consequences of doing so, regardless of whether the criminal *deserves* to be punished, is one which is very rarely held. Much more common is a 'mixed' theory of punishment, which asserts that punishment is *justified* by its beneficial consequences, but with the desert of the offender acting as a constraint on who can be justifiably punished. Even a 'pure' utilitarian theorist is likely to have something to say about why punishing people who do not deserve to be punished does not in fact have beneficial consequences, and therefore desert should act as a constraint even if the consequences of punishment are the only thing that matters ultimately. In terms of the law as it is

[2] Hemphill et al. (1998), Salekin (2008).

actually constituted, as well, tests for criminal responsibility are tests of whether the offender deserves punishment rather than tests of whether the consequences of punishing them would be beneficial. I will turn shortly to the principles embodied in these tests, and will consider in particular how they might be applied to the case of psychopaths. First, though, I will acknowledge and consider a view based on the point that I have already noted, that the criminal law is in some sense an embodiment of democratic norms.

6.2   Criminal Responsibility and Public Norms

Samuel Pillsbury has defended the position that psychopaths are criminally responsible based on a conception of criminal responsibility (or 'liability') according to which it 'depends on the social meaning of interactions, not on the moral or emotional resources of the individual harm doer'. According to Pillsbury, it is enough that the acts of psychopaths are harmful and are 'committed for reasons that demonstrate basic disregard for the value of human beings'.[3] For Pillsbury:

> Criminal law judges the social/moral character of the accused's conduct, based on the reasons for which the accused acted. The reasons for the conduct matter, because they are critical to determining whether the conduct violated fundamental public norms. It's the character of the conduct that matters, not that of the individual.[4]

If the accused acted for reasons which are contrary to such 'public norms', for Pillsbury, this is enough to demonstrate criminal responsibility. It is not necessary also to enquire whether they could have understood the moral reasons speaking against their conduct.

Pillsbury's argument for this view is, as he acknowledges, not complete; it forms part of a broader view of criminal responsibility which would need considerable fleshing out. According to this view:

> The criminal law must resolve particular disputes – accusations of serious individual wrongdoing – according to legal principles that accord with the most important values of the population. Criminal law expresses and defends baseline moral principles, setting out what conduct is fundamentally prohibited in society. Its condemnations must have moral weight with the public to have full effect. This means that the criminal law *must reflect a general public ethos*, not just that of certain groups and individuals. Over

---

[3] Pillsbury (2014), p. 298.   [4] Ibid., p. 303.

the long term, criminal law must retain the public's respect to succeed. To this extent, its work is political as well as moral.[5]

What does it mean for a set of laws and legal practices to 'reflect a general public ethos'? Whatever it means, it must presumably not amount to the idea that a given individual, or category of individuals, is criminally responsible if a large enough proportion of the public believes that they are criminally responsible. The 'baseline moral principles' Pillsbury has in mind may ultimately be answerable to public opinion, but disputes about their correct application must surely be settled through rational argument, and not by surveying the public.

Pillsbury, of course, understands this, and his argument is not that the law is answerable to the public – at least directly – on the question of how moral principles should be applied in specific cases, but on the question of what moral principles it would be appropriate to seek to apply. His central claims, roughly, are that acts which are intentional, intentionally harmful and expressive of malice, should be punishable by the law, that a legal doctrine which sought to excuse a category of person who committed such acts would not 'have moral weight with the public', and that it would therefore be illegitimate on democratic grounds.

Pillsbury is probably correct that a majority of the public would reject a legal doctrine which seeks to excuse psychopaths. However, it is reasonable to question whether this rejection would be based on an informed, reflective understanding of moral or criminal responsibility, or indeed of psychopathy. As I have argued previously in this book, it may be that most people would have the intuition that someone who fails to show basic regard for others in their conduct is morally responsible for this failure, but it is not clear that they would have the same intuition about someone who was *incapable* of feeling such regard. People's intuitions in this area are simply not clear, and nor are there available simple parallels in which intuitions are clearer. For example, Pillsbury suggests that 'to excuse for moral capacity in criminal law would be like excusing a musician for being tone deaf, or a painter for being colour-blind.'[6] But surely we *would* excuse someone in one of these predicaments for their poor artistic or musical performance, or if we would not, this is because we would think that they should have known that their lack of the relevant capacity disqualified them from being a painter or musician, and therefore should not have put themself in the position of being a candidate for assessment of their artistic

[5] Ibid. (my italics).   [6] Ibid., p. 307.

or musical merits. No such consideration applies in the case of psycho-paths, who are inescapably candidates for moral assessment, and are subject to the law, simply because they are human beings who exist in society.

Pillsbury is also concerned that the capacity to appreciate and act on moral reasons would be difficult or impossible to prove either way to a standard which would be acceptable in court. He supports this claim by setting up a dichotomy between physical and moral capacity. Proving physical capacity or incapacity is usually quite a simple matter, whereas it is unclear how we would measure moral capacity in a similar way. Not through 'brain scanning technology' whose 'documentation of brain states cannot quantify *moral* capacity'.[7] However, this is surely a false dichotomy. Moral capacity is, after all, a type of mental capacity, and judgments of mental capacity in relation to criminal responsibility have to be made in court all the time. In practice, this typically becomes a matter of, not evidence from brain scanning technology, but testimony from experts as to the mental capacities of the accused. No doubt this process does not work perfectly, and as long as it remains necessary to adjudicate criminal responsibility in this way, there is always likely to be debate over the proper way to translate medical categories of mental illness into legal criteria of responsibility which are, in Stephen Morse's words, 'resolutely folk psychological'.[8] But for other types of mental illness, the law recognises that these choppy waters must be navigated. It is not immediately clear why the mental capacities necessary to recog-nise and respond to moral reasons should be hopelessly recalcitrant to expert testimony, as long as the work is done to define what is meant by moral reasons, and what mental capacities should be thought necessary to recognise and respond to them.

Nonetheless, it would need to be demonstrated that this could be done effectively and in a way that delivers justice, and worries about the practical difficulty of adjudicating moral capacity in a court of law can certainly not be dismissed. One particular concern has to do with the incentives that would be introduced by including capacities relating to psychopathy in anything akin to the current 'insanity defence'. Because of the dangerous-ness of psychopaths, particularly those who have committed violent crimes, it is unlikely that a psychopath who successfully entered an insanity defence would be released following acquittal. More likely, the trial would result in admittance to secure accommodation (as through the 'special verdict' in English law). The psychopath's eventual release would then be

[7] Ibid., p. 304.   [8] Morse (2008), p. 206.

contingent, not on their having served a determinate sentence, but purely on their having proved that they were no longer dangerous. Given that psychopathy does not appear to be a condition which is amenable to treatment or change, this might in practice mean a long and indeterminate sentence with a very unsure prospect of eventual release. Rather than subject their client to this, a psychopath's attorney might be more likely to advise them to take their chances in the regular criminal justice system. Even if a modified insanity defence contained provisions for psychopaths, then, it might simply never be used by them.

6.3   Do Psychopaths Deserve Punishment?

As noted earlier, it is already recognised in law that mental illness can often present a legitimate excuse from moral responsibility. The job of criminal courts is to determine whether the particular form of mental illness that a defendant manifests is sufficient to excuse them from (criminal) responsibility for the particular crime of which they are accused. In the categorisation given by legal theorist Michael S. Moore,[9] there are four ways in which criminal responsibility might be determined in cases of mental illness, at least three of which find some expression in current legal tests:

1. Negation of *mens rea*. It is argued that the mentally ill offender does not act intentionally, which is what is required for the *mens rea* or 'guilty mind' component of the most serious offences, and therefore should not be convicted of these offenses.
2. Negation of free will. It is argued that the actions of mentally ill people are *caused*, and are therefore not free. This idea is perhaps reflected in the 'Durham Test', according to which mentally ill people should not be found responsible for acts which are the *products* of their illness.
3. Irrationality. This is Moore's view. It holds that the mentally ill offender should be excused because their actions are unintelligible, in the sense that they cannot be explained in terms of the agent's desires, beliefs and intentions.
4. Compulsion or ignorance. According to this view, mental illness is only excusing insofar as it interferes with the two traditional Aristotelian conditions of moral responsibility: control or knowledge. The idea that a mentally ill offender might have acted through compulsion is

---

[9] Moore (1997). In this section, I will follow Moore's categorisation and much of his reasoning, but will not agree with his ultimate conclusion.

reflected in the 'Irresistible Impulse Test', while the idea that they might have acted through ignorance is reflected in both the M'Naghten and Model Penal Code tests.

The first of these, the negation of *mens rea*, is perhaps the simplest to deal with, in terms of mental illness in general but particularly in terms of psychopathy. It is, as Moore points out, 'manifestly false'[10] that mentally ill people do not act intentionally, at least in most cases. Moore is right to argue that even the most restrictive of the disputed legal criteria for intentional action – that the consequences of the action must be intended, and not just foreseen – would be met by the majority of criminal acts performed by the mentally ill. For example, the 'M'Naghten ruling' of 1843, which established the precedent for the way insanity pleas are dealt with in English law today, followed the case of Daniel M'Naghten. M'Naghten had attempted to kill the Prime Minister of England, Sir Robert Peel, believing that Peel intended to kill him, M'Naghten. Believing him to be Peel, M'Naghten instead shot and killed his secretary, Edward Drummond. Medical experts testified that M'Naghten was psychotic, and he was acquitted. In the aftermath of the trial, the Lords of Justice of the Queen's Bench formulated the definition of criminal insanity which remains the basis of the insanity defence in English law. There is no doubt that M'Naghten met the criteria for *mens rea*, since he fully intended to cause death when he pulled the trigger, though he was deluded as to the reasons he might have for doing so. A standard which provided an excuse only in the absence of *mens rea* would mean that only those cases in which the action and its consequences were not intended (imagine M'Naghten's delusion led to him believing he was holding a water pistol instead of a gun, and he only intended to soak his victim) would result in an excuse. This is surely too restrictive a standard.

The second possible standard is the negation of free will. Here too I agree with Moore that there is little prospect of this forming a coherent criterion that can be applied to cases of mental illness. The problem is that, if an action cannot be freely willed in the sense relevant to criminal responsibility if it is caused by factors outside the agent's control, then we may be forced to the conclusion that *nobody's* actions are freely willed in the relevant way, because of familiar concerns about the supposed incompatibility of physical determinism with free will. All of our actions are, it

---

[10] Ibid., p. 600.

would seem, caused by the movement of particles within and outside our bodies, factors which are surely outside our control.

Of course, it is entirely possible to reject such incompatibilist concerns, but if we do this, we are left with the task of picking out some other form of causation which is relevant to responsibility ascriptions. It is true that there is a colloquial sense in which we might say that someone's schizophrenia, for example, 'caused' them to act in a particular way. Perhaps the most promising way of making sense of this idea is counterfactually: when we say that 'their schizophrenia caused them to act like that', what we mean is that, if they had not been schizophrenic, they would have acted otherwise. However, this is an equally natural way to talk about non-pathological psychological features of the agent, for example their anger, enthusiasm or jealousy. We might well say that their actions were 'caused' by their anger, and by this we might well mean that, had they not been angry, they would not have done what they did. Ordinarily, this would not be to excuse them from moral responsibility. In some extreme cases, however, it might be. How do we distinguish such cases from the more typical cases in which responsibility is intact? It is surely by looking for evidence that their anger not only caused their behaviour, but caused it by producing ignorance (they were so blinded by rage that they did not know what they were doing) or compulsion (the emotion overwhelmed them and caused them to lose control over their actions). And as I have argued previously in this book, we apply, or should apply, a similar test to cases of mental illness. If schizophrenia, for example, is excusing, it is because it prevents the agent from properly understanding the reasons they have for acting in certain ways, or from coordinating their actions in response to those reasons. If addiction is excusing, it is because it overwhelms the agent's self-control and leads them to act under compulsion. But if it will be necessary in any case to look for conditions such as these in our assessments of mental illness cases in regard to the law, then it is unclear what the notion of someone's actions being 'caused' by their illness adds that is not already supplied by these conditions themselves.

As I have said, Moore's view is that, where the mentally ill are to be excused from criminal responsibility, this should be on grounds of irrationality. Moore's argument for this is complex, and involves an analysis of rational action which it will not be possible to set out in full here.[11] In short, he classifies behaviour as irrational when it exhibits any of the following features:

---

[11] See ibid., pp. 604–9.

1. Where it is unrelated to any beliefs or desires which 'we can reasonably ascribe to the agent', for example 'the bodily motions of epileptics during a *grand mal* seizure, or the word salads of schizophrenics'.[12]

2. Where an individual 'decides firmly on a course of conduct A, believes if he performs some routine M then he will accomplish A, nothing prevents him from doing M, and yet refuses to do M'. In cases like this, something like extreme weakness of will appears to prevent the agent from doing what they must do by their own lights.

3. Where the agent believes, desires or intends something which it is irrational for them to believe, desire or intend, and their actions stem from these irrational beliefs, desires or intentions.[13]

There is little doubt that the forms of irrationality Moore describes can be excusing. Given the overall question we are seeking to answer here – why should some mentally ill people be excused from criminal responsibility? – it is important to consider whether they are reducible to instances of compulsion or ignorance since, if they are, there will be no difference between Moore's suggestion and the final possibility listed earlier: that mental illness is excusing because it issues in compulsion or ignorance. Cases of excusing irrational belief, at least, do seem to represent a sub-category of excusing ignorance.[14] If I have formed the irrational belief that I am made of glass, and as a result I fail to rescue someone who is drowning because I am worried that I will sink or shatter in the attempt, then I have seemingly become ignorant of the circumstances in which I am acting in a way that plausibly excuses me from moral responsibility.

Cases of irrational desires or intentions, however, are more difficult to make sense of as instances of ignorance of compulsion. The example of an irrational desire given by Moore is 'wishing to expose one's green books to the sun'.[15] It may be that the irrationality of such a desire depends on some irrational, delusional belief, for example that the books in question will be

---

[12] Ibid., p. 605.

[13] Not every instance of an irrational belief, desire or intention is presumably sufficient to ground non-responsibility. For example, it might be irrational for me to believe that I can beat you in a tennis match, given your superior skill and fitness. But ordinary delusions of this kind are not enough to block responsibility, unlike the belief, to use Moore's example, 'that one is made of glass' (ibid., p. 606.). It is a little unclear how we are to distinguish cases of the former type from cases of the latter type, since both involve 'the epistemic situation of the actor and the degree to which that situation gives her warrant for believing what she does' (ibid.). Perhaps there is simply a spectrum of irrationality of belief with only cases at the extreme end counting as responsibility-blocking.

[14] Only a sub-category, because there are cases in which the agent has a false belief which is excusing, but which is nonetheless rational in relation to their other beliefs, desires and intentions, as when the agent has been deceived by someone whom they have, as far as they know, good reason to believe.

[15] Moore (1997), p. 606.

improved in some way by this action. In these cases, we are again faced with an excusing condition which is, at bottom, attributable to a form of ignorance. However, it might be that the desire has sprung fully formed, so to speak, and that its irrationality is really attributable to its not being intelligible in terms of any beliefs, desires or intentions of the agent, whether delusional or otherwise. In cases like this, there does not appear to be any excusing ignorance. Nor is there obviously any compulsion: the agent need not be compelled to open their green books to the sun; they need only have the irrational desire to do so. Something similar applies to cases of irrational intention: I need not have any irrational beliefs to form an irrational intention, and that intention need not be compelling or compelled.

Although it seems to be true that some forms of irrationality can be explained in terms neither of ignorance nor of compulsion, it does seem to me that all of the forms of irrationality considered by Moore can be expressed in terms of the agent's responsiveness to reasons. Moreover, thinking in these terms helps to make sense not only of these cases, but also of cases of ignorance or compulsion that do not fall into any of Moore's categories of irrationality.

In cases which belong to the first category, the agent appears unable to conform their actions to the reasons they have, or to the reasons they take themself to have. (In fact, we do not typically know in such cases what reasons the agent takes themself to have, but whatever they are it is fairly clear that they are unrelated to the action in question in any meaningful way.) In category 2 cases, the agent also appears unable to conform their behaviour to their own perceived reasons. In category 3 cases, or at least in those where the degree of irrationality of the desire, belief or intention is sufficient to render the agent non-responsible, the lack of responsibility is plausibly attributable to unresponsiveness to reasons. To have an irrational belief, on this interpretation, is to believe something which one does not have good reason to believe, given one's other beliefs, desires, intentions and so on. Cases in which irrational beliefs are excusing are those in which the beliefs in question interfere with the agent's view of what reasons they have. An irrational desire is one which is directed at something which one has no reason to desire. If the desire is responsibility-blocking, it is because it interferes with the agent's ability to see rightly what reasons they have, or to direct their behaviour in pursuit of those reasons. Irrational intentions, meanwhile, are intentions that are unaffected by, or contrary to, the reasons they take themself to have, and they are excusing to the extent that they interfere with their ability to conform their behaviour to those reasons. If an agent's mental illness has led them to form the intention to do something which is contrary to the reasons that bear on their choices, there is a sense in which this intention has apparently overwhelmed their ability to apply those reasons in their conduct. We would expect a fully responsible agent to recognise that the intention in question was irrational and to reject it. But in the case where the intention is a result of mental illness, this does not seem to be something we can expect.[16]

Where does this leave psychopaths? Might they be excused from criminal responsibility because of compulsion, ignorance or the more general forms of irrationality described by Moore?

To take the last of these first, it is, I think, unlikely that psychopaths would be excused from criminal responsibility on the grounds that they exhibit the kind of general irrationality that Moore has in mind. While the motivations of psychopaths can sometimes present a puzzle, this appears to be because they have an alien set of values, rather than because we cannot make sense of their actions in the light of those values. Why does a violent psychopath who is on parole kill a man in a bar fight in retaliation for a minor slight, in front of multiple witnesses? On one level, this action is surely irrational: we assume the psychopath values their freedom – certainly a lengthy prison sentence would make them unhappy – and this is exactly what they are risking, for something which seems bizarrely trivial. But action which is irrational in this sense – in the sense of being against our own considered opinion of what is in our interests – is not automatically irrational in a sense that would remove our moral responsibility. Indeed we all act in this general way sometimes, and are morally responsible for doing so. The psychopath in my example's desire to hurt the man in the bar, and his intention to cause him harm, are intelligible in terms of his emotional state at the time and his overall motivational structure. They do not spring fully formed and unrelated to his existing set of desires and beliefs.[17]

There are some descriptions of psychopaths' behaviour which might lead us to believe that it is in some sense directed by compulsion. In

[16] Schopp's example of 'Mary' (Schopp (1991), pp. 160–2, also considered in Duff (2010), pp. 205–6) is also an interesting illustration of irrationality that appears not to be equivalent either to simple ignorance or compulsion. Mary stabbed a stranger leaving a church service because 'she believed that criminals were going to kill her unless she could show them that she was as bad as them: she believed this because she had heard them talking to her on the telephone; and she killed someone leaving church because she found a dollar bill and was struck by the "In God We Trust" printed on it' (ibid., p. 205). Mary's irrationality is not correctly described as ignorance or compulsion: it is a radical and thoroughgoing breakdown in her ability to grasp and apply reasons.

[17] See Haksar (1965) for a discussion of psychopaths' values and responsibility.

describing his case studies in his book *The Mask of Sanity*, Cleckley in particular frequently emphasises the sense that psychopaths chafe under the disguise that they must adopt in order to pass in society. Cleckley's psychopaths appear to be able to wear this mask only for a certain length of time before it inevitably slips and they begin again to indulge in extreme forms of behaviour: bouts of drunkenness and/or violence, for example. The sense that this behaviour can only be kept in check through an effort which cannot be sustained beyond a certain point might suggest that it is compulsive. It does not follow from the fact that it is uncomfortable for a person to avoid indulging in a form of behaviour, however, that that form of behaviour is compulsive in ways that would remove either moral or criminal responsibility. We might just as easily want to describe this phenomenon in terms of the behaviour's being natural or unnatural. The psychopath, to fit in to society, must behave in a way that is unnatural to them, and ultimately they will return to a form of behaviour that is more natural. It cannot be that we are excused from responsibility simply for adopting forms of behaviour that are natural to us. We must also take into account the fact that psychopaths apparently do not see any reason for refraining from socially or morally transgressive behaviour beyond the fact that it is advantageous for them to pass as a normal member of society. It is not that the psychopath struggles in vain to refrain from behaving in a way that they know is wrong. Rather, they naturally behave in ways in which they take themself to have every reason to behave.

This just leaves the possibility that psychopaths might be excused through ignorance, a possibility which depends, more than anything, on what type of ignorance is necessary for absolution of criminal responsibility.

6.4 Ignorance and Criminal Responsibility

The M'Naghten test, which is still influential, in different forms, in many jurisdictions, uses ignorance as the criterion to judge whether a defendant is mentally ill in a way that excuses them from moral responsibility. This ruling states that someone is 'insane' in a way that exempts them from criminal responsibility if, 'at the time of the committing of the act, the party accused was labouring under such a defect of reason, from disease of the mind, as not to know the nature and quality of the act he was doing; or, if he did know it, that he did not know he was doing what was wrong'.[18] While it may appear from this wording that a psychopath would have

---

[18] M'Naghten's Case (1843).

a good chance of successfully employing the defence, the standard interpretation of the ruling which has emerged from case law suggests otherwise. According to this interpretation, 'nature and quality' is taken only to
refer to the physical aspects of the act, so that 'the insanity defence is
unavailable if the defendant has knowledge of the physical aspects of the act
alleged even if he or she does not have knowledge of the moral aspects of his
or her act'.[19] Meanwhile, the requirement that the accused must 'know he
was doing what was wrong' is taken to refer only to knowledge that the act
was legally wrong, as opposed to morally wrong.[20] There is no reason to
think that psychopaths would be unable to fulfil either criterion: their
condition does not prevent them from understanding either what they
have physically done or whether it was, or was not, against the law.

The question we must answer then is whether these are in fact the
criteria which ought to be applied in such cases. Is it only ignorance of
the physical circumstances in which one acts, or of the fact that one's
actions are illegal, that ought to be excusing, or should some forms of moral
ignorance also be taken to be excusing in a similar way?

The idea that moral ignorance should be excusing in a criminal context has
been debated among legal practitioners as well as philosophers. In 2013, the
English Law Commission published a discussion paper which argued for the
replacement of the insanity defence with a new defence of 'not criminally
responsible by reason of a recognised medical condition'. This defence would
have two 'limbs', each describing a capacity which a defendant would need to
be shown to lack if they wanted to avail themselves of the defence. Each of
these conditions could be seen as being relevant to psychopaths, given the
kind of imperviousness to some reasons that I have argued they display.

The first condition is 'the capacity rationally to form a judgment about
the relevant conduct or circumstances.' It could be argued that someone
who is not capable of seeing the rights, interests and concerns of other
people as presenting a reason for action, could not 'rationally form
a judgment' about matters upon which such reasons bear. In its discussion
of this issue, the Law Commission report cites an account by Schopp of the
capacities necessary for practical reasoning, as a definition of what is meant
by 'the capacity rationally to form a judgment'.[21] One of these is 'the ability
to form accurate beliefs'.[22] If it is true that the rights, interests and concerns

---

[19] Law Commission (2013), p. 10.   [20] Ibid.
[21] Schopp (1991), cited in Law Commission (2013), p. 54.
[22] Ibid. The other capacities are 'an ability to draw on existing wants and beliefs that the actor has, and
    "an accurate reasoning process that allows him to draw warranted conclusions about the probable
    relationships among various wants, acts, and consequences"'.

of others present reasons for action, and psychopaths are incapable of knowing this, then there are at least some relevant, accurate beliefs which they are unable to form. However, we are in danger here of entangling ourselves in meta-ethical controversies about the nature of moral claims and moral beliefs, and it would be preferable if the law could avoid committing itself to positions in these controversies. Moreover, it is clear from the discussion in the Law Commission report that this limb is intended to refer to common or garden beliefs about physical states of affairs rather than metaphysical beliefs about what reasons one has.

The more promising limb, then, is the second one, which stipulates that a defendant must have the capacity to understand 'the wrongfulness of the act'.[23] This formulation is close to that in the M'Naghten ruling, with the difference being that in this case, wrongfulness is apparently intended to refer to what is morally wrong, and not just to what is legally wrong. This, it might seem, must include psychopaths. If a psychopath is unable to understand that they have a reason not to harm another person, for example, then they cannot understand that it is morally wrong to harm that person. Therefore, we might think, they must lack the capacity indicated by this limb of the proposed defence.

Unfortunately, the Law Commission report takes an approach to the task of defining 'morally wrong', which seemingly conflates it with what is *generally considered to be* morally wrong. The report notes that, 'It would obviously not be desirable for a court to have to conduct an inquiry into what was generally regarded as morally wrong; on the other hand, the standard cannot be wholly subjective to the accused.'[24] Rejecting the 'subjective' alternative, the authors of the report apparently settle on what they see as the only other alternative, endorsing a practice in Canadian law whereby understanding that something is illegal is taken as evidence that one understands that it is generally considered to be morally wrong. However, not having resolved the difficulty they themselves identify as attending the attempt to define 'what is generally considered to be morally wrong', namely that this seemingly requires the court to have knowledge of complex empirical facts about public moral opinion, the authors of the report appear to have taken us back to the original M'Naghten standard, with the difference that understanding the illegality of an act is now taken to be a sufficient condition of understanding its 'wrongness', but is perhaps no longer taken to be a necessary condition.

---

[23] Law Commission (2013), p. 59.   [24] Ibid., p. 56.

In reality, understanding that an act is illegal is neither a necessary nor a sufficient condition of understanding whether it is morally wrong. Plenty of acts are morally wrong without being illegal, and it is at least possible that some things that are illegal are morally permissible. Nor is something's being generally considered to be morally wrong sufficient for its being, in fact, morally wrong. The public can be mistaken about moral matters. These are theoretical problems, but they are not without practical implications. By employing these proxies for moral understanding, the authors of the report are limiting the ability of their proposed law to discriminate accurately between cases of responsibility and non-responsibility.

To see this, and to examine how the capacity to understand moral wrongness might be made a condition of criminal responsibility, it will be useful to consider some cases. In discussing the limitations of the existing insanity defence, the report rightly points out that restricting interpretation of 'wrong' to 'legally wrong' means that the defence will exclude some cases that look like clear cases of non-responsibility. One such case is that of Andrea Yates:

> 'Yates, a woman with a history of mental illness, drowned all five of her children in a bath. Believing that Satan had been conversing with her, she concluded she needed to kill her children while they were still innocent to save them from an eternity of torment in hell.'[25]

Under existing law, Yates would not be able to present an insanity defence, because her mental condition did not, as far as we know, prevent her from understanding that killing her children was against the law. It did, however, prevent her from understanding that killing her children was morally wrong, because it resulted in a mistaken conviction that she was acting in their interests. The authors of the report are surely right to conclude that this case demonstrates the limitations of the current law, since (I take it) her inability to understand that her actions were morally wrong is enough to establish her lack of responsibility, while her ability to understand that they are legally wrong does not disprove this. However, it is far from clear that changing the requirement to an understanding that one's actions are *generally considered* to be morally wrong delivers the right verdict in this case either. It is not obvious that Yates would have been of the belief that her actions would be generally considered to be morally permissible. In any case, this is surely not the point. The point is that, regardless of what

---

[25] Ibid., p. 10. It should be noted, however, that Yates was found not guilty by a Texas court, using a version of the M'Naghten test. I am grateful to an anonymous reviewer for pointing this out.

anyone else would have thought of what she was doing, she was convinced, because of her mental condition, that what she was doing *was in fact morally right*.

Consider also the hypothetical case of Larry. Larry suffers from a paranoid delusion that everyone else in the world has had a chip implanted in their brain by an evil alien who is bent on killing Larry. The chips, in Larry's imagination, are designed so that they will activate whenever their host sees Larry, at which point they will take over the host's body in order to attack Larry, with the aim of killing him. Larry locks himself in his house and proceeds to attack everyone who knocks on his door, in what he believes to be self-defence, and imprison them in his cellar. In this scenario, Larry presumably understands that his actions would generally be considered to be morally wrong. After all, the people do not know that they have chips in their heads, and therefore do not know that their presence puts Larry in danger, and therefore that he has a right to imprison them. If we think Larry is not morally responsible, and should not be held criminally responsible, for his actions, this cannot be on the basis of his beliefs about what is generally considered to be morally wrong. As with Andrea Yates, the delusional belief held by Larry which is relevant to both his moral and criminal responsibility is surely just the belief that what he does *is* morally permissible.

It could be thought that the Law Commission's proposal could be rescued here by refining the relevant criterion somewhat. The question might be, not simply whether the act in question would generally be considered to be morally wrong, but whether most people would, in a world in which they had the same set of relevant beliefs as the accused, consider the act to be morally wrong. Thus, it might be that most people who were in Andrea Yates's position, and who shared her beliefs about the mortal danger to her children's souls, would also share her conclusion that drowning them was morally justified. It might also be that most people who were in Larry's position, and who shared his beliefs about the supposed chips in people's heads, would also conclude that imprisoning them was permissible.

However, even a condition of this nature fails to attend to the mental condition of the accused in the right way. Let us imagine another hypothetical person, Larry's brother Barry. Barry has a condition which is much simpler than that of his brother. Let us imagine that Barry, perhaps because of some brain injury, is gripped by a powerful conviction that beheading innocent people is a morally worthy act. Barry's condition, let us say, does not result in his holding any particular beliefs other than this one, or upon which this one might depend. He does not think that other people are aliens, or have chips in their heads, or are zombies, or are possessed by Satan. He just thinks that beheading them is a good thing to do, morally speaking. Now, it seems clear to me that Barry is no more morally responsible for his actions than is Larry, and it also seems equally clear that he should not be held criminally responsible. But Barry would not fit the criterion of failing to understand that what he did was generally considered to be morally wrong, on either of the possible construals we have discussed. He need not, first of all, be under any misapprehension that other people share his view of the moral rectitude of beheading innocent people. Perhaps he considers himself to be a moral hero, akin to someone in a slave-owning society who helps slaves to escape, that is someone who refuses to go along with prevailing norms and sticks instead to what he knows is right as a matter of deep moral conviction. But it also cannot be said that he fails to understand that other people, given a set of relevant beliefs identical to his own, would consider what he does to be morally wrong. This is because either we take the set of relevant beliefs to include his conviction that what he does is right, in which case it is not true that other people with those beliefs would consider what he does to be wrong, or else we take the set of relevant beliefs not to include that belief, in which case it is true that most people would consider what he does to be wrong, but this is not something that Barry's condition causes him to have any difficulty understanding.

It is hard to escape the conclusion, I think, that the criminal law cannot be on a sure footing unless it is acknowledged that criminal responsibility should, like moral responsibility, depend on the ability to understand the moral features of one's actions. Specifically, it seems to me, the capacity to see the rights, interests and concerns of other people as presenting the defendant with reasons for action should be made a condition of criminal responsibility.

I have already argued for this capacity being a necessary condition of moral responsibility. But am I right that it should also be considered a necessary condition of criminal responsibility? First, it should be noted that, in practice, in the vast majority of cases, conditions of criminal responsibility already track those of moral responsibility. Cases in which a defendant might be criminally responsible without being morally responsible are relatively rare and are marked out as special cases. The largest category of such cases is that of 'strict liability'. The justification for such cases is somewhat obscure and controversial,[26] but it appears to be,

---

[26] See, for example, Keating (2014).

essentially, that there are certain offences whereby it is thought desirable to place an increased responsibility on individuals to avoid any risk that their behaviour might lead them to commit the offence. Thus, offences which may be categorised as strict liability offences, depending upon the jurisdiction (it is important to note that some jurisdictions contain many more strict liability defences than others), include parking offences, offences concerning the environmental impacts of business and, at least in the United States, statutory rape of a minor. In each case, the intention behind the application of strict liability is to place additional responsibility on those engaging in activities that might put them at risk of committing the offence, to take extra pains to ensure that they do not do so. So, for example, in the case of statutory rape, it is thought desirable to incentivise people to know beyond doubt that their sexual partners are above the age of consent – the defence that a reasonable person would have thought that someone was above the age of consent is not enough to establish non-responsibility.

Now, it is hard to see how this kind of intention could play any role in setting legal principles for the treatment of psychopaths, for whom *every* offence would presumably have to become, in effect, a strict liability offence. If this is right, then the particular harm arising from a given offence, or the difficulty of securing a conviction for that particular offence given normal standards of criminal responsibility, could not be justifying grounds for stipulating that psychopaths, for all possible offences, need not be morally responsible for the act in order to be criminally responsible for it.

However, there is a way in which it might more plausibly be thought that moral and criminal responsibility might come apart in certain cases, which is if it were true that the knowledge that what one has done was illegal was the only knowledge requirement attaching to criminal responsibility – that moral knowledge was irrelevant. After all, strict liability laws concern cases in which the defendant's knowledge that they have done something illegal is in doubt – if it could be established that the defendant knew this, then there would be no need to apply strict liability. Even if cases such as that of Andrea Yates suggest that, for some mental conditions at least, a delusory belief that what one does is morally right is enough to absolve one of criminal responsibility, one might argue, it is not clear that cases involving psychopaths are relevantly similar to these cases. Andrea Yates acted as she did because she believed, wrongly but through no fault of her own, that she had a supervening moral reason to do what she did, which was important enough to outweigh her reasons – arising from the fact that her actions were illegal – not to do so. In fact, the law makes provision for cases in which the accused genuinely has such reasons, so that, for example, someone who breaks a minor law to prevent a much worse event from taking place is unlikely to be convicted of breaking the minor law. Perhaps it is something like this that accounts for our intuition that Andrea Yates should not be held criminally responsible for what she did. (Of course, killing one's children is not a minor offence, but still it might plausibly be outweighed by the prospect of their suffering an eternity of torment.) Cases involving psychopaths are not like this. It is not that they mistakenly believe that they have some supervening reason to do what they do; they simply believe that they have no moral reason not to.

The idea of making responsiveness to moral reasons a condition of criminal responsibility has worried some writers, who suspect that to go down this route would end in the absolution of a great many people, perhaps even most criminals, from responsibility. This is a worry worth taking seriously. Larry Alexander and Kimberley Kessler Ferzan summarise the problem thus:

> If pure psychopaths cannot be blamed for their failure to see that others' interests are reasons for them to take into account in acting, how can ordinary criminals be blamed for their failure to see that others' interests are as weighty as they in fact are? In short, is culpability deserving of punishment restricted to the akratic – those who correctly perceive the weight of others' interests but nonetheless knowingly act against the balance of reasons?[27]

The idea underpinning this worry is that our beliefs about the reasons presented by others' interests, and their relative weight, are no more under our control than are our beliefs about straightforward, factual matters. We do not have 'direct control over how things appear to us, including reasons and their strength. Like our other beliefs, our beliefs about reasons come to us unbidden'.[28]

Leaving aside the empirical question of what proportion of criminals' actions may be genuinely akratic in the way described, the view that our moral beliefs are outside the scope of our control, and hence our culpability, can certainly be questioned. While it might be true that we cannot change our beliefs about moral matters by a simple act of will, it does not follow from this that we bear no responsibility for the beliefs of this kind that we have. William Fitzpatrick, in an argument which Alexander and

[27] Alexander and Ferzan (2018), p. 99.   [28] Ibid., p. 100.

Ferzan discuss but ultimately dismiss, suggests that mistaken moral beliefs may be the result of vices which are, or have been, within the power of the criminal to change.[29] In cases where the criminal has had the opportunity to correct their moral ignorance, and where their failure to do so has been the result of vices such as arrogance, laziness and so on, we can reasonably expect the criminal to have the correct moral beliefs, and the fact that they do not have these beliefs is not excusing. They are, one might say, responsible because they have been morally negligent. Whether one agrees with this view perhaps at least partly depends on whether one believes in moral luck. The criminal thus described is in a situation akin to that of the drunk-driver who runs over and kills a child. If one believes that the drunk-driver is responsible, not only for drinking and driving, but also for killing the child, then one might also believe that the morally negligent criminal is responsible for the acts that are the result of their moral ignorance, and not only for their failure to correct that ignorance at an earlier time.

Alexander and Ferzan reject this possibility on the following grounds:

> That one could correct one's mistaken views, factual or moral, is immaterial, for one would need to perceive a sufficiently strong reason to investigate whether one's views are correct. And at the moment of decision, the negligent actor does not perceive such a reason. The fact that there is such a reason – namely, that the actor's views are mistaken – cannot guide the actor who does not perceive it.[30]

But perceiving that other people have interests that present reasons of significant relative weight is not something that simply happens by chance. As I tried to explain in Chapter 5, it has something to do with our ability to empathise with others, to see the world from their point of view and to feel some analogue of the impact of our immoral actions on them. In cases where these abilities are intact, but where the individual has nevertheless neglected to take seriously the possibility that other people's interests have value and present reasons for action that must be taken into account, it is reasonable to suppose that the individual bears some responsibility for their actions. Only in cases where these abilities are entirely absent, which is to say in psychopaths, should we conclude that responsibility is also entirely absent.

If we are to establish that responsiveness to moral reasons should be made a condition of criminal responsibility, of course, we do not need only to establish that such a condition would not inadvertently excuse the

---

[29] Fitzpatrick (2008).   [30] Alexander and Ferzan (2018), p. 102.

majority of criminals. We also need to establish that the mere recognition of a legal reason, as opposed to a moral reason, against one's actions, is not enough to establish criminal responsibility on its own. In his discussion of criminal responsibility and psychopaths, Stephen Morse argues against this view:

> If a person does not understand the point of morality and has no conscience or capacity for empathy, only fear of punishment will give the person good reason not to violate the rights of others. As has been recognized at least since Hobbes, however, social cooperation and safety cannot be secured solely by the fear of state punishment. Internalized conscience and fellow feeling are the best guarantors of right action. The psychopath is not responsive to moral reasons, even if they are responsive to other reasons. Consequently, they do not have the capacity for moral rationality, at least when their behavior implicates moral concerns, and thus they are not responsible. They have no access to the most rational reasons to behave well.[31]

This discussion helpfully clarifies the terms of the debate. For the majority of people, compliance with the law is not in practice secured merely by the law's existence and the potential for its enforcement through criminal sanctions. Most of us comply with the law partly because we recognise the norms that the law codifies as being of moral value in themselves. The fact that it is illegal might be one reason why we do not attack random strangers on the street, but it is not as important a reason as the fact that to do so would be wrong – would violate the rights of those strangers and cause them harm – regardless of whether it was illegal or not. To this we can perhaps add the point that many of us take the law to supply moral reasons itself. Assuming I buy into the legitimacy of whatever legislative system is in place to create laws, and assuming I do not think the law in question is so egregious as to require me to break it as a form of civil disobedience, it seems to me that the very fact that a law exists gives me a moral reason to comply with it.

But neither moral reasons arising from moral requirements that coincide with legal ones, nor moral reasons arising from the legitimacy of the legal system overall, are available to psychopaths, assuming (as Morse believes, and I do) that they are unresponsive to reasons stemming from the rights, interests and concerns of other people. This is obviously true of the first type of reason, but it is true of the second type as well since, however a legislative system derives its legitimacy, it is surely partly due to its role in

---

[31] Morse (2008), p. 208.

protecting the rights, interests and concerns of citizens. If I was unable to care about these, it is hard to see how I would take laws to supply me with moral reasons, as opposed to prudential reasons arising from the possibility of punishment.

For Morse, the unavailability of these moral reasons to psychopaths is enough to establish that they are not criminally responsible. However, this does not automatically follow from the fact that 'internalized conscience and fellow feeling are the best guarantors of right action'. I should acknowledge before closing that nothing I have argued in this chapter should convince someone who believes that the notion of desert plays no role in justifying the punishment of criminals. The only way to shut down this possibility would be to engage with the deep and philosophically vexed questions concerning the role of the state in punishing offenders, and what justification there might be for this role, to which I alluded briefly at the start of this chapter. If the justification for punishment is purely based on its beneficial consequences overall, then it might be that the fact that the law presents, in Morse's words, 'a "pricing" system'[32] to psychopaths, which may be effective in deterring them from criminal acts, might be enough to justify including psychopaths within the scope of criminal responsibility. However, if the justification for punishment does rest on their deserving to be punished, or indeed if it rests on something like the desirability of a form of moral communication between the state and the offender, through which the latter is brought face to face with the moral import of their actions, then this may be less appropriate in the case of psychopaths (or at least those who are at the higher end of the scale for psychopathic traits including the capacity for empathy). Resolving these questions is beyond the scope of what I am attempting here, and so this is where my discussion should end.

6.5 Conclusions

Psychopaths present a significant problem for the criminal law, which is both moral and practical in nature. As a philosopher with only limited understanding of the law, it would be inappropriate for me to offer firm conclusions as to how the law should seek to deal with offenders who, after all, present a significant danger to the public. However, I do believe there are good reasons to think that the law as it currently stands is on a shaky theoretical footing with regard to psychopaths, even if (as I do not assume)

[32] Ibid.

most jurisdictions have found ways of dealing with them, that work on a practical level. I have tried to present some of these reasons in this chapter, and to point towards the further theoretical difficulties which would need to be resolved if firmer conclusions about the proper treatment of psychopaths were to be found.

Conclusions

I have argued that psychopaths are not responsive to certain reasons and are therefore not morally responsible for failing to act on those reasons. Being responsive to the reasons in question, I have argued, depends on the ability to value others. More accurately, it depends on the ability to recognise something other than oneself as an ultimate source of value, since (1) psychopaths might be able to see others as valuable instrumentally, insofar as they can serve the psychopath's end, and (2) they are blind to the value not just of other people, but also of such things as animals, the environment or justice. I think psychopaths are unresponsive to these reasons because they have a general emotional deficiency which stunts their ability to engage evaluatively with the world, and a specific deficiency of empathy which prevents them from achieving an ability to value others. I think because these deficiencies are already well established in childhood and appear to be irreversible, psychopaths are not morally responsible for being in this state of unresponsiveness to the reasons in question – this is beyond their control.

The reasons to which I think psychopaths are unresponsive are therefore all those reasons that depend on the value of entities other than oneself. I have focused primarily on reasons stemming from the rights, interests and concerns of other people, for example reasons to refrain from harming people which are due to their having a right not to be harmed, or an interest in not being harmed. However, as I argued in Chapter 3, psychopaths are also unresponsive to any reasons which may stem from the rights, interests and concerns of animals, and from considerations such as fairness and justice, which also depend on the value of entities that must be treated fairly or justly.

In Chapter 1, I argued that one can be morally responsible for morally good, bad and neutral acts. I think that psychopaths, insofar as they have failed to develop the ability to value others, are not morally responsible for morally bad acts, since morally bad acts depend on the ability to value others. I also think that psychopaths are not morally responsible for morally *good* acts, insofar as morally good acts depend on the ability to value entities other than oneself. Imagine a psychopath gives money to a homeless person in the street. Unless they have some ulterior motive for doing so, and given the premise that they do not think that person valuable (so, for example, they could just as happily kill the person if they wanted to), then they act without reason, and do not understand the reasons which would ordinarily make this a morally good act. Therefore, the verdict that the psychopath is not morally responsible for the act (and does not deserve praise for it, for example) seems to me to be the right one. Morally neutral acts are unaffected by reasons based on the value of others, and therefore psychopaths (*qua* psychopaths) are morally responsible for these acts.

Acts are not the only things we can be morally responsible for. We can also be morally responsible for choices, for states of affairs which are the result of our acts or of our negligent inaction, for attitudes and for emotions. Insofar as reasons based on the value of others bear on these things, psychopaths are not morally responsible for them either.

As I noted in Chapter 2, psychopaths exist on a continuum, or rather on several continua. The features that make up a diagnosis of psychopathy according to the Hare checklist exist in a great many people to a greater or lesser extent. However, what the review of clinical and scientific literature in Chapter 2, together with the developmental picture set out in Chapter 5, hopefully makes clear is that there is a group of people whose genetic inheritance, upbringing or both renders them truly incapable of seeing others as valuable. This set of people may only be a subset of people who would be assessed as psychopathic using Hare's scale, including only those who score at the high end for emotional deficiencies and lack of empathy specifically. It is these people to whom my verdict of moral non-responsibility applies. There are, of course, likely to be difficult borderline cases. In such cases, the criterion for ascribing moral responsibility implied by my account would be the ability to value others. Secondary evidence for this ability, or its lack, could in principle be sought by considering the individual's neurological resources and the extent to which they had an upbringing characterised by the encouragement and exploitation of empathy by a caring parent. In practice, of course, making confident judgements on the basis of this evidence is likely to be a difficult endeavour. An opportunity for further research would be to consider in depth how we should think about borderline cases. Common sense would suggest that responsibility is not 'all or nothing', but admits of degrees (as in the parallel legal concept of 'diminished responsibility'). But what exactly is the relationship between a diminished capacity for empathy, a diminished capacity for valuing others and diminished moral responsibility? How does each lead to the next? Finally, what should be our attitudes and practices towards someone who has diminished, but not absent, responsibility? These are interesting and non-trivial questions which would require further work.

It also remains to be stated what the implications of a verdict of non-responsibility ought to be for our practices and attitudes in respect of the clearer cases of psychopathy, and of the actions of these psychopaths. It is implied by the conclusions of Chapter 1 that lacking moral responsibility for an act (say) invalidates a whole range of practices and attitudes towards that act, including blame or praise, and the reactive emotions such as resentment. In Chapter 6, I made some preliminary observations concerning whether a verdict of non-responsibility for psychopaths invalidates punishment of the agent by the state. Answering this question definitively would require a thorough analysis of the purposes of punishment, which is beyond the scope of this book.

Commentators[1] have sometimes worried that verdicts of non-responsibility may have the effect of excluding people from the moral community, and therefore of validating forms of treatment towards them which would ordinarily be considered unjust or illiberal. I have stated some actions and attitudes which I believe are inappropriate when directed at psychopaths, but which would be appropriate when directed at non-psychopaths. I have not said whether there are actions which would be justified when directed at psychopaths and which would not be justified when directed at non-psychopaths, such as pre-emptive incarceration. Again, disentangling these issues would require significant additional argument.

The waters around both moral and criminal responsibility are further muddied by the use of diagnostic categories different from, but supposedly related to, psychopathy. Significantly, my conclusions in this thesis say nothing about how we should treat people who have been diagnosed using the DSM-V classification of Antisocial Personality Disorder(APD). Indeed, due to the issues with this diagnosis that I explored in Chapter 2, it is difficult to say anything very useful about how we should treat people in this category, who are unlikely to be a homogenous group at the level of personality. Given that APD is a very widely used diagnostic category, this obviously raises difficulties

[1] For example, Benn (1999).

for anyone who would want to draw firm conclusions about how such people should be treated as a matter of judicial policy.

In practical terms, the conclusions I have presented in this thesis tell us something about how we should think about psychopaths, and point the way towards how we should interact with them, both as individuals and from a societal standpoint. In theoretical terms, they add to our understanding of what moral responsibility, understood on the reasons-responsiveness model, requires. It turns out that psychopaths, though not irrational in the sense that their condition does not render them factually mistaken about anything, are nonetheless unable to grasp a significant set of reasons which are available to non-psychopaths, and indeed which do apply to psychopaths as well. Moral responsibility, it turns out, requires not just the ability to grasp and apply moral concepts, but also the ability to value others.

References

Adolphs, R. 2010. What does the amygdala contribute to social cognition? *Annals of the New York Academy of Sciences.* 1191(1), pp. 42–61.

Adshead, G. 1999. Psychopaths and other-regarding beliefs. *Philosophy, Psychiatry and Psychology.* 6(1), pp. 41–4.

Alexander, L. and Ferzan, K. K. 2018. *Reflections on crime and culpability: Problems and puzzles.* Cambridge: Cambridge University Press.

American Psychiatric Association. 2013. *Diagnostic and statistical manual of mental disorders: DSM-5.* Washington, D.C.: American Psychiatric Association.

Appelbaum, P. S. 1999. Ought we to require emotional capacity as part of decisional competence? *Kennedy Institute of Ethics Journal.* 8(4), pp. 377–87.

Aristotle. 1985. *Nicomachean ethics.* Indianapolis, Indiana: Hackett.

Arrington, R. L. 1979. Practical reason, responsibility and the psychopath. *Journal for the Theory of Social Behaviour.* 9(1), pp. 71–89.

Austin, J. L. 1956. A plea for excuses. *Proceedings of the Aristotelian Society.* 57, pp. 1–30.

Bandura, A. and Walters, R. H. 1959. *Adolescent aggression.* New York: Ronald Press.

Barker, E. 1980. The penetanguishene program: A personal review. In: Toch, H. ed. *Therapeutic communities in corrections.* New York: Praeger, pp. 73–81.

Barker, E. T. and Mason, M. H. 1968. Buber behind bars. *Canadian Psychiatric Association Journal.* 13, pp. 61–72.

Barker, E. T., Mason, M. H. and Wilson, J. 1969. Defence-disrupting therapy. *Canadian Psychiatric Association Journal.* 14(4), pp. 355–9.

Barker, E. T. and McLaughlin, A. J. 1977. The total encounter capsule. *Canadian Psychiatric Association Journal.* 22(7), pp. 355–60.

Barry, P. B. 2010. Saving Strawson: Evil and Strawsonian accounts of moral responsibility. *Ethical Theory and Moral Practice.* 14(1), pp. 5–21.

Bartlett, P. 2010. Stabbing in the dark: English law relating to psychopathy. In: Malatesti, L. and McMillan, J. eds. *Responsibility and psychopathy: Interfacing law, psychiatry and philosophy.* Oxford: Oxford University Press.

Ben-Ze'Ev, A. 2004. Emotions are not mere judgments. *Philosophy and Phenomenological Research.* 68(2), pp. 450–7.

Benn, P. 1999. Freedom, resentment and the psychopath. *Philosophy, Psychiatry and Psychology.* 6(1), pp. 29–39.

Blair, J., Mitchell, D. and Blair, K. 2005. *The psychopath: Emotion and the brain.* Oxford: Blackwell.

Blair, R. J., Jones, L., Clark, F. and Smith, M. 1997. The psychopathic individual: A lack of responsiveness to distress cues? *Psychophysiology.* 34(2), pp. 192–8.

Blair, R. J. R. 1995. A cognitive developmental approach to morality: Investigating the psychopath. *Cognition.* 57, pp. 1–29.

Blair, R. J. R. 1997. Moral reasoning and the child with psychopathic tendencies. *Personality and Individual Differences.* 22(5), pp. 731–9.

Blair, R. J. R. 2001. Neurocognitive models of aggression, the antisocial personality disorders, and psychopathy. *Journal of Neurology, Neurosurgery & Psychiatry.* 71(6), pp. 727–31.

Blair, R. J. R. 2003. Neurobiological basis of psychopathy. *The British Journal of Psychiatry.* 182, pp. 5–7.

Blair, R. J. R. 2008. The cognitive neuroscience of psychopathy and implications for judgments of responsibility. *Neuroethics.* 1(3), pp. 149–57.

Blair, R. J. R. 2010. Neuroimaging of psychopathy and antisocial behavior: A targeted review. *Current psychiatry reports.* 12(1), pp. 76–82.

Blair, R. J. R. 2011. Moral judgment and psychopathy. *Emotion Review.* 3(3), pp. 296–8.

Blair, R. J. R., Colledge, E. and Mitchell, D. G. V. 2001a. Somatic markers and response reversal: Is there orbitofrontal cortex dysfunction in boys with psychopathic tendencies? *Journal of Abnormal Child Psychology.* 29(6), pp. 499–511.

Blair, R. J. R., Colledge, E., Murray, L. and Mitchell, D. G. 2001b. A selective impairment in the processing of sad and fearful expressions in children with psychopathic tendencies. *Journal of Abnormal Child Psychology.* 29(6), pp. 491–8.

Blair, R. J. R., Jones, L., Clark, F. and Smith, M. 1995. Is the psychopath 'morally insane'? *Personality and Individual Differences.* 19(5), pp. 741–52.

Blair, R. J. R., Mitchell, D. G. V., Peschardt, K. S., Colledge, E., Leonard, R. A., Shine, J. H., Murray, L. K. and Perrett, D. I. 2004. Reduced sensitivity to others' fearful expressions in psychopathic individuals. *Personality and Individual Differences.* 37, pp. 1111–22.

Blair, R. J. R., Mitchell, D. G. V., Richell, R. A., Kelly, S., Leonard, A. and Newman, C. 2002. Turning a deaf ear to fear: Impaired recognition of vocal affect in psychopathic individuals. *Journal of Abnormal Psychology.* 111, pp. 682–6.

Bloom, P. 2016. *Against empathy: The case for rational compassion.* New York: Ecco Press.

Bok, H. 2002. Wallace's 'normative approach' to moral responsibility. *Philosophy and Phenomenological Research.* 64(3), pp. 682–6.

Botterell, A. 2009. A primer on the distinction between justification and excuse. *Philosophy Compass.* 4(1), pp. 172–96.

Brandt, R. B. 1969. A utilitarian theory of excuses. *The Philosophical Review.* 78(3), pp. 337–61.

Brody, G. H. and Shaffer, D. R. 1982. Contributions of parents and peers to children's moral socialization. *Development Review*. 2, pp. 31–75.

Calder, A. J., Young, A. W., Rowland, D., Perrett, D. I., Hodges, J. R. and Etcoff, N. L. 1996. Facial emotion recognition after bilateral amygdala damage: Differentially severe impairment of fear. *Cognitive Neuropsychology*. 13(5), pp. 699–745.

Caldwell, M. F. 2011. Treatment related changes in behavioral outcomes of psychopathy facets in adolescent offenders. *Law and Human Behavior*. 35, pp. 275–87.

Caldwell, M. F., McCormick, D. J., Umstead, D. and Van Rybroek, G. J. 2007. Evidence of treatment progress and therapeutic outcomes among adolescents with psychopathic features. *Criminal Justice & Behavior*. 34, pp. 573–87.

Caldwell, M. F., McCormick, D. J., Wolfe, J. and Umstead, D. 2012. Treatment related changes in psychopathy features and behavior in adolescent offenders. *Criminal Justice & Behavior*. 39, pp. 144–55.

Caldwell, M. F., Skeem, J. L., Salekin, R. L. and Van Rybroek, G. J. 2006. Treatment response of adolescent offenders with psychopathy features: A two-year follow-up. *Criminal Justice and Behaviour*. 33, pp. 571–96.

Calhoun, C. 1989. Responsibility and reproach. *Ethics*. 99(2), pp. 389–406.

Chakhssi, F., de Ruiter, C. and Bernstein, D. 2010. Change during forensic treatment in psychopathic vs. nonpsychopathic offenders. *The Journal of Forensic Psychiatry and Psychology*. 21, pp. 660–82.

Ciaramelli, E. and di Pellegrino, G. 2011. Ventromedial prefrontal cortex and the future of morality. *Emotion Review*. 3(3), pp. 308–9.

Ciocchetti, C. 2003. The responsibility of the psychopathic offender. *Philosophy, Psychology and Psychiatry*. 10(2), pp. 175–83.

Cleckley, H. M. 1941. *The mask of sanity: An attempt to clarify some issues about the so-called psychopathic personality*. St Louis: Mosby.

Coid, J., Yang, M., Ullrich, S., Roberts, A., Moran, P., Bebbington, P., Brugha, T., Jenkins, R., Farrell, M., Lewis, G., Singleton, N. and Hare, R. 2009. Psychopathy among prisoners in England and Wales. *International Journal of Law and Psychiatry*. 32, pp. 134–41.

Cooke, D. J. and Michie, C. 2001. Refining the construct of psychopathy: Towards a hierarchical model. *Psychological Assessment*. 13(2), pp. 171–88.

Coplan, A. and Goldie, P. eds. 2011. *Empathy: Philosophical and psychological perspectives*. Oxford: Oxford University Press.

Craft, M., Stephenson, G. and Granger, C. 1964. A controlled trial of authoritarian and self-governing regimes with adolescent psychopaths. *American Journal of Orthopsychiatry*. 34(3), pp. 543–54.

Crockenberg, S. B. and Litman, C. 1990. Autonomy as competence in 2-year-olds: Maternal correlates of defiance, compliance and self-assertion. *Developmental Psychology*. 26, pp. 961–71.

Damasio, A. 2006. *Descartes' error: Emotion, reason and the human brain*. London: Vintage.

Davies, S. 2011. Infectious music: Music-listener emotional contagion. In: Coplan, A. and Goldie, P. eds. *Empathy: Philosophical and psychological perspectives*. Oxford: Oxford University Press.

Davis, M. H. 1996. *Empathy: A social psychological approach*. Boulder, CO: Westview Press.

de Oliveira-Souza, R., Hare, R. D., Bramati, I. E., Garrido, G. J., Azevedo, I. F., Tovar-Moll, F. and Moll, J. 2008. Psychopathy as a disorder of the moral brain: Fronto-temporo-limbic grey matter reductions demonstrated by voxel-based morphometry. *Neuroimage*. 40(3), pp. 1202–13.

De Sousa, R. 1987. *The rationality of emotion*. Cambridge: MIT Press.

De Sousa, R. 2002. Emotional truth. *Proceedings of the Aristotelian Society*. **supp. vol. 76**, pp. 247–63.

De Veer, A. 1991. *Parental disciplinary strategies and the child's moral internalization*. Unpublished doctoral dissertation, University of Nijmegen.

Debes, R. 2009. Which empathy? Limitations in the mirrored "understanding" of emotion. *Synthese*. 175(2), pp. 219–39.

Decety, J., Chen, C., Harenski, C. and Kiehl, K. A. 2013a. An FMRI study of affective perspective taking in individuals with psychopathy: Imagining another in pain does not evoke empathy. *Frontiers in Human Neuroscience*. 7, p. 489.

Decety, J., Skelly, L. R. and Kiehl, K. A. 2013b. Brain response to empathy-eliciting scenarios involving pain in incarcerated individuals with psychopathy. *JAMA Psychiatry*. 70(6), pp. 638–45.

Decety, J., Skelly, L., Yoder, K. J. and Kiehl, K. A. 2014. Neural processing of dynamic emotional facial expressions in psychopaths. *Social Neuroscience*. 9(1), pp. 36–49.

Deeley, Q., Daly, E., Surguladze, S., Tunstall, N., Mezey, G., Beer, D., Ambikapathy, A., Robertson, D., Giampietro, V., Brammer, M. J., Clarke, A., Dowsett, J., Fahy, T., Phillips, M. L. and Murphy, D. G. 2006. Facial emotion processing in criminal psychopathy. Preliminary functional magnetic resonance imaging study. *British Journal of Psychiatry*. **189**, pp. 533–9.

Deigh, J. 1995. Empathy and universalizability. *Ethics*. 105(4), pp. 743–63.

Deonna, J. A. 2006. Emotion, perception and perspective. *Dialectica*. 60(1), pp. 29–46.

Ditto, P. H. and Koleva, S. P. 2011. Moral empathy gaps and the American culture war. *Emotion Review*. 3(3), pp. 331–2.

Döring, S. A. 2004. *Gründe und gefühle. Rationale motivation durch emotionale vernunft*. Habilitationschrift, Universität Essen-Duisburg.

Douglas, K. S., Ogloff, J. R., Nicholls, T. L. and Grant, I. 1999. Assessing risk for violence among psychiatric patients: The HCR-20 violence risk assessment scheme and the psychopathy checklist: screening version. *Journal of consulting and Clinical Psychology*. 67(6), pp. 917–30.

Duff, A. 1977. Psychopathy and moral understanding. *American Philosophical Quarterly*. 14(3), pp. 189–200.

Duff, A. 2010. Psychopathy and answerability. In: Malatesti, L. and McMillan, J. eds. *Responsibility and psychopathy: Interfacing law, psychiatry and philosophy*. Oxford: Oxford University Press, pp. 199–212.

Dutton, K. 2012. *The wisdom of psychopaths: Lessons in life from saints, spies and serial killers*. London: Random House.

Eisenberg, N. and Strayer, J. 1987. *Empathy and its development*. Cambridge: Cambridge University Press.

Ekman, P. and Friesen, W. V. 1971. Constants across cultures in the face and emotion. *Journal of Personality and Social Psychiatry*. 17(2), pp. 124–9.

Elliott, C. 1992. Diagnosing blame: Responsibility and the psychopath. *Journal of Medicine and Philosophy*. 17(2), pp. 199–214.

Elliott, C. 1994. Puppetmasters and personality disorders: Wittgenstein, mechanism and moral responsibility. *Philosophy, Psychiatry and Psychology*. 1(2), pp. 91–100.

Elliott, C. 1996. *The rules of insanity: Moral responsibility and the mentally ill offender*. Albany: State University of New York Press.

Ellis, H. 1890. *The criminal*. London: Walter Scott.

Eshleman, A. 2009. *Moral responsibility*. [Online]. Stanford Encyclopedia of Philosophy. Available from: http://plato.stanford.edu/entries/moral-responsibility/

Eslinger, P. J. and Damasio, A. R. 1985. Severe disturbance of higher cognition after bilateral frontal lobe ablation: Patient EVR. *Neurology*. 35(12), pp. 1731–41.

Farrington, D. P. 2006. Family background and psychopathy. In: Patrick, C. J. ed. *Handbook of psychopathy*. New York: The Guilford Press, pp. 229–50.

Farrington, D. P., Ullrich, S., Salekin, R. T. and Lynam, D. R. 2010. Environmental influences on child and adolescent psychopathy. In: Salekin, R. T. and Lynam, D. R. eds. *Handbook of child and adolescent psychopathy*. New York: The Guilford Press, pp. 202–32.

Fawcett, C., Wesevich, V. and Gredeback, G. 2016. Pupillary contagion in infancy: Evidence for spontaneous transfer of arousal. *Psychological Science*. 27 (7), pp. 997–1003.

Feinberg, J. 1986. *Harm to self: The moral limits of the criminal law*. New York: Oxford University Press.

Felthous, A. R. 2011. The 'untreatability' of psychopathy and hospital commitment in the USA. *International Journal of Law and Psychiatry*. 34, pp. 400–5.

Field, T. M., Woodson, R., Greenberg, R. and Cohen, D. 1982. Discrimination and imitation of facial expressions by neonates. *Science*. 218, pp. 179–81.

Fine, C. and Kennett, J. 2004. Mental impairment, moral understanding and criminal responsibility: Psychopathy and the purposes of punishment. *International Journal of Law and Psychiatry*. 27(5), pp. 425–43.

Fischer, J. M. 1999. Recent work on moral responsibility. *Ethics*. 110(1), pp. 93–139.

Fischer, J. M. and Ravizza, M. 1998. *Responsibility and control: A theory of moral responsibility*. Cambridge: Cambridge University Press.

Fitzpatrick, W. J. 2008. Moral responsibility and normative ignorance: Answering a new skeptical challenge. *Ethics*. 118(4), pp. 589–613.

Flor, H., Birbaumer, N., Hermann, C., Ziegler, S. and Patrick, C. J. 2002. Aversive Pavlovian conditioning in psychopaths: Peripheral and central correlates. *Psychophysiology.* 39(4), pp. 505–18.

French, P. A. 1979. The corporation as a moral person. *American Philosophical Quarterly.* 16(3), pp. 297–317.

French, P. A. 1984. *Collective and corporate responsibility.* New York: Columbia University Press.

Gabbard, G. O. 2005. Mind, brain and personality disorders. *American Journal of Psychiatry.* 162, pp. 648–55.

Gacono, C. B. 2005. *The clinical and forensic interview schedule for the Hare psychopathy checklist: Revised and screening version.* Mahwah, New Jersey: Lawrence Erlbaum Associates.

Gao, Y., Glenn, A. L., Schug, R. A., Yang, Y. and Raine, A. 2009. The neurobiology of psychopathy: A neurodevelopmental perspective. *Canadian Journal of Psychiatry.* 54(12), pp. 813–23.

Gao, Y. and Raine, A. 2010. Successful and unsuccessful psychopaths: A neurobiological model. *Behavioral Sciences and the Law.* 28(2), pp. 194–210.

Gardner, J. 2007. *Offences and defences: Selected essays in the philosophy of criminal law.* Oxford: Oxford University Press, pp. 77–89.

Gibbons, J. 2010. Things that make things reasonable. *Philosophy and Phenomenological Research.* 81, pp. 335–61.

Gillberg, C. 2007. Non-autism childhood empathy disorders. In: Farrow, T. and Woodruff, P. eds. *Empathy in mental illness.* Cambridge: Cambridge University Press, pp. 111–25.

Glannon, W. 1997. Psychopathy and responsibility. *Journal of Applied Philosophy.* 14(3), pp. 263–75.

Glannon, W. 2008. Moral responsibility and the psychopath. *Neuroethics.* 1(3), pp. 158–66.

Glenn, A. L., Raine, A. and Laufer, W. S. 2011. Is it wrong to criminalize and punish psychopaths? *Emotion Review.* 3(3), pp. 302–4.

Glenn, A. L., Raine, A. and Schug, R. A. 2009. The neural correlates of moral decision-making in psychopathy. *Molecular Psychiatry.* 14(1), pp. 5–6.

Glover, J. 1970. *Responsibility.* London: Routledge and Keegan Paul.

Glover, J. 2008. *LSE meeting with Alan Ryan, part II. "Antisocial personality disorder" interviews in Broadmoor.* Available from: http://www.jonathanglover.co.uk/philosophy-beliefs-and-conflicts/lse-meeting-with-alan-ryan

Goldie, P. 2004. Emotion, feeling, and knowledge of the world. In: Solomon, R. C. ed. *Thinking about feeling: Contemporary philosophers on emotions.* Oxford: Oxford University Press, pp. 91–106.

Goldie, P. 2005. Imagination and the distorting power of emotion. *Journal of Consciousness Studies.* 12(8-10), pp. 127–39.

Goldie, P. 2007a. Emotion. *Philosophy Compass.* 2(6), pp. 928–38.

Goldie, P. 2007b. Seeing what is the kind thing to do: Perception and emotion in morality. *Dialectica.* 61(3), pp. 347–61.

Goldie, P. 2011. Anti-empathy. In: Coplan, A. and Goldie, P. eds. *Empathy: Philosophical and psychological perspectives*. Oxford: Oxford University Press, pp. 304–31.

Gordon, R. M. 1987. *The structure of emotions: Investigations in cognitive philosophy*. Cambridge: Cambridge University Press.

Greenspan, P. S. 2003. Responsible psychopaths. *Philosophical Psychology*. 16(3), pp. 417–29.

Griffiths, P. E. 2004. Is emotion a natural kind? In: Solomon, R. C. ed. *Thinking about feeling*. Oxford: Oxford University Press, pp. 233–49.

Habel, U., Kuhn, E., Salloum, J. B., Devos, H. and Schneider, F. 2002. Emotional processing in psychopathic personality. *Aggressive Behavior*. 28(5), pp. 394–400.

Haji, I. 1998. On psychopaths and culpability. *Law and Philosophy*. 17(2), pp. 117–40.

Haji, I. 2003. The emotional depravity of psychopaths and culpability. *Legal Theory*. 9, pp. 63–82.

Haji, I. 2005. Introduction: Semi-compatibilism, reasons-responsiveness, and ownership. *Philosophical Explorations*. 8(2), pp. 91–3.

Haksar, V. 1964. Aristotle and the punishment of psychopaths. *Philosophy*. 39 (150), pp. 323–40.

Haksar, V. 1965. The responsibility of psychopaths. *The Philosophical Quarterly*. 15 (59), pp. 135–45.

Hamilton, G. 2008. Mythos and mental illness: Psychopathy, fantasy, and contemporary moral life. *The Journal of Medical Humanities*. 29(4), pp. 231–42.

Hare, R. D. 1965. Psychopathy, fear arousal and anticipated pain. *Psychological Reports*. 16(16), pp. 499–502.

Hare, R. D. 1970. *Psychopathy: Theory and research*. New York: Wiley.

Hare, R. D. 1980. A research scale for the assessment of psychopathy in criminal populations. *Personality and Individual Differences*. 1(2), pp. 111–9.

Hare, R. D. 1982. Psychopathy and physiological-activity during anticipation of an aversive stimulus in a distraction paradigm. *Psychophysiology*. 19(3), pp. 266–71.

Hare, R. D. 1991. *The psychopathy checklist-revised*. Toronto: Multi-Health Systems.

Hare, R. D. 1995. *Without conscience: The disturbing world of the psychopaths among us*. New York: The Guilford Press.

Hare, R. D. 1998. The Hare PCL-R: Some issues concerning its use and misuse. *Legal and Criminological Psychology*. 3, pp. 99–119.

Hare, R. D., Clark, D., Grann, M. and Thornton, D. 2000. Psychopathy and the predictive validity of the PCL-R: An international perspective. *Behavioural sciences and the law*. 18, pp. 623–45.

Hare, R. D., Frazelle, J. and Cox, D. N. 1978. Psychopathy and physiological responses to threat of an aversive stimulus. *Psychophysiology*. 15(2), pp. 165–72.

Hare, R. D. and Neumann, C. S. 2008. Psychopathy as a clinical and empirical construct. *Annual Review of Clinical Psychology*. 4, pp. 217–46.

Hare, R. D. and Neumann, C. S. 2010. Psychopathy: Assessment and forensic implications. In: Malatesti, L. and McMillan, J. eds. *Responsibility and psychopathy: Interfacing law, psychiatry and philosophy.* Oxford: Oxford University Press, pp. 121–63.

Harenski, C. L. and Kiehl, K. A. 2011. Emotion and morality in psychopathy and paraphilias. *Emotion review.* 3(3), pp. 299–303.

Harlow, J. M. 1868. Recovery from the passage of an iron bar through the head. *Publications of the Massachusetts Medical Society.* 2, pp. 327–47.

Harold, J. and Elliott, C. 1999. Travelers, mercenaries and psychopaths. *Philosophy, Psychiatry and Psychology.* 6(1), pp. 45–8.

Harpur, T. J., Hakstian, A. R. and Hare, R. D. 1988. Factor structure of the psychopathy checklist. *Journal of Consulting and Clinical Psychology.* 56(5), pp. 741–7.

Harris, G. T. and Rice, M. E. 2006. *Treatment of psychopathy: A review of empirical findings.* In: Patrick, C. J. ed. *Handbook of psychopathy.* New York: The Guilford Press.

Harris, T. *The silence of the lambs.* 1999. London: Arrow (Random House).

Hart, C. H., DeWolfe, D. M., Wozniak, P. and Burts, D. C. 1992. Maternal and paternal disciplinary styles: Relations with preschoolers' playground behavioural orientations and peer status. *Child Development.* 63, pp. 879–92.

Hart, H. L. A. 1968. IX. Postscript: Responsibility and retribution. *Punishment and responsibility.* Oxford: Clarendon Press, pp. 210–37.

Hatfield, E., Cacioppo, J. T. and Rapson, R. L. 1992. Primitive emotional contagion. In: Clarke, M. ed. *Review of personality and social psychology: Emotion and social behaviour.* Thousand Oaks, CA: Sage, pp. 151–77.

Hatfield, E., Cacioppo, J. T. and Rapson, R. L. 1994. *Emotional contagion.* Cambridge: Cambridge University Press.

Haviland, J. M. and Lelwica, M. 1987. The induced affect response: 10-week-old infants' responses to three emotion expressions. *Developmental Psychology.* 23, pp. 97–104.

Hemphill, J. F., Hare, R. D. and Wong, S. 1998. Psychopathy and recidivism a review. *Legal and Criminal Psychology.* 3, pp. 737–45.

Hobson, J. and Shines, J. 1998. Measurement of psychopathy in a UK prison population referred for long-term psychotherapy. *British Journal of Criminology.* 38(3), pp. 504–15.

Hoffman, M. L. 1960. Power assertion by the parent and its impact on the child. *Child Development.* 31, pp. 129–43.

Hoffman, M. L. 2000. *Empathy and moral development: Implications for caring and justice.* New York: Cambridge University Press.

Howe, D. 2013. *Empathy: What it is and why it matters.* Basingstoke: Palgrave Macmillan.

Howe, M. L. and Courage, M. L. 1997. The emergence and early development of autobiographical memory. *Psychological Review.* 104(3), pp. 499–523.

Jaffee, S. R., Caspi, A., Moffitt, T. E. and Taylor, A. 2004. Physical maltreatment victim to antisocial child: Evidence of an environmentally mediated process. *Journal of Abnormal Psychology.* 113(1), pp. 44–55.

James, W. 1884. What is an emotion? *Mind.* 9(34), pp. 188–205.

Judisch, N. 2005. Responsibility, manipulation and ownership. *Philosophical Explorations.* 8(2), pp. 115–30.

Kane, R. 2002a. Free will: Reflections on Wallace's theory. *Philosophy and Phenomenological Research.* 64(3), pp. 693–8.

Kane, R. 2002b. Responsibility, reactive attitudes and free will: Reflections on Wallace's theory. *Philosophy and Phenomenological Research.* 64(3), pp. 693–8.

Kant, I. 2005. *Groundwork for the metaphysic of morals.* Available at http://www .earlymoderntexts.com/pdf/kantgrou.pdf.

Keating, G. C. 2014. Strict liability wrongs. In: Oberdiek, J. ed. *Philosophical foundations of the law of torts.* Oxford: Oxford University Press, pp. 292–311.

Kennett, J. 2006. Do psychopaths really threaten moral rationalism? *Philosophical Explorations.* 9(1), pp. 69–82.

Kiehl, K. A., Smith, A. M., Hare, R. D., Mendrek, A., Forster, B. B., Brink, J. and Liddle, P. F. 2001. Limbic abnormalities in affective processing by criminal psychopaths as revealed by functional magnetic resonance imaging. *Biological Psychiatry.* 50(9), pp. 677–84.

Kirsch, L. G. and Becker, J. V. 2007. Emotional deficits in psychopathy and sexual sadism: Implications for violent and sadistic behavior. *Clinical Psychology Review.* 27(8), pp. 904–22.

Knausgaard, K. O. 2013. *My struggle book 2: A man in love.* London: Random House.

Knobe, J. 2003a. Intentional action and side effects in ordinary language. *Analysis.* 63, pp. 190–3.

Knobe, J. 2003b. Intentional action in folk psychology: An experimental investigation. *Philosophical Psychology.* 16, pp. 309–24.

Kohlberg, L. 1981. *Essays on moral development, vol. I: The philosophy of moral development.* San Francisco, CA: Harper & Row.

Korsgaard, C. M. 1986. Skepticism about practical reason. *The Journal of Philosophy.* 83(1), pp. 5–25.

Kosson, D. S., Suchy, Y., Mayer, A. R. and Libby, J. 2002. Facial affect recognition in criminal psychopaths. *Emotion.* 2(4), pp. 398–411.

Krevans, J. and Gibbs, J. C. 1996. Parents' use of inductive discipline: Relations to children's empathy and prosocial behavior. *Child Development.* 67(6), pp. 3263–77.

Kringelbach, M. L. and Rolls, E. T. 2004. The functional neuroanatomy of the human orbitofrontal cortex: Evidence from neuroimaging and neuropsychology. *Progress in Neurobiology.* 72(5), pp. 341–72.

Kroner, D. G., Forth, A. E. and Mills, J. F. 2005. Endorsement and processing of negative affect among violent psychopathic offenders. *Personality and Individual Differences.* 38(2), pp. 413–23.

Kuczynski, L. 1983. Reasoning, prohibitions and motivations for compliance. *Developmental Psychology.* 19, pp. 126–34.

Kutz, C. 2004. Chapter 14: Responsibility. In: Coleman, J. and Shapiro, S. eds. *Jurisprudence and philosophy of law.* Oxford: Oxford University Press, pp. 548–87.

Law Commission. 2013. *Criminal liability: Insanity and automism*. Law Commission.

Leichsenring, F., Leibing, E., Kruse, J., New, A. S. and Leweke, F. 2011. Borderline personality disorder. *The Lancet*. 377(9759), pp. 74–84.

Levenson, R. W., Ekman, P. and Friesen, W. V. 1990. Voluntary facial action generates emotion-specific autonomic nervous system activity. *Psychophysiology*. 27(4), pp. 363–84.

Levenston, G. K. and Patrick, C. J. 2000. The psychopath as observer: Emotion and attention in picture processing. *Journal of abnormal psychology*. 109(3), pp. 373–85.

Levy, N. 2008. The responsibility of the psychopath revisited. *Philosophy, Psychology and Psychiatry*. 14(2), pp. 129–38.

Levy, N. 2011. Expressing who we are: Moral responsibility and awareness of our reasons for action. *Analytic Philosophy*. 52(4), pp. 243–61.

Levy, N. 2014. Psychopaths and blame: The argument from content. *Philosophical Psychology*. 27(3), pp. 351–68.

Lieb, K., Zanarini, M. C., Schmahl, C., Linehan, M. M. and Bohus, M. 2004. Borderline personality disorder. *The Lancet*. 364(9432), pp. 453–61.

Lilienfeld, S. O., Watts, A. L. and Francis Smith, S. 2015. Successful psychopathy: A scientific status report. *Current Directions in Psychological Science*. 24(4), pp. 298–303.

List, C. and Pettit, P. 2011. *Group agency: The possibility, design, and status of corporate agents*. New York: Oxford University Press.

Litton, P. 2008. Responsibility status of the psychopath: On moral reasoning and rational self-governance. *Rutgers Law Journal*. 39, pp. 349–92.

Lykken, D. T. 1957. A study of anxiety in the sociopathic personality. *Journal of Abnormal and Social Psychology*. 55(1), pp. 6–10.

M'Naghten's Case [1843–1860] ALL ER Rep 229.

Maibom, H. L. 2005. Moral unreason: The case of psychopathy. *Mind and Language*. 20(2), pp. 237–57.

Maibom, H. L. 2008. The mad, the bad, and the psychopath. *Neuroethics*. 1(3), pp. 167–84.

Malatesti, L. and McMillan, J. eds. 2010. *Responsibility and psychopathy: Interfacing law, psychiatry and philosophy*. Oxford: Oxford University Press.

Mason, M. 2011. Blame: Taking it seriously. *Philosophy and Phenomenological Research*. **LXXXIII**(2), pp. 473–81.

Maudsley, H. 1873. *Body and mind*. London: Macmillan and Co.

Maudsley, H. 1874. *Responsibility in mental disease*. London: H.S. King.

Maxwell, B. and Sage, L. L. 2009. Are psychopaths morally sensitive? *Journal of Moral Education*. 38(1), pp.75–91.

McKenna, M. S. 1998. The limits of evil and the role of moral address: A defense of Strawsonian compatibilism. *The Journal of Ethics*. 2(2), pp. 123–42.

McMillan, J. R. 2003. Dangerousness, mental disorder, and responsibility. *Journal of Medical Ethics*. 29(4), pp. 232–5.

Meffert, H., Gazzola, V., den Boer, J. A., Bartels, A. A. and Keysers, C. 2013. Reduced spontaneous but relatively normal deliberate vicarious representations in psychopathy. *Brain*. 136(8), pp. 2550–62.

Mikhail, J. 2011. Emotion, neuroscience, and law: A comment on Darwin and Greene. *Emotion Review*. 3(3), pp. 293–5.

Millgram, E. 1996. Williams' argument against external reasons. *Nous*. 30(2), pp. 197–220.

Millon, T., Simonsen, E., Birket-Smith, M. and Davis, R. D. eds. 1998. *Psychopathy: Antisocial, criminal and violent behaviour*. New York: The Guilford Press.

Minzenberg, M. J. and Siever, L. J. 2006. Neurochemistry and pharmacology of psychopathy and related disorders. In: Patrick, C. J. ed. *Handbook of psychopathy*. New York: Guilford, pp. 251–77.

Mitchell, D. G. V., Colledge, E., Leonard, A. and Blair, R. J. R. 2002. Risky decisions and response reversal: Is there evidence of orbitofrontal cortex dysfunction in psychopathic individuals? *Neuropsychologia*. 40, pp. 2013–22.

Montmarquet, J. A. 2002. Wallace's 'Kantian' Strawsonianism. *Philosophy and Phenomenological Research*. 64(3), pp. 687–92.

Moore, M. S. 1997. *Placing blame: A theory of the criminal law*. Oxford: Oxford University Press.

Morse, S. J. 2008. Psychopathy and criminal responsibility. *Neuroethics*. 1(3), pp. 205–12.

Motzkin, J. C., Newman, J. P., Kiehl, K. A. and Koenigs, M. 2011. Reduced prefrontal connectivity in psychopathy. *Journal of Neuroscience*. 31(48), pp. 17348–57.

Muller, J. L., Sommer, M., Dohnel, K., Weber, T., Schmidt-Wilcke, T. and Hajak, G. 2008. Disturbed prefrontal and temporal brain function during emotion and cognition interaction in criminal psychopathy. *Behavioral Sciences and the Law*. 26(1), pp. 131–50.

Muller, J. L., Sommer, M., Wagner, V., Lange, K., Taschler, H., Roder, C. H., Schuierer, G., Klein, H. E. and Hajak, G. 2003. Abnormalities in emotion processing within cortical and subcortical regions in criminal psychopaths: Evidence from a functional magnetic resonance imaging study using pictures with emotional content. *Biological Psychiatry*. 54(2), pp. 152–62.

Murphy, J. G. 1972. Moral death: A Kantian essay on psychopathy. *Ethics*. 82(4), pp. 284–98.

Nagel, T. 1986. *The view from nowhere*. Oxford: Oxford University Press.

Newman, J. P., Patterson, C. M. and Kosson, D. S. 1987. Response perseveration in psychopaths. *Journal of Abnormal Psychology*. 96(2), pp. 145–8.

Nichols, S. 2002. How psychopaths threaten moral rationalism: Is it irrational to be amoral? *Monist*. 85(2), pp. 285–303.

Nussbaum, M. 2001. *Upheavals of thought*. Cambridge: Cambridge University Press.

Nussbaum, M. 2004. Emotions as judgments of value and importance. *Thinking about feeling: Contemporary philosophers on emotions*. Oxford: Oxford University Press, pp. 183–99.

Ogloff, J. R. P. and Wong, S. 1990. Electrodermal and cardiovascular evidence of a coping response in psychopaths. *Criminal Justice and Behavior.* 17(2), pp. 231–45.

Oksenberg Rorty, A. 2004. Enough already with 'theories of the emotions'. In: Solomon, R. C. ed. *Thinking about feeling.* Oxford: Oxford University Press, pp. 269–78.

Oshana, M. A. L. 1997. Ascriptions of responsibility. *American Philosophical Quarterly.* 34(1), pp. 71–83.

Oshana, M. A. L. 2004. Moral accountability. *Philosophical Topics.* 32(1), pp. 255–74.

Owens, D. 2008. Rationalism about obligations. *European Journal of Philosophy.* 16(3), pp. 403–31.

Parfit, D. and Broome, J. 1997. Reasons and motivation. *Proceedings of the Aristotelian Society.* **Supp. Vol.** 71(May), pp. 99–146.

Patrick, C. J. ed. 2006. *Handbook of psychopathy.* New York: The Guilford Press.

Patrick, C. J., Bradley, M. M. and Lang, P. J. 1993. Emotion in the criminal psychopath: Startle reflex modulation. *Journal of Abnormal Psychology.* 102(1), pp. 82–92.

Patrick, C. J., Cuthbert, B. N. and Lang, P. J. 1994. Emotion in the criminal psychopath: Fear image processing. *Journal of Abnormal Psychology.* 103(3), pp. 523–34.

Pickard, H. 2012. *Philosophy bites: Hannah Pickard on responsibility and personality disorder.* Warburton, N. July 7. Available at: http://philosophybites.com/2012/07/hanna-pickard-on-responsibility-and-personality-disorder-originally-on-bioethics-bites.html

Pillsbury, S. H. 2014. Why psychopaths are responsible. In: Kiehl, K. A. and Sinnott-Armstrong, W. P. eds. *Handbook on psychopathy and law.* Oxford: Oxford University Press, pp. 297–318.

Polaschek, D. L. L. and Daly, T. E. 2013. Treatment and psychopathy in forensic settings. *Aggression and Violent Behavior.* 18, pp. 592–603.

Preston, S. D. and de Waal, F. B. M. 2002. Empathy: Its ultimate and proximate bases. *Behavioural and Brain Sciences.* 25, pp. 1–72.

Prinz, J. J. 2004a. Embodied emotions. In: Solomon, R. C. ed. *Thinking about feeling: Contemporary philosophers on emotions.* Oxford: Oxford University Press, pp. 44–60.

Prinz, J. J. 2004b. *Gut reactions: A perceptual theory of emotion.* Oxford: Oxford University Press.

Prinz, J. J. 2011. Is empathy necessary for morality? In: Coplan, A. and Goldie, P. eds. *Empathy: Philosophical and psychological perspectives.* Oxford: Oxford University Press, pp. 211–29.

Pritchard, J. C. 1835. *A treatise on insanity.* London: Sherwood, Gilbert and Piper.

Pritchard, M. S. 1974. Responsibility, understanding, and psychopathology. *The Monist.* 58, pp. 630–45.

Pujol, J., Batalla, I., Contreras-Rodriguez, O., Harrison, B. J., Pera, V., Hernandez-Ribas, R., Real, E., Bosa, L., Soriano-Mas, C., Deus, J., Lopez-

Sola, M., Pifarre, J., Menchon, J. M. and Cardoner, N. 2012. Breakdown in the brain network subserving moral judgment in criminal psychopathy. *Social Cognitive and Affective Neuroscience*. 7(8), pp. 917–23.

Reidy, D. E., Kearns, M. C. and DeGue, S. 2013. Reducing psychopathic violence: A review of the treatment literature. *Aggression and Violent Behavior*. 18, pp. 527–38.

Rice, M. E., Harris, G. T. and Cormier, C. A. 1992. An evaluation of a maximum security therapeutic community for psychopaths and other mentally disordered offenders. *Law and Human Behavior*. 16, pp. 399–412.

Richman, K. A. 2018. Autism and moral responsibility: Executive function, reasons responsiveness, and reasons blockage. *Neuroethics*. 11(1), pp. 23–33.

Robinson, J. 2004. Emotion: Biological fact or social construction? In: Solomon, R. ed. *Thinking about feeling*. Oxford: Oxford University Press, pp. 28–43.

Robinson, P. 1996. Competing theories of justification: Deeds v. Reasons. In: Simester, A. P. and Smith, A. T. H. eds. *Harm and culpability*. Oxford: Clarendon Press, pp. 45–70.

Rollins, B. C. and Thomas, D. L. 1979. Parental support, power and control techniques in the socialization of children. In: Burr, W. R., et al. eds. *Contemporary theories about the family: Vol. 1, research-based theories*. New York: Free Press, pp. 317–64.

Rolls, E. T. 2004. The functions of the orbitofrontal cortex. *Brain Cogn*. 55(1), pp. 11–29.

Rönnegard, D. 2015. *The fallacy of corporate moral agency*. New York: Springer.

Rosen, G. 2014. Culpability and duress: A case study. *Proceedings of the Aristotelian Society*. **Supp. Vol. 88**(1), pp. 69–90.

Roskies, A. L. 2003. Are ethical judgments intrinsically motivational? Lessons from "acquired sociopathy" [1]. *Philosophical Psychology*. 16(1), pp. 51–66.

Roskies, A. L. 2011. A puzzle about empathy. *Emotion Review*. 3(3), pp. 278–80.

Salekin, R. T. 2002. Psychopathy and therapeutic pessimism. Clinical lore or clinical reality? *Clinical Psychology Review*. 22(1), pp. 79–112.

Salekin, R. T. 2008. Psychopathy and recidivism from mid-adolescence to young adulthood: Cumulating legal problems and limiting life opportunities. *Journal of Abnormal Psychology*. 17(2), pp. 386–95.

Salekin, R. T., Worley, C. and Grimes, R. D. 2010. Treatment of psychopathy: A review and brief introduction to the mental model approach for psychopathy. *Behavioral Sciences & the Law*. 28, pp. 235–66.

Salmela, M. 2011. Can emotion be modelled on perception? *Dialectica*. 65(1), pp. 1–28.

Sawin, D. B. and Parke, R. D. 1980. Empathy and fear as mediators of resistance-to-deviation in children. *Merrill-Palmer Quarterly of Behaviour and Development*. 26, pp. 123–34.

Scanlon, T. M. 1998. *What we owe to each other*. Cambridge, MA: Harvard University Press.

Scanlon, T. M. 2008. *Moral dimensions: Permissibility, meaning, blame*. Cambridge, Mass.: Harvard University Press.

Schachter, S. and Singer, J. E. 1962. Cognitive, social, and physiological determinants of emotional state. *Psychological Review.* **69**(5), pp. 379–99.

Schopp, R. F. 1991. *Automatism, insanity, and the psychology of criminal responsibility: A philosophical inquiry.* Cambridge: Cambridge University Press.

Schroeder, M. 2007. Reasons and agent-neutrality. *Philosophical Studies.* **135**(2), pp. 279–306.

Seara-Cardoso, A. and Viding, E. 2014. Functional neuroscience of psychopathic personality in adults. *Journal of Personality.* **83**(6), pp. 723–37.

Seto, M. C. and Barbaree, H. 1999. Psychopathy, treatment behaviour, and sex offender recidivism. *Journal of Interpersonal Violence.* **14**, pp. 1235–48.

Shand, A. F. 1918. Emotion and value. *Proceedings of the Aristotelian Society.* **19**, pp. 208–35.

Shoemaker, D. 2007. Moral address, moral responsibility, and the boundaries of the moral community. *Ethics.* **118**(October), pp. 70–108.

Shoemaker, D. 2009. Responsibility and disability. *Metaphilosophy.* **40**(3–4), pp. 438–61.

Shoemaker, D. 2011a. Attributability, answerability, and accountability: Toward a wider theory of moral responsibility. *Ethics.* **121**(3), pp. 602–32.

Shoemaker, D. 2011b. Psychopathy, responsibility, and the moral/conventional distinction. *The Southern Journal of Philosophy.* **49**, pp. 99–124.

Shoemaker, D. 2015. *Responsibility from the margins.* New York: Oxford University Press.

Sifferd, K. and Hirstein, B. 2013. On the criminal culpability of successful and unsuccessful psychopaths. *Neuroethics.* **6**(1), pp. 129–40.

Skodol, A. E., Siever, L. J., Livesley, W. J., Gunderson, J. G., Pfohl, B. and Widiger, T. A. 2002. The borderline diagnosis II: Biology, genetics, and clinical course. *Biological Psychiatry.* **51**, pp. 951–3.

Slobogin, C. 2000. An end to insanity: Recasting the role of mental disability in criminal cases. *Virginia Law Review.* **86**(6), pp. 1199–247.

Smart, J. J. C. 1969. Free-will, praise and blame. *Mind.* **78**(3), pp. 337–61.

Smith, G. T. and Oltmanns, T. F. 2009. Scientific advances in the diagnosis of psychopathology: Introduction to the special section. *Psychological Assessment.* **21**(3), pp. 241–2.

Smith, M. 1995. Internal reasons. *Philosophy and Phenomenological Research.* **55**(1), pp. 109–31.

Smith, R. J. 1984. The psychopath as moral agent. *Philosophy and Phenomenological Research.* **45**(2), pp. 177–93.

Sneddon, A. 2005. Moral responsibility: The difference of Strawson, and the difference it should make. *Ethical theory and moral practice.* **8**(3), pp. 239–64.

Sobel, D. 2001. Subjective accounts of reasons for action. *Ethics.* **111**(3), pp. 461–92.

Solomon, R. 1976. *The passions: Emotions and the meaning of life.* New York: Doubleday.

Solomon, R. 2004. Emotions, thoughts and feelings: Emotions as engagements with the world. In: Solomon, R. ed. *Thinking about feeling.* Oxford: Oxford University Press, pp. 76–88.

Sommer, M., Sodian, B., Dohnel, K., Schwerdtner, J., Meinhardt, J. and Hajak, G. 2010. In psychopathic patients emotion attribution modulates activity in outcome-related brain areas. *Psychiatry Research*. 182(2), pp. 88–95.

Southwood, N. 2011. The moral/conventional distinction. *Mind*. 120(479), pp. 761–802.

Speak, D. 2005. Semi-compatibilism and stalemate. *Philosophical Explorations*. 8 (2), pp. 95–102.

Stiles, J. and Jernigan, T. L. 2010. The basics of brain development. *Neuropsychology Review*. 20(4), pp. 327–48.

Stocker, M. 1987. Emotional thoughts. *American Philosophical Quarterly*. 24(1), pp. 59–69.

Stocker, M. 1994. Emotions and ethical knowledge: Some naturalistic connections. *Midwest Studies in Philosophy*. 19(1), pp. 143–58.

Stout, M. 2005. *The sociopath next door*. New York: Random House.

Strawson, P. F. 1980. P. F. Strawson replies. In: Straaten, Z.V. ed. *Philosophical subjects: Essays presented to P. F. Strawson*. Oxford: Clarendon Press, pp. 260–7.

Strawson, P. F. 2008. Freedom and resentment. *Freedom and resentment and other essays*. Abingdon, Oxon: Routledge, pp. 1–25.

Strayer, J. 1989. What children know and feel in reponse to witnessing affective events. In: Saarni, C. and Harris, P. eds. *Children's understanding of emotions*. New York: Cambridge University Press, pp. 259–89.

Talbert, M. 2008. Blame and responsiveness to moral reasons: Are psychopaths blameworthy? *Pacific Philosophical Quarterly*. 89, pp. 516–35.

Talbert, M. 2012. Accountability, aliens, and psychopaths: A reply to Shoemaker. *Ethics*. 122(3), pp. 562–74.

Todd, C. 2014. Emotion and value. *Philosophy Compass*. 9(10), pp. 702–12.

Torgerson, S., Czajkowski, N., Jacobson, K., Rechborn-Kjennerud, T., Roysamb, E., Neale, M. C. and Kendler, K. S. 2008. Dimensional representations of DSM-IV Cluster B personality disorders in a population-based sample of Norwegian twins: A multivariate study. *Psychological Medicine*. 38, pp. 1617–25.

Vargas, M. and Nichols, S. 2007. Psychopaths and moral knowledge. *Philosophy, Psychiatry and Psychology*. 14(2), pp. 157–62.

Viding, E. and Larsson, H. 2010. Genetics of child and adolescent psychopathy. In: Salekin, R. T. and Lynam, D. R. eds. *Handbook of child and adolescent psychopathy*. New York: The Guilford Press, pp. 113–34.

Vitacco, M. J. 2007. Psychopathy. *The British Journal of Psychiatry*. 191, p. 357.

Waldman, I. D., Rhee, S. H., LoParo, D. and Park, Y., 2006. Genetic and environmental influences on psychopathy and antisocial behavior. In: Patrick, C. J. ed. *Handbook of Psychopathy*. New York: The Guilford Press, pp. 205–28.

Wallace, R. J. 1994. *Responsibility and the moral sentiments*. Cambridge, MA: Harvard University Press.

Wallace, R. J. 2002. Replies to reviews of 'Responsibility and moral sentiments'. *Philosophy and Phenomenological Research*. 64(3), pp. 707–27.

Wallace, R. J. 2007. The argument from resentment. *Proceedings of the Aristotelian Society.* **CVII**(3), pp. 295–318.

Ward, T. 2010. Psychopathy and criminal responsibility in historical perspective. In: Malatesti, L. and McMillan, J. eds. *Responsibility and psychopathy: Interfacing law, psychiatry and philosophy.* Oxford: Oxford University Press, pp. 8–30.

Waters, S. F., West, T. V. and Mendes, W. B. 2014. Stress contagion: Physiological covariation between mothers and infants. *Psychological Science.* 25(4), pp. 934–42.

Watson, G. 1987. Responsibility and the limits of evil: Variations on a Strawsonian theme. In: Schoeman, F. ed. *Responsibility, character and the emotions: New essays in moral psychology.* Cambridge: Cambridge University Press, pp. 256–86.

Watson, G. 1996. Two faces of responsibility. *Philosophical Topics.* 24, pp. 227–48.

Watson, G. 2013. Psychopathic agency and prudential deficits. *Proceedings of the Aristotelian Society.* 113(3pt3), pp. 269–92.

Werhane, P. H. 1985. *Persons, rights, and corporations.* Englewood Cliffs, NJ: Prentice-Hall.

Whiting, D. 2012. Are emotions perceptual experiences of value? *Ratio.* 25(1), pp. 93–107.

Williams, B. 1981. Internal and external reasons. *Moral luck: Philosophical papers 1973–1980.* pp. 101–13.

Wispé, L. 1987. History of the concept of empathy. In: Eisenberg, N. and Strayer, J. eds. *Empathy and its development.* Cambridge: Cambridge University Press, pp. 17–37.

Woodworth, M. and Porter, S. 2002. In cold blood: Characteristics of criminal homicides as a function of psychopathy. *Journal of Abnormal Psychology.* 111(3), pp. 436–45.

Wootton, B. 1959. *Social science and social pathology.* London: G. Allen and Unwin.

Yang, Y., Raine, A., Colletti, P., Toga, A. W. and Narr, K. L. 2010. Morphological alterations in the prefrontal cortex and the amygdala in unsuccessful psychopaths. *Journal of Abnormal Psychology.* 119(3), pp. 546–54.

Yang, Y., Raine, A., Colletti, P., Toga, A. W. and Narr, K. L. 2011. Abnormal structural correlates of response perseveration in individuals with psychopathy. *The Journal of Neuropsychiatry and Clinical Neurosciences.* 23(1), pp. 107–10.

Yang, Y., Raine, A., Lencz, T., Bihrle, S., LaCasse, L. and Colletti, P. 2005. Volume reduction in prefrontal gray matter in unsuccessful criminal psychopaths. *Biological Psychiatry.* 57(10), pp. 1103–8.

Yang, Y., Raine, A., Narr, K. L., Colletti, P. and Toga, A. W. 2009. Localization of deformations within the amygdala in individuals with psychopathy. *Archives of General Psychiatry.* 66(9), pp. 986–94.

Yen, S., Shea, M. T., Battle, C. L., Johnson, D. M., Zlotnick, C., Dolan-Sewell, R., Skodol, A. E., Grilo, C. M., Gunderson, J. G., Sanislow, C. A., Zanarini, M. C., Bender, D. S., Rettew, J. B. and McGlashan, T. H. 2002. Traumatic exposure and posttraumatic stress disorder in borderline, schizo-typal, avoidant, and obsessive-compulsive personality disorders: Findings from the collaborative longitudinal personality disorders study. *The Journal of Nervous and Mental Disease.* 190(8), pp. 510–8.

Zanarini, M. C., Yong, L., Frankenburg, F. R., Hennen, J., Reich, D. B., Marino, M. F. and Vujanovic, A. A. 2002. Severity of reported childhood sexual abuse and its relationship to severity of borderline psychopathology and psychosocial impairment among borderline inpatients. *Journal of Nervous and Mental Disease.* 190(6), pp. 381–7.

Zarpentine, C. 2007. Michael Smith, rationalism, and the moral psychology of psychopathy. *Florida Philosophical Review.* 7(1), pp. 1–15.

Zavaliy, A. G. 2008. Absent, full and partial responsibility of the psychopaths. *Journal for the Theory of Social Behaviour.* 38(1), pp. 87–103.

Index

For EU product safety concerns, contact us at Calle de José Abascal, 56–1°,
28003 Madrid, Spain or eugpsr@cambridge.org.

www.ingramcontent.com/pod-product-compliance
Ingram Content Group UK Ltd.
Pitfield, Milton Keynes, MK11 3LW, UK
UKHW020352140625
459647UK00020B/2424